# FRAIL DREAM OF TIMBUKTU

# FRAIL DREAM OF TIMBUKTU

Bettina Selby

JOHN MURRAY

© Bettina Selby 1991

First published in 1991
by John Murray (Publishers) Ltd
50 Albemarle Street, London W1X 4BD

The right of Bettina Selby to be identified
as the author of this work has been
asserted by her in accordance with the
Copyright, Designs and Patents Act, 1988

**British Library Cataloguing in Publication Data**
Selby, Bettina
 Frail dream of Timbuktu.
 1. Sahara Desert. Description & travel
 I. Title
 916.604

ISBN 0–7195–4838–1

Printed and bound in Great Britain by
Butler & Tanner Ltd, Frome and London

# Contents

# Illustrations

*All photographs taken by the author.*

vi

# Acknowledgements

THIS JOURNEY THROUGH the Sahel – the land on the fringes of the great desert – has been one of the most physically demanding I have ever made, and without the help and encouragement of many people it would certainly not have been as pleasurable and rewarding; indeed it might well have proved impossible. Certainly without their assistance I would not have been able to see nearly as much of the area as I did.

The unfailing cheerfulness of the West African people themselves, in spite of the harshness of their conditions, provided a constant example when the going was tough. And I found their friendly acceptance of the stranger in their midst wonderfully sustaining.

Particular thanks are due to David Sanders and to all the staff of UTA French Airlines who looked after both me and the bicycle in London, Paris, Niamey and Bamako, and who could not have done more to help – even to the extent of the entire staff of the Bamako office setting to with cardboard, scissors and sticky tape to construct a special travelling box for Evans' homeward journey.

A very special thank you is also due to Diallo Dienaba (Abou), to Mano Dayak and his wife of Temet Tours, Agadez; to the American Ambassador to Niger, Carl Cundiff and his wife Jackie; to Paul, Christina, Jean Claude and Laurence, Denise, Bettina, Aaron, and to all the people, too numerous to mention by name, who offered lifts, food and succour in those dry lands.

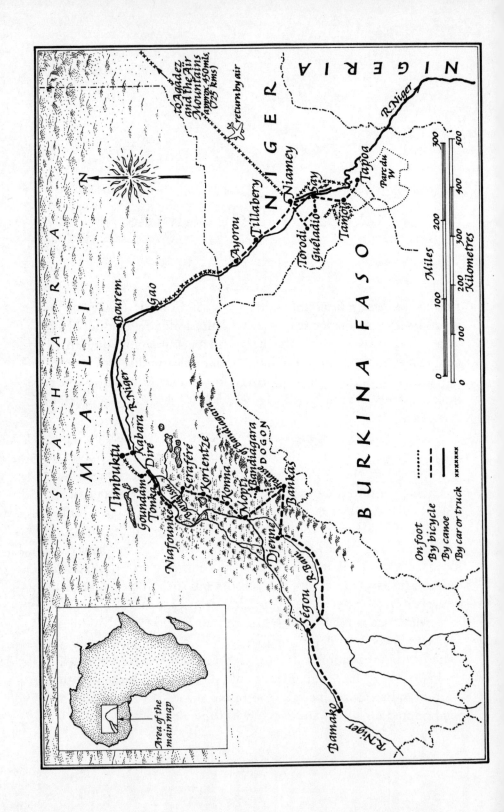

*This book is dedicated to the nomads of Niger and Mali
whose life centres on the Great Water.*

Wide Afric, doth thy sun
Lighten, thy hills unfold a city as fair
As those which starred the night o' the elder world?
Or is the rumour of thy Timbuctoo
A dream as frail as those of ancient time?
... the time is well nigh come
When I must render up this glorious home
To keen Discovery: soon your brilliant towers
Shall darken with the waving of her wand;
Darken, and shrink and shiver into huts,
Black specks amid a waste of dreary sand,
Low-built, mud-wall'd, barbarian settlements.

Tennyson

# 1

# The Strong Brown God

*I do not know much about gods; but I think that the river*
*Is a strong brown god*

Four Quartets    *T. S. Eliot*

I FIRST SAW THE River Niger from the terrace of the Grand Hotel
in Niamey. It was at that perfect and all too brief hour in the tropics,
when the sun is relinquishing its white hot grip on the day, and
beginning the swift descent into the African night. The luminous
sky was growing ever more darkly red, and long trailing skeins of
black tree duck drifted across it flying low over the water. Across
the bridge came lines of women in long brightly-coloured wraps,
little towers of calabashes, painted enamel bowls, or baskets of fruit
balanced effortlessly upon their richly swathed heads. Strings of
disdainful-looking brown camels, loaded high with bristly stacks of
wood for the city's cooking fires, swayed through the traffic. At the
water's edge naked men and boys bathed – ebony silhouettes, their
newly-washed clothes spread out drying on the banks behind them.
Several canoe-like craft whose long attenuated prows and sterns
rose clear above the water were being poled slowly upstream,
keeping close in to the banks where the shallow reed-filled water
moved more slowly.

The river reflected back none of these scenes. It was a solid
golden-brown flood, immensely wide, flowing strongly and silently
southwards. In spite of the charm and the novelty of all that was

1

going on around, it was the river itself that drew and finally held my attention. For what had been until then only a thin black line drawn on a map, along which my finger had so often and casually passed in the preceding months, measuring distances, noting details, was now suddenly translated into an immensely powerful presence, a primal force eclipsing totally the notion of being bound within an atlas. Looking at the Niger I suddenly remembered Eliot's 'strong brown god' and wondered if the attraction I felt was what he had meant by 'The river is within us ... His rhythm was present in the nursery bedroom'.

Long before I had grown tired of sitting there, the sky had become a canopy of stars, the river had all but faded into invisibility, and the air was pulsing and throbbing with the noise of stridulating crickets. It was high time to return to my more modest quarters, and catch up on some sleep. As I wheeled my bicycle away through the dusty streets, between the pools of light that spilled out from cooking fires and from stall holders' hurricane lamps, smells of unfamiliar food wafted up around me, and the soft murmur of voices rose from the shadows where people had begun the evening's eating and talking. After the cold impersonal streets of London which I had so recently left, it seemed to me an extraordinarily tender scene, and one that filled me with happiness. Suddenly the full realization was there, I was in Africa once again at the start of a new journey.

At the Catholic Mission, where I had earlier secured a room, instead of sinking immediately into much needed sleep, I found myself among a party of Belgian adventurers. The Catholic Mission's guest house was really intended for visiting clergy and the like. That it was currently full of non-ecclesiastical Westerners was because the good Fathers, realizing that ordinary travellers on limited budgets couldn't afford the current inflated prices charged by the city's hotels, practised hospitality and swelled their funds at the same time by letting out any unoccupied accommodation. Clad in a weird selection of brightly flowered shirts, baggy shorts and strange hats, these French Fathers were not in the least in keeping with the normally accepted monkish mode. But in spite of their own rather rackety appearance they were reputed to be selective about which wandering Westerners they took in. Arriving with a bicycle (although not actually riding it, as I had been given a lift in from the airport) I had experienced no problems, but was welcomed with wide-flung Gallic arms and warm expressions of approval, so that I could see that bicyclists were as highly regarded in this francophone area of Africa as they are in France itself.

In addition to my small concrete cell, furnished with two metal cots hung with mosquito nets, a shower and a key to the outside lavatory, I had been shown a room where guests could prepare their own food. It was here that I found the Belgians having a celebratory meal, and was invited to join them. They had recently driven a collection of old cars across the Sahara, they told me, nursing them carefully all the way to Niamey in order to sell them there. Used vehicles of all types were much sought after in Niger, as the import duty on new ones was as prohibitive as the price of hotels. The Belgians had made a good profit on theirs, hence the celebration. Explaining in return what I was doing alone except for my bicycle in the capital city of Niger was not nearly so easy.

The idea of exploring a part of the Sahel – that broad strip of West Africa that fringes the Sahara Desert to the north, and gradually gives way to verdant savannah and steamy jungle on its western and southern borders – had been maturing slowly over many years. It had been sparked off in the first place, I suppose, by the siren call of cities like Timbuktu, Djenné and Gao: cities which were so remote as to seem almost legendary, but which had once been the centres of great empires; centres too of a web of ancient overland trade routes that had stretched to all points of the known world. Gold, silks, frankincense, spices, slaves, religion and learning, and the many strange and diverse articles and commodities that merchants think worth transporting over thousands of miles, and through all the dangers of deserts and oceans, had flowed through these cities, making their names known throughout the civilized world.

Timbuktu, the most famed of them all, had been the market where for centuries gold had changed hands, pound weight for pound weight with salt, an equally precious substance which came from mines deep in the desert, the location of which was as closely guarded a secret as was the source of the gold in the jungles. This West African gold had once fed the royal mints of most of Europe, including that distant small kingdom of medieval England. Even in obscurity Timbuktu preserved its allure. It was not a city that had become suddenly accessible in the days of jet travel, and I anticipated no easy passage in getting there.

But if the romance of Timbuktu was the starting point, it was only one of many magnets that had been gradually drawing me towards this particular journey. An equally great attraction was the diversity of people who lived in the Sahel. The countries of Niger and Mali are home to Bozo, Dogon, Fulani, Peul and Tuareg to mention but a few, most of them leading lives very different to our comfortable technically-orientated western existence. The accidents of geography that had created the vast land-locked region of semi-arid plains, deserts and oases, remote cliffs and mountains in the interior of the huge continent of Africa has also helped to preserve the traditional way of life of many nomadic tribes long after those ways had been destroyed or abandoned in more fertile and accessible lands. Perhaps some small residue of our distant wandering ancestors lingers on in most of us; I, at any rate, have always been fascinated by dwellers in tents, and, in the fast-changing, cluttered world of the late twentieth century, I was particularly eager to see what I could of the life of the nomads of the Sahel before they disappeared.

The first casual glance at the map showed me my main route. The river Niger runs through both Niger and Mali like a giant ox-bow; a royal road, as it must always have been both for trade and conquest; the way followed by kings, merchants and explorers. The great river, the third longest in Africa, is unique. Rising only a hundred and fifty miles from the Atlantic coast in Guinea, it runs northwards for a thousand miles into the edges of the Sahara Desert, spreading out before it gets there to form a huge inland delta – flooding for half the year an area the size of England. Not far from Timbuktu, in the edges of the sandy wastes, the river again gathers into a single force, gradually curving back upon itself, to run south westerly for another fifteen hundred miles until it empties by way of a multitude of small channels into the Bight of Benin – a fact unknown to the map makers until the nineteenth century.

I became so taken up with the geography of this magnificent river, and with the stirring accounts of the eighteenth- and nineteenth-century explorers like Mungo Park, Clapperton and the Lander brothers who had, at no small cost to themselves, finally unravelled the mystery of its course, that at one point I considered making the entire journey on the Niger, in an antique pirogue like the ones I had just seen from the terrace of the Grand Hotel and which cannot have been very different from the one in which Mungo Park had made his historic descent of the Niger in 1805.

Mungo Park had been a hero of mine for as long as I could remember. A young Scottish doctor, he had first been sent out to West Africa in 1795 by the newly-founded *Association for Promoting the Discovery of the Inland Parts of the Continent of Africa*. His particular task was to explore the course of the River Niger, and, if possible, to 'find its rise and termination'; also 'to use the utmost exertions to visit the principal towns in its neighbourhood, particularly Timbuktu'. Since ancient times the Niger, whose course doubles back upon itself in the most confusing way, was thought to be a tributary of the Nile, and a medieval traveller, Leo Africanus, added to the confusion by stating, quite wrongly, that it flowed in a westerly direction. With the great interest of the age in scientific matters and in the opening up of new trading areas, it had become a pressing matter to solve these perplexing geographical questions. It was not, however, the best of times for such exploration. The conquest of the last of the great Negro empires by the Moors had reduced the Sahel to a chaos of warring states, and the horrid and prolific slave trade further aggravated the general lawlessness. Park was often attacked and robbed, and his life was constantly threatened. He suffered particularly from the attentions of the Moors, who were hostile to all Christians, and, in Mungo Park's opinion, 'studied mischief as an art'.

In spite of all the difficulties, the illnesses, starvation and ill-treatment, Park finally succeeded in reaching the banks of the Niger at Segou, where he was able to ascertain that there was indeed a mighty river and that it flowed *eastward*. That was the full extent of his exploration of the Niger, but the two-year expedition was considered a great success because of the wealth of detail he collected about a part of the world entirely unknown to the West. His *Travels* which was published on his return to England shows him to have been a resilient, resourceful and observant explorer bearing the frightful rigours of the journey with a fortitude that was spiced with humour.

Like many other great explorers before and after him, Mungo Park's experiences in Africa made it difficult for him to settle to a more mundane existence. Although he married and took up medical practice once more, in 1804, when he was invited by the British Government to lead another expedition to the River Niger, he accepted the commission with alacrity. This second journey was very different to the first and had a single objective – 'to pursue the course of the river to the utmost possible distance to which it can be traced'. A large expedition was assembled for the purpose, consisting of Park, his brother-in-law, a junior officer, thirty-six soldiers, and four carpenters and a draughtsman whose job would be to build boats for the expedition when the Niger was reached.

From the outset this second journey went badly. Instead of the six weeks they had reckoned on, it took nearly four months to reach the Niger at Bamako, by which time all but Park himself, the junior officer Martyn and three of the soldiers had succumbed to local diseases or to the rigours of the trek. Exhausted though he was, Mungo Park refused to acknowledge defeat. Resourceful as ever, he sold off what surplus European goods he had with him, and with the money bought a native pirogue, which the five remaining members of the expedition spent eighteen days converting into 'his Majesty's schooner *Joliba*'. Before setting off down river in this craft Mungo Park wrote home to his wife 'I do not intend to stop or land anywhere, till we reach the coast ... I think it not unlikely that I will be in England before you receive this'. It was the last anyone was to hear from him.

The story of Mungo Park's passage down the Niger filtered

through by degrees over the next few years, corroborated finally by a native who had accompanied the little party, and having left it just before the final fatal attack, had been the sole survivor. Mungo Park had stuck firmly to his intention of landing nowhere, and if native craft pursued him too closely he fired upon them, killing several men on different occasions. He was repeatedly threatened from the shore and from canoes by the warriors of the various little kingdoms through which he passed without presenting the customary tribute. The chief of one such territory set an ambush for the *Joliba* at the falls of Bussa in present-day Nigeria. As the boat was being negotiated through the tortuous channels it stuck fast, and the natives, standing on rocks among the rapids, hurled spears and rocks into it until it was about to sink. At that point, the account claimed, both Martyn and Park each seized one of the other white men, who were either injured or who could not swim, and jumped with them into the water. All perished while trying to reach the safety of the bank. Mungo Park had brought his hybrid craft to within four hundred miles of his goal.

In spite of Mungo Park's example, I soon abandoned the idea of making my journey entirely by water, mainly because the world of a boat is a tight, self-contained one, cut off from what lies beyond the narrow margins of the river. I certainly looked forward to spending some time afloat, but I also wanted a wider picture of the Sahel, particularly of the spectacular Aïr Mountains, the cliff dwellings of the Dogon, and the more fertile areas of Niger to the south of Niamey. It would be impossible to combine everything I hoped to see into one continuous journey, so I planned to make Niamey the base to which I could return from preliminary excursions, before I finally set off northwards to follow the course of the Niger towards Timbuktu.

Being a confirmed bicyclist, I had finally decided once again to make the journey on a sturdy 'all-terrain' cycle. All things considered, no other form of transport seemed to offer half the independence and convenience, not to mention the delight that I find in simply being on a bicycle. The Belgian explorers expressed both awe and doubt at the thought of a cyclist tackling some of the sandy areas they had had difficulty traversing with four-wheel drive vehicles. But as I explained, although an 'all terrain' bicycle is built expressly for tackling rough country, if the going gets too hard you can always take it on some other form of transport, this wonderful flexibility being another of its advantages. I am certainly no masochist, and contemplating the nature of the terrain, I anticipated many stretches of the journey where both I and the bicycle would be playing the role of passenger.

The Belgians, like the French Fathers, were actually greatly impressed by my bicycle, as well they might be, for it was a little masterpiece, and so new that its red paintwork gleamed with a deep rich lustre. It had been built especially for this journey, and incorporated all the very latest technology. The frame was made of the same lightweight tubing as was used in *Tour de France* racing cycles, so it was both strong and responsive, and there were twenty-one gears, operated by the merest flick of a button. I usually design my own bicycles, but this one reflected more of the maker's ideas than mine, and although it was a real joy to ride, I did wonder if it would prove robust enough for what was bound to be a very tough trip for anything mechanical. It was certainly a more complicated machine than I needed for a trek through the Sahel, but the shop that built it viewed my travels as admirable opportunities for a thorough testing of new ideas and equipment. They didn't mind if the paintwork suffered and parts got knocked about and broken. I did though, because on a long journey there is a tendency to grow rather fond of your one constant companion, even if it is an inanimate one. The name on the down tube of this exotic bicycle was in a more modern script than on previous models, but still read Evans. For the first few weeks while I was becoming used to it on the streets of London, I referred to it as the 'Mark Five', to distinguish it from its predecessors, but by the time we had arrived in Africa, I thought of it simply and affectionately as Evans, as I had done with all the others.

That the first duty of travellers is to survive to tell their tale was not something I needed to be reminded of as, much later that same morning, with the heat hitting me like the blast from an oven, I cautiously edged out into the colourful, pungent mêlée of the capital's traffic. Still feeling somewhat disorientated by jet lag, and by the too abrupt transition from a Europe locked in frost-bound November, I viewed this first ride through the centre of Niamey with some trepidation.

Niger, like Mali, is a francophone country. In the nineteenth century, when Britain and the European nations were engaged in carving up the African continent between them, Britain had initially expressed great interest in the interior of West Africa. Following the exploration of the Niger, trading enterprises – mostly in palm oil for soap-making – had started at the easily accessible coastal end. White men died like flies there, however, mainly from malaria which no one then connected with mosquitoes, and the initial enthusiasm waned, which was perhaps why Britain's territorial ambitions in the lands of the Niger stopped at the borders of present-day Nigeria.

France had entered the arena from the north, and had she not had an army seemingly full of expendable young men eager to make a name for themselves, the interior of West Africa might never have become a colonial possession. Conquering the marauding Tuaregs, the nomad warriors of the desert, cost France dear; conquering the Sahara itself cost far more. Whole regiments vanished, swallowed up in the vast inhospitable fastnesses, dying of thirst and heat, their weapons swelling the arsenals of the Tuaregs. But with the rest of Africa already parcelled out, the French persevered, and apart from a few coastal territories, the whole of Western Africa was under French control by the end of the nineteenth century.

The French conquest of Niger and Mali was swift and brutal, particularly so in Niger, where black mercenaries from Senegal were used to suppress uprisings, and there were several bloody massacres in the closing years of the century. The French interest in the Sahel was largely a matter of producing cheap exports for France, particularly cotton and rice, and they employed forced labour to establish monoculture farming on soil which was unsuitable for such exploitation. Both the people and the marginal land suffered, as the age-old delicate balance between pastoralist and cultivator, and the land that both depended upon, was broken.

But the French also brought peace in the wake of conquest, putting an end to slavery and to the perpetual tribal fighting that had characterized the life of the Sahel since the seventeenth century, when the last of the great Negro empires had broken up. Unlike the British, whose policy was to administer their colonies and protectorates at a distance, and not to interfere with local customs, the French permeated West Africa with their own culture and language, as though they had the conscious intention of creating so many new Frenchmen. This has had one distinct advantage for a traveller, since it meant that everywhere I went I would find people with whom I could communicate, even though my own French was not particularly fluent. Niger achieved its independence in 1960, but French is still the official language, and the currency is firmly linked to the French franc.

Being a francophone country, I had expected vehicles to drive on the right, but many drivers in Niamey seemed to prefer the centre of the road, or even the left, going for any space that appeared, and relying on their horns to force a passage. Bicyclists appeared to follow no rules at all, except that of 'see who gives way first'. Most of the roads were unpaved and full of holes and dust rose in clouds. Non-mechanized traffic added to the noisy confusion: herds of sheep and goats, some of them pulled along on pieces of string, bleated vociferously in protest; tough stubborn donkeys almost invisible under their loads refused to move in spite of their drivers belabouring them with huge clubs; men and women weaving perilously in and out of the traffic with enormous burdens balanced on their heads, stopped wherever they felt the need to exchange lengthy greetings. Fortunately nothing was able to move with any great speed or it would have proved quite lethal. As it was, it was merely dangerous, but in an essentially good-humoured way. No-one seemed to lose their temper, and anyone whose eye I caught always called out a '*Ça va?*' or '*Bonjour*'. And although there were many beggars about, some of whom appeared to have their own permanent pitches at traffic lights, in front of banks, shops and the like, there seemed, nonetheless, an air of light-heartedness about the city, a sort of gaiety that was quite different to anything I had encountered in East Africa. As had happened with my first view of the river, riding through the bustle of Niamey's traffic made me feel happy about the journey ahead.

This was just as well, as my first full day there did not promise much in the way of either excitement or relaxation. I had several tedious visits to make to various official agencies before I was legally entitled to be in Africa, or to travel in any direction. Although I had been submitted to the usual chaotic bureaucratic procedures of a Third World airport upon my arrival the day before, when several pages of my passport had been rubber-stamped and extensively written over, I still had to go to the tourist police in order to have further pages stamped to show that I had arrived in Niamey. After which, still further endorsements were needed to grant permission for me to proceed upon my way. I was glad I had opted for a jumbo-sized passport.

The imperious young policeman who was wielding the rubber stamp was not pleased when I tried to explain that I didn't really know where I would go to first in Niger, or exactly when, as the whole point of travelling by bicycle is to be free to change one's mind and drift off wherever and whenever the fancy takes one. He said in that case I couldn't go anywhere outside Niamey, and snapped shut his ink pad with a dismissive gesture. While I was pondering this impasse he suggested I fill in time by going to another building to obtain my photographic permit and white tourist card, and to return when I had made up my mind where I wanted to go.

This second visit was also destined to be not entirely successful; neither white tourist cards nor photo permits were any longer available or necessary, I was told. I said the police had informed me that I must have them. The patient young man behind the counter agreed that this was very possible as the documents had only just been discontinued, and he thought that it would take many months before most police in the country became aware of this fact. Since he seemed sympathetic, I asked if he would write a letter explaining that the documents were no longer necessary. He said he couldn't do that, but that if I wrote the note he would sign it. The result did not make a very convincing document but I added it to other useful papers I had with me, and hoped for the best.

I had already had occasion to use some of my unofficial *carnets de passage* the previous day when the customs official at the airport seemed unable to believe that I was seriously intending to ride the new-looking bright red Evans to Timbuktu. He was convinced that I had brought it into Niger for the express purpose of selling it there at a profit, and demanded that I pay him a large sum in import tax. The difficulty of dissuading him from this idea was compounded by having to plead my case in French. When the spoken word finally failed me, I produced a letter from The Royal Geographical Society which begged the reader (in rather more grammatical French than I had at my fingertips) to aid their Fellow in her journey along the Niger, which journey she was undertaking for the serious and proper purpose of researching the routes of the great nineteenth-century explorers. Adding to this suitably embossed document a few covers from previous books, which showed me riding bicycles through other parts of the world, I was able to set the seal on my truthfulness, and the official had begun the lengthy process of filling up several pages of my passport with evidence of his country's approval of me.

The only remaining difficulty had been to persuade him to return the book jackets which he said he wanted to keep to decorate his wall. While I was charmed at the unlikely notion of becoming a pin-up in an African customs office, I also felt sure that I would need the covers again before the journey was over. Eventually he agreed to wait for his 'cadeau' until I flew out, which I fear was not in keeping with the image of veracity I had striven so hard to convey, since my intention was to leave Africa from an airport in Mali, many hundreds of miles away.

It was Mali, or rather its Consulate in Niamey that was the object of the last visit of the day. Unlike Niger, Mali required me to have a visa to enter the country, and I had been forewarned by the guide book to expect further difficulties in obtaining one. This was because the Malian authorities were reluctant to grant a visa of more than one month's duration, and although an extension could be obtained in the capital, Bamako, I would not reach that city until the end of the journey, in about four months' time.

The effort to track down the Malian Consulate gave me further opportunity to practice my French, though when I was finally directed to the dingy little house in an obscure street behind the market, I feared my grip on the language must be worse than I thought, for I could not believe that any Consulate could be housed in so humble a place. However I found the elderly and rather wizened Consul sitting in state with his lady on a small sofa in a tiny inner room, while all around them men bustled about with pots of paint, piles of books, and a welter of assorted objects, trying, rather ineffectually I thought, to create order out of the chaos. I left nothing to chance but presented him with the Royal Geographical letter, all the book covers and my jumbo-sized passport for good measure. He passed them on one by one to his companion, and said 'as one scholar to another' he would be pleased to grant me a three months visa effective from the date of entry. If I thought my Arabic was up to it, I was also welcome to read about the Niger and Timbuktu in his many volumes on the subject. The actual inscribing of the visa into my passport had to wait until his corpulent secretary had returned from her siesta, and then was further delayed by everyone gathering their robes about them and finding a space on the cluttered floor where they could perform the prostrations of the mid-afternoon prayers. A final delay was occasioned by the Consul consulting an enormous Arabic/French dictionary, after which he wrote painstakingly over my visa in his own hand. He showed me the result with a glow of pride. Half printed, half in cursive script was the word *Exceptionnel*; the 'i' bearing a little circle above it instead of a dot. I wondered afterwards whether perhaps I was expected to tip him; the secretary, as she gave me my change, certainly intimated that I was welcome to make her a little *'cadeau'*. But from the price the honorary consul had told her to charge me, I decided it might well have been included.

The *'cadeau'* was a subject that needed to be faced up to straight away on this journey, and some policy about it decided upon if the constant demands were not to twist me into knots. *'Donne moi un*

13

*cadeau*' or even '*Il faut donner moi un cadeau*' was a constant cry. The people of the Sahel are among the poorest in the world, and beggars were everywhere, from the blind, the crippled, lepers with hands, feet or features gone, to those who were whole but destitute. It seemed to me that in such a situation a traveller from the affluent West had no choice but to give, even if it made no difference to the sum total of the suffering. It was necessary for one's own sake, and from a basic sense of justice and decency. In any case, this was a predominantly Moslem country where alms-giving was an accepted way of life, and where not to give was incomprehensible. The problem was that the demands were insatiable, and my purse strictly limited. I decided finally to settle on a daily amount that I thought I could afford, and having disposed of it to say, 'I'm sorry, I have already given today'. In practice it seldom proved as straightforward as this, but I was surprised at how well it did work.

That night I celebrated my partial success with bureaucracy by having dinner in the garden restaurant of a downtown hotel. It was simple food, steak skewered and cooked over charcoal, but it was hormone-free and delicious. Every so often the electric current failed, and the buzz of conversation died down as the African night was suddenly switched on, with huge stars leaping out of the deep blue, only to vanish again just as suddenly when the neon flickered back into life. Bone-thin elongated cats mewed softly and twined themselves between the legs of the diners, or sat like Egyptian statues, their over-long tails wrapped around their paws with a little curl left standing and twitching slightly from time to time. The lean young waiters in their white jackets and gloves contrasted sharply with the plumper figures and softer features of the casually dressed European diners, sharing something of the cats' air of timeless and effortless superiority.

# 2

# Niamey

AT ABOUT 4.30 A.M. in Niamey the crowing of roosters rose in pitch and volume to compete with the muezzin's first morning call to prayer. The town was full of fresh food on the hoof or on the wing – pigeons in wicker crates, chickens and guinea fowl tethered by the leg or hanging upside down in great feathery bunches from the handlebars of bicycles, goats, sheep and cattle trotting down the thoroughfares in herds and by twos and threes, bleating and lowing in bewilderment at the noisy unfamiliar scenes. After they had been sold, they were kept beside their new owners in courtyards or on the pavements until the day of their slaughter arrived, fed and watered meanwhile between the cooking fires and the open drains that were conveniently, if malodorously placed for the disposing of waste and the rinsing of pots. Succulent skewers of the roasted pieces of their erstwhile companions scented the air around them as they learnt to adapt to city ways. Together with the many working donkeys and camels, all these creatures added their cries to the dawn chorus until the last full-throated assertion that 'God is great and Mohammed is His prophet' had finally faded away and the roosters had the stage to themselves. Strangely, after this concert had ended, and I lay there gathering my energies to begin the day, I had the distinct sense of having just attended Morning Prayer in an Anglican church, and my head was ringing with the words of the great canticle – O All ye Fowls of the Air . . . .O all ye Beasts and Cattle . . . ye Winds of God . . . ye Sun and Moon . . . ye Children of Men

... O all ye Works of the Lord, Bless ye the Lord: Praise Him and magnify Him for ever'.

Niamey, while having nothing that was particularly attractive about it apart from the river, was a place I could happily have stayed in for quite a while. For a capital city that had been growing rapidly in recent years, it was still agreeably small; a town in which a traveller could quickly get to know her way around, yet still find enough variety to maintain the excitement of discovery. It was largely a place of single-storey mud-brick houses and dirt streets, with a sprinkling of smart western-style banks, office blocks and luxury hotels scattered around the centre, a growth that had slowed down soon after it had begun, when the price of the country's recently discovered uranium slumped on the world markets. Now each tall new building was, like the bridge which had been built at the same time, a distinct landmark rising uncharacteristically pale and angular above everything else. There was no distinct pattern to the city, it had simply spread outwards from the tree-lined boulevards of the original small French Colonial settlement, which had been sited on the plateau above the east bank of the river. A pleasant feeling of cohesion and continuity did exist however, and I think this was because of the wide streets and the many tall shady trees which lent a touch of elegance to the meanest quarters. But the reason that I felt so contented in Niamey had much to do with the fact that I quickly built up a wide circle of friends and acquaintances, so that I did not feel the loneliness that is so often the lot of a solitary traveller in a strange town.

Through passing by on my distinctive bicycle I became known to large numbers of people in the streets, people who were always sitting in the same spots, by their stalls, or beside little piles of produce, and whose greetings and smiles of recognition gave me a warm feeling of being welcome. There were paraplegics with hand-pedalled tricycles who haunted the entrance to the museum, the tourist office and anywhere else that foreigners might be found and persuaded to buy postcards, guide books and the like. These men were particularly interested in 'la bicyclette rouge' and when I sometimes came upon them away from their usual working patches they used to initiate races along the sandy thoroughfares. Being very competitive and braver than I was at flouting traffic regulations, wins were about even, in spite of Evans being much the fastest machine.

Every foot of downtown pavement was a pitch for someone trying to sell something to Westerners. The most persistent were the veiled and robed Tuareg men with their medieval weapons, jewellery, and the charms they called *gri-gris*, but they too soon grew to recognize me and to know that I wasn't in the market for souvenirs. It was a relief when these warriors ceased to follow me waving a beautiful curved knife or a sharp sword, persistently and urgently intoning 'I give you very good price'.

When I shopped at the supermarket, which was full of imported luxury food at ruinous prices, and which was the one landmark in Niamey known to all expatriates, Evans had its regular minder. I had brought a lock, but the first time I was fastening it two street urchins told me 'a thief can still easily steal your bicycle' graphically miming two men lifting it up and carrying it away on their heads. The sum they demanded to act as guards seemed a small price to pay for peace of mind, but when I emerged with my shopping I found that the boys had wandered off and a leper had taken their place. Every time I came to the store after that the same leper appeared beside me, and was hovering watchfully over Evans when I came out. He always accepted without comment whatever I placed in his fingerless stump of a hand, and although we usually exchanged a few pleasantries – he liked to make use of an English phrase he had picked up somewhere 'A vair good day Mistah' – he gave the impression of being a busy man with other customers to look after.

Most mornings around ten o'clock I had a glass of lemon tea on the terrace of an hotel with Abou, a very beautiful Fulani girl who worked at UTA, the airline that had flown me out. I had met her on my first day in Niamey when I had gone to her office to finalize some travel details. The staff were all very friendly and interested in my bicycle journey through the Sahel, and several of them invited me home for meals and introduced me to their friends. In this way I came to meet some of the wealthier and more influential Nigeriens, and also gained an entrée into the expatriate community, which was mainly American and French, though nearly every other nationality was also represented, engaged for the most part in the mega-world of International Aid. But it was Abou I came to know best. She was the daughter of an ex-diplomat, had travelled widely, and spoke excellent English as well as half a dozen other languages. Apart from enjoying her company, and her waspish views about Niger, I came to value her greatly as a talented and creative fixer. Getting anything done in Niger depended upon whom you knew. Abou seemed to know everyone, and the advice she gave me during these morning tea breaks was invaluable.

Between twelve and four the city closed down. Every patch of shadow held its group of supine figures and dozing animals, and the air seemed to have congealed into a more solid medium. Most people who had a home or a hotel room took a siesta at this time, but I was still too fascinated by the novelty of everything to want to do that. A corniche ran alongside the west bank of the river, and I soon decided that riding this tree-hung shady path was the ideal way to escape the heat and the dust of the afternoons. One of the advantages cycling has over walking is that a slight refreshing flow of air is created by the speed.

The stretch upstream from the solitary bridge soon became my favourite place. I found another world here, where the corniche gave way to an intermittent ribbon development of rough cabins set among small gardens. Closely planted beds of intensely green lettuce made a startling contrast with the grey hovels and the rubbish heaps. Refugees from neighbouring Burkina Faso tended these gardens, and there was always someone at work there splashing the crops with sparkling arcs of water. Small boys in ragged tunics whose task was to fill the calabashes with water from the river leaned against the rickety fences between trips, in attitudes of uncon-scious grace, one arm above their head, the hand loosely curled in the wire, one bare foot resting on the knee of the other leg. Half-naked round-eyed toddlers tumbled about the middens, breaking into instant beaming smiles and calling out shy '*Ça va?*s' as I passed. If I stopped, one of them would usually come and trustingly slip a grubby little hand into mine. The place was full of contrasts, beauty and filth side by side, and over it all a sense of peace I found nowhere else in the city.

Downstream of the bridge the way led eventually to an abattoir and tannery, but it was not only the horrid stench that assailed one there that made me decide that once was enough to cycle in that direction. The problem was that many of the town's men and older boys took their daily bath and washed their clothes in this stretch of the river. I hadn't known this, but in any case it would not have occurred to me to think twice about it, as from just below the bridge, only feet away from constant passing traffic and in full view of tourists drinking or dining on hotel terraces the men bathed quite openly. It seemed no different here; the men stood knee-deep in the water, leisurely soaping their bodies and heads until they were covered with a thick white lather and then ducked their heads down beneath the water, blowing like hippos. They appeared to be having a lovely time, and were in no hurry to get out, but continued to stand naked in the water pounding their clothes clean while women and young girls walked close by without taking any notice. They seemed not in the least embarrassed by their own nakedness, so it hadn't occurred to me that they might resent the presence of strangers. But the men of Niamey clearly had their own ideas of modesty, and it seems that in recent years they have felt harassed by tourists stalking them with cameras, so that they now suspect any Westerner, male or female, of being around expressly to take photographs of them in the nude. As it happened I didn't have a camera with me that day, otherwise I would certainly have wanted a picture. There was not one of the bathers, young or old, who did not have a beautiful physique, and they would have made a fine classical study with the great river in the background. Clearly some of the men decided this could be my only object in cycling that way, and they left me in no doubt of their feelings on the subject. One old man even ran naked into the road to shake his fist at me as I rode past, so that on my return to the bridge I felt compelled to travel at a rather brisker pace, and with my head firmly turned in the other direction.

About a week after I had arrived, Abou and I were sitting over tea on the terrace, discussing how to get myself and Evans down to the W Game Park, on the southern borders of Niger. The park is named after the distinctive triple bend on the River Niger, and I had already decided to visit it, when an invitation had come from the Minister of Tourism, another of Abou's acquaintances, to attend the official opening of the tourist season there. As this was to be a grand affair, celebrated with junketing and entertainment for the benefit of all the Nigerien ministers, foreign diplomats and leading businessmen, it sounded too good an occasion to be missed.

The party was on the following day but one, and it wasn't really practical to ride down. Although it was no more than eighty miles to the entrance of the park, it was by way of badly corrugated dirt roads on which a bicycle can move only slowly if machine and rider are not to be shaken to bits. It was also necessary to arrive looking reasonably respectable, which was certainly not possible when bicycling on Niger's dirt roads, where every vehicle that passed created thick clouds of clogging dust that quickly transformed one into a cross between a tramp and a coal miner.

There would have been no problem at all about my getting a lift down with a minister or one of the businessmen, as Abou knew most of them. The difficulty was Evans. I wanted to take it too, so that I could ride back to Niamey slowly through the bush. The idea was not only to spend a week or so seeing something of the more verdant part of the Sahel, before I set off northwards towards the desert, but also to have a preliminary ride with a well-laden Evans to see how it performed over rough ground. If anything was to prove inadequate to the task I could probably get it fixed when I got back to Niamey. Once I had finally left the capital and was on my way to Timbuktu I doubted if there would be any mechanical help available, apart from my own rudimentary skills.

Ministerial vehicles, however, even the four-wheel drive ones which African terrain demands, were not geared up to carrying bicycles, it seemed. It was only after several visits and many telephone calls that Abou received a third-hand invitation for me to join the German director of a European aid agency who was taking the German Ambassador down. There was plenty of room in their Landrover, apparently, and I was to present myself at the agency on the morning in question at 6.30 a.m. An escort would pick me up from the Catholic Mission to make sure I didn't get lost. As I was still naïve about West African arrangements, I thought it all sounded most efficient.

With departure imminent, life changed gear, and the austere little cell which had become home to me was transformed into temporary chaos as I checked over my kit and re-packed it carefully in what I hoped would be dust-proof plastic bags. Now that I was about to become peripatetic for a while, and dependent for life and comfort upon what I carried with me, it was important to know exactly where every piece of equipment was, so that if necessary I could get at it in the dark with the minimum delay and expenditure of energy.

I had seven separate pieces of luggage; two large panniers which fitted onto a rack at the back, two smaller ones for the front, a small bag for bicycle tools which fastened snugly under the saddle, a narrow cylindrical bag containing the tent poles and ground sheet, which went along the top of the rear pannier rack, and a bag with a shoulder strap, which hung on the front of the handlebars. The handlebar bag contained all my valuables, and the idea was to remove it every time I left the bicycle, even if only for a moment. I had spent a lot of time modifying the interior of it, making compartments to organize the plethora of small objects I needed frequently, like torch, compass, penknife, notebook and pen, sun cream, sunglasses and so forth. There were also several hidden zipped pockets for money, passport and documents. Earlier that day I had visited the bank in Niamey and, discovering the iniquitous charge exacted for changing travellers' cheques – the same amount for twenty pounds as for several hundred – I had cashed all the cheques I had, and was now carrying large wads of Central African francs distributed among these secret pockets. As long as I remembered to remove this bag from the bicycle whenever I halted anywhere, and always to carry it with me, I would not be rendered destitute in the event of Evans being stolen.

In the right-hand rear pannier I packed most of the camping gear,

21

lightweight tent, sleeping bag, three-quarter-sized self-inflating mattress, and a small wedge-shaped mosquito net for using indoors where a net wasn't supplied. The greatest danger to health in this part of Africa is still malaria, and the best way to safeguard against it is not to get bitten by mosquitoes. In the outside pocket, conveniently to hand, went the pump for filtering drinking water – another necessary precaution for staying healthy. Ten rolls of colour film were packed inside the sleeping bag in order to keep them as cool as possible.

At the bottom of the left-hand pannier went two sets of spare tyres and two spare inner tubes. On top of those was the part of my wardrobe that I wasn't wearing – a pair of dark-blue reinforced poly-cotton trousers, two shirts, a light cotton cagoule, socks, underwear, sandals, and a nylon wind jacket. The shirt, trousers and underwear I had on rotated with the other set, washed out each day whenever possible. The third shirt was to make sure that I had at least one respectable garment for wearing on formal occasions. I kept the clean clothes in a drawstring bag which made a handy pillow to use in the tent. The outside pocket held my toilet bag, together with a 'traveller's towel' which weighed almost nothing but also proved little better than useless, and a large flannel, which I was forced to use in place of the inadequate towel.

The left front pannier became the commissariat, and held the small petrol stove, two light aluminium pans, a kettle, a plastic mug, two plastic spoons and forks, plastic containers of coffee, tea and salt, and waterproof matches. There was room for a little food too which I intended to buy as I went along.

In the front right pannier were the maps, reading material, relevant pages from guide and reference books, spare notebooks, sun hat, a net bag for putting over the sun hat in case of attacks by swarms of vicious insects, a medicine bag containing antibiotics, anti-malarial pills, vitamins, aspirin, and ointments, another bag containing a first aid kit of sutures, plasters, sealed gauze swabs, and some hypodermic needles. These last were most advisable in Africa, I was told, as there was a high risk of contracting AIDS by being injected or put on a drip with a needle used many times before.

Though how, in the case of a serious accident, where I was rendered unconscious, I was to let anyone know I was carrying my own needles was not something I had yet worked out. There was a further little bag in this pannier with all the oddments that had no other place, like safety pins, spare laces, batteries, bits of nylon string and wax earplugs.

Water I would carry in two plastic bottles which fitted into cages on the frame, and in a few other plastic bottles stuffed under the flaps of the panniers. The sort of temperatures I would be cycling through would mean that I needed a minimum of two gallons a day to replace lost body fluid. As I could only manage the weight of about four pints, the rest would have to be found in villages along the way. As long as my water pump continued to function there would be no problem about purifying it.

I was also carrying a few items that were not strictly necessary but which were either farewell presents, or what I considered permissible luxuries. A litre of good scotch in half litre plastic flasks was amongst the latter. A small dram before retiring, especially when camping in wild places is a universal catholicon against most known ills; at least this was the belief handed down to me by my Scottish forebears. And if it did nothing else it certainly helped to relax aching muscles at the end of a long day of hard cycling.

I had an amulet made of jet, the traveller's stone, which was supposed to ensure a safe return if given by a friend. It was in three pieces hanging from a single ring – a cross, an anchor, and a heart – signifying faith, hope and charity. I had no reason to question its efficacy, never having come a serious cropper so far on my journeys, and I kept it pinned to the inside of my shoulder bag for safe-keeping. In Niamey I found it had an additional use, for when I passed the stalls of the sorcerers, where they sat surrounded by their stock in trade of lions' skulls, eagles' wings, dried furry animal remains, powdered snakes and a hundred other unrecognizable ingredients for their spells, and I was pressed by these gentlemen to let them make me a *gri gri* to protect me against evil spirits, I could pull out my jet charms and show them that I already had a Christian *gri gri*. At this the sorcerers usually narrowed their eyes and looked thoughtful, and I am convinced that I could probably have sold them my amulet had I been in need.

A pair of miniature binoculars which was an advance Christmas present from my husband had their own case which fitted onto my belt, handy for getting at quickly to spot the many exotic birds I hoped to see. My new camera, with the built-in twin lenses would balance it on the other side. There was also a bag of crystallized ginger which a friend had given me because she knew I suffered from sea sickness, and her mother had told her that ginger was an excellent remedy for this complaint. But as the only sea I had had to cross in order to get to Paris to pick up my flight had been the English Channel, and as that two-hour crossing had been flat calm, I had forgotten this gift until I was organizing my things in the mission. Not knowing quite what to do with it, I tucked it in with the cooking things and forgot about it until later in the journey, when I discovered its true worth.

Having finished the packing and sat for a while making sure I could remember where everything was, I wiped the city's dust off Evans so that it would look respectable for the German Ambassador in the morning, and went to bed to prepare for the early start. As I lay there cocooned under my net, I could hear faint sounds of drums, marimbas and singing, barely audible above the eternal sound of the cicadas, while from the huge old acacia tree just outside my door came the dry scurrying of lizards still active in the hot African night.

# 3

# The Edge of Paradise

THE DAY DID NOT begin well. The kind person who had decided that the Germans' Landrover was just the thing for taking the English-woman's bicycle had neglected to acquaint the Germans of the fact. Matters were not improved by my objections to the idea of tying Evans to the roof of the Landrover, where I knew it would be battered into scrap metal long before arrival. What had been only a hint of impatience on the Germans' part began to take on shades of national rivalry; German bicycles, it seemed, always travelled on roofs without damage. Only when I demonstrated how easy it was to take off Evans' panniers and remove the front wheel did they bow to English eccentricity. A little rearrangement of the interior, and everything was fitted in, without undue reduction in passenger comfort.

Once across the Niger and heading south we began to make up for lost time, while I held onto the prone Evans to stop it hitting the roof at every bump. Very soon we began overtaking a stream of cars, whose flags of office proclaimed the occupants, white or black, to be bound for the jamboree, and the Ambassador and his friend visibly relaxed, and made complimentary remarks about the quality of Landrovers compared with Japanese bush waggons. An air of European solidarity warmed the atmosphere.

But this was not to be the Germans' day. With a couple of lurches, and a stutter or two from the engine, we rolled to a halt. The driver had the bonnet up in a trice and was poking about underneath, while the rest of us got out and stood around aimlessly. All the cars we had so recently overtaken now began to pass us, leaving us gasping in clouds of choking dust. None of them stopped.

The driver announced that the coil had gone, and that we must return to Niamey and pick up a new one, but with the Landrover refusing to start no one had any idea of how we could do this. Other vehicles bound for the park continued to stream past, the occupants, it seemed, trying hard not to look smug, but barely succeeding. One car, carrying a black military gentleman with lots of braid and medals did stop, and, much to our driver's annoyance, insisted that his driver inspect the engine. Having confirmed the diagnosis they then drove off without further comment, leaving us in the same state as before.

Another half-hour passed and the American Ambassador and his party drew up in a shiny black safari vehicle, the size of a small bus. I was keeping well back out of the dust and didn't hear the exchange, but afterwards the Germans told me that the Americans had offered us all a lift, but that they had refused because they knew I wouldn't have agreed to Evans travelling on the Americans' roof. I thought it very noble of them not to have abandoned both me and Evans, but I also got the impression that they were glad of the excuse, and had no wish to be rescued by Americans.

The impasse was ended by the Minister of Roads, a man with enviable eyelashes who pulled up in a neat Suzuki waggon, and with charm and diplomacy had everyone organized in minutes. We would ride to the fête with him, and the Germans' driver would be given money to arrange a tow back to the city, rejoining us later at the park with the mended Landrover. There was nothing I could do but concur, though the realization that I was parting company with all my possessions at the very beginning of the trek was not a comfortable one, not to mention the thought of the unfortunate Evans being thrown about in the back of the Landrover without the aid of a restraining hand.

Several hours later, hot, cramped, thirsty and very dusty, we arrived at the reception in the hotel at the entrance to the game park, only to find that the last of the much-needed refreshment of

26

coffee, cold drinks and sandwiches was being cleared away. Already events were running behind schedule, and guests were being urged to assemble for the official welcome.

One hundred and fifty assorted black and white dignitaries were far too many to fit under the awning provided. People spilled out into the blinding midday sunshine on either side, and the neat rows of assorted chairs broke rank and became squashed together, as those at the rear pushed forward. It was difficult to understand the protocol employed in the seating arrangements; many of the ambassadors and ministers were sitting on hard chairs at the back, while body-guards and personal assistants were occupying the armchairs in the places of honour at the front. The black guests were by far the most impressive. Those who were not in military uniform were dressed in traditional robes, long and full, and wonderfully patterned, with pillbox hats that enhanced their tall stature. Their ladies were also tall, and, unlike the splendid men, they were also very plump, as this was the fashion for women. They were dressed in even more flamboyantly patterned peignoirs, with matching cloths wound artfully round their heads, the projecting folds and pleats greatly increasing the size, and giving balance to the overall bulk, so that they had the appearance of stately galleons sailing through the crowds. They were very successful at clearing a path for themselves, and really took up quite a lot more than their fair share of the seats. The whites appeared very pallid in comparison with all this rich colour, and as there could not be said to be any snappy dressers amongst them I for once did not feel out of place in my cycling clothes.

Three groups of dancers, each with their own band, competed for the audience's attention while we waited for proceedings to commence. One group of young girls dancing with impressive vigour were uniformly dressed in bright yellow cotton cloths which were wrapped tightly round their bodies from armpit to mid-calf and patterned all over with large cameo portraits of the President of Niger in military dress. Nicely positioned over each mercurial bottom and breast the stern heavy features under the peaked cap rippled and broke in blissful parody. All too soon soldiers appeared to chase the dancers away, and the most important black leaders arrived, preceded by other soldiers carrying armchairs. As soon as these dignitaries were seated, the three bands each broke into a slightly different version of the Nigerien national anthem, and, when the audience finally realized what it was, they struggled to their feet, taking up deeply reverent stances till it ended, as the awning was too low for any but the shortest guest to stand upright.

Some brief and suitably optimistic speeches about the country's forthcoming elections followed – there was only one party, so no one had to work too hard. Our printed programmes now showed that we had a choice of either a tour of the park, or a spectacle of racing pirogues on the river. The Germans and I, still lacking our own transport, were to be passengers in the American's sedan. The hand of friendship had been proffered once again, and this time it had been accepted. Our party had unanimously opted for the river which was supposed to be only about fifteen minutes away, but after an hour we were still part of an endless line of official cars that streamed along in a pall of dust, clearing the jungle of animals and birds for miles around. Everyone had had enough of driving after the long ride down, and even the vast interior of the Ambassador's car seemed cramped with the three extra passengers, but we had the joint blessings of air-conditioning and ice-cold coke.

River spectacle and tour had combined, it seemed, for after two hours of driving through the depopulated forest, the convoy came to a halt under open skies, on the banks of the fast-flowing brown Niger. Chauffeurs jockeyed for parking space, while the passengers faced the difficult decision of whether to take a much-needed pit stop in the surrounding jungle, opt for one of the limited number of seats on the launch, or make for a buffet table set out with beer and soft drinks. I missed out on the last two having just seen my first wild creatures of the day, a black kite and a splendid-looking vulture perched high in the trees. By the time I had got my binoculars out and taken a good look at them, the pirogue race was almost finished, and the muscular sweating crews, as competitive as the paraplegic tricyclists of Niamey, were straining over their paddles, driving the narrow craft towards the shore at such a rate that they grounded them high up the bank, scattering the watching dignitaries.

The whole thing was over in fifteen minutes, including more congratulatory speeches and the presentation of cash prizes to the winning crews. The briefly glimpsed magic of the jungle and the river running between green banks were again shrouded as the convoy rolled back to the hotel for a very late luncheon.

Although our party was last into the dining room, the Americans having decided that a thorough wash was more important than food, the number of guests and the recruitment of unskilled local people to serve them meant that the first course was still going its rounds. The Ambassador was quickly served with a plate of cucumber and tomatoes which his wife said he wasn't allowed, as the last time he'd had such things at a function he had been sick for days afterwards. He passed it to me saying he was sure his wife was right in these matters, although he reassuringly added that it probably wouldn't do me any harm. I was too hungry to refuse, though the alternative dish of beans and rice which he *was* allowed looked more sustaining. Large plates of couscous and goat meat followed, which calmed my fears that I was going to remain in a state of permanent hunger, and having got away to a head start on the first course, I was also served tinned fruit salad of which there proved to be not enough to go around.

Wine was available for infidels, and fizzy drinks for the Moslems, but the availability of the former depended upon whom one sat next to. I was alright because although the Americans had foresworn alcohol while they were in Africa, the Germans were seated on my other side, and they were adroit at reaching for the bottle. It was therefore a far more relaxed and happy party that eventually left the dining room. The Germans and I were perhaps the happiest of all because the first thing we saw as we emerged was the Landrover up and running again.

The joy of being reunited with Evans, albeit an Evans almost unrecognizable under a thick coat of dust, was enhanced by a Frenchman coming up to admire it as I was refitting the wheel and the luggage. The look in the Frenchman's eyes was one I had seen often before, it was the sudden yearning for the freedom that a bicycle represents, especially one loaded up with all the paraphernalia for a carefree self-sufficient existence. Yes indeed, I did know I was lucky, if only not to have to face the long boring drive back through the dust-veiled countryside. I would be able to see it all at my leisure, as a free agent. But not yet. Now that the junketing was over, it was time to take a proper look at the park.

Staying as the guest of a Peace Corps worker in the W Park, an invitation organized by the American Ambassador's wife, had very real advantages. Visitors could only travel through the game reserve by vehicle, with a guide in tow to make sure they stayed on the trails. But as I was already in the park and didn't have to pass through the entrance gates, I was able to go about alone, on foot, and didn't have to stick to tracks. Emily, the Peace Corps volunteer, showed me some basic routes, and then left me to my own devices.

Away from the squalor of the small village that had sprung up around the hotel, the powerful beauty of the land was suddenly apparent, bringing a moment of intense happiness like a physical shock. And yet beauty seemed a strange quality to apply to this harsh bright world of rock and scrub that stretched away into the far distance over endless low jumbled hills and valleys. Gone was the close-grown jungle I had glimpsed earlier. This was a landscape of gaunt twisted acacia trees and thorny bushes, each bearing millions of barbs to rip and tear. Underfoot was a red laterite that the dry air and relentless sun had crusted into a jagged, rock-like surface that bruised the feet and through which every growing thing had pushed its way into the light only with difficulty. It was a landscape reduced to essentials; its beauty a thing of skeletal austerity, inimical to all but the toughest life forms.

After walking for an hour over this punishing surface, feeling the moisture being drawn out of me by the relentless dry heat, I came to the edge of a steep slope. Below me, in a bowl-shaped depression, was a sudden vision of paradise – a place of rich dark-green where a large still pool lay surrounded by rocky bluffs. I made my way down to it with some trepidation: it seemed so magical a place that I half expected some monster, or an angel with flaming sword to appear and bar my way. The cool thick water was shaded by densely-leafed trees in which sat innumerable birds. Later, when the first sense of awe had somewhat moderated, I was able to identify a river eagle, a bird almost identical to the American bald eagle, several sorts of heron, including a Goliath heron which is enormous and very rare; a hammercap – a large brown bird aptly named for its distinctively-shaped head, a jewel-bright red-throated bee eater, hooded vultures, a little stint, and some delicate rock pigeons. There were many more I couldn't name, even with the help of Emily's bird book, including flocks of sparrow-like birds clowning about at the water's edge.

The pond was the centre of teeming life, and the surface was marked all over with widening circles as fish leaped repeatedly after the insects that hovered inches above them. Baboon and antelope spoor were neatly imprinted in the soft black mud around the edges, and lions' pug marks were set like plaster casts in the dried mud higher up. A sudden tremendous flurry and furious splashing at the far side of the pool accompanied by a quick glimpse of a huge crocodile shape was not as frightening as it might have been had I not been warned to expect it, and to know that it was only a harmless giant monitor lizard; but it was deeply thrilling none the less.

This was an important water hole for the park. Part of the River Tapoa, a tributary of the Niger, it remained a source of drinking water for the animals long after the rest of the river had dried up. For the last few months before the rains began, I was told, one could find more game here than anywhere in the park. Now, just two months after the end of the rainy season, there were still plenty of other watering places and the game was scattered.

To explore further around the pool meant taking to the water to avoid the dense thorny vegetation and the steep rocks blocking the shore line. Having removed my trousers and shoes to wade across a shallow neck I was suddenly conscious of how good it was to have cool mud oozing up between my toes and to feel my skin coming to life, freed from the clogging dust. From there it was but a step to throw off my shirt as well and to swim out into the middle of the lake. As I floated in the thick soupy brown water a frisky pack of baboons traversed the low red cliff face opposite, and a herd of water buck, all females with young, moved off uphill through a belt of trees.

Later, when I was telling Emily about the day's events, she said I had taken a risk in swimming because of the prevalence of bilharzia in the river. This is a nasty condition in which tiny worms get into the bloodstream through the feet and then multiply in the pelvic region. It is passed on through the urine of an infected person, but needs a particular water snail to act as intermediate host to the parasite, and can only occur where an infected person pees in the water where these snails live. As local people seldom visited the water hole I reckoned I was reasonably safe, and in any case bilharzia is easily cured these days, as long as one can obtain the medication. Even so I wouldn't have risked bathing where all the boys of the village took their daily swim, in the dramatic rocky gorge just below the hotel.

Emily was the first Peace Corps volunteer I had met, and I was interested to hear how the service functioned. It seemed not unlike the English Voluntary Service Overseas idea had once been – an opportunity for young people to gain an understanding of a Third World culture, and to do a bit to help in a small local way. VSO had long since decided that the Third World was more in need of skilled help than mere good will, and recruited people with trades like bricklayers and plumbers. The Peace Corps however had stuck to its original, more amateur leaning, and ran on a very low budget. Volunteers were expected to live in conditions as close as possible to those of the host community, with the idea that both sides would benefit from the cultural exchange. The best that I found most outsiders had to say about the service was that it seemed to do very little harm, and must at the very least help Americans themselves gain a wider understanding of geography and history. At the worst it was accused of being an insult to the intelligence of the people amongst whom the volunteers lived, for no one, said the detractors, certainly not the villagers themselves, would choose to live in those conditions if they could afford better.

For two nights I slept under my mosquito net in Emily's tiny compound and spent the days wandering through the paradise of the park, a paradise made somewhat less than perfect by the thorns and barbs that lurked everywhere, ripping clothing and skin and bringing the unwary back to earth. There were not the enormous numbers and varieties of big game animals that are found in the East African parks, though to my huge delight I had my first ever face-to-face meeting with a lioness, an incident I related to no one in case it was decided that I shouldn't be wandering about there alone after all. There was nothing frightening about the encounter, rather the opposite; it felt more like the vision in Isaiah of the eventual harmony of all creation. She was sprawled out in the dust in a sun-dappled clearing, with four half-grown cubs around her, and perhaps it was because the River Tapoa, some fourteen feet wide at that point, was between us, that neither they nor I felt any sense of threat. It was quite a few minutes before they moved, so I was able to stare my fill at the magnificent creatures. Even then they were in no hurry, but yawned once or twice before lazily getting to their feet, stretching slowly and luxuriously, and finally turning and padding off slowly into the thick woods behind them.

Baboons in troops of thirty or forty could usually be found patrolling the banks of the river, endlessly busy and always fun to watch, the young ones possessing a great sense of humour of the practical joke kind, pulling their elders' tails, and the like. They too seemed not to feel threatened as long as the water was between us. Antelope were plentiful, especially water buck, and there were some small gazelle I couldn't identify, but they were all very shy, and I could never get close to them.

While I was thrilled with all these sightings of animals, especially the lions, it was the birds that gave me the greatest pleasure, for they were everywhere in amazing variety such as I had seen nowhere else. With my wonderful little binoculars I could study them in a detail that hadn't been possible on previous journeys. The showiest were the long-tailed starlings, large birds with tail feathers a yard long, and whose glossy plumage was like shot silk, changing from purple to emerald as the light struck them. There were red-billed hornbills whose small black and white bodies seemed too frail for the weight of the huge red beaks, and who flew from tree to tree in a series of dipping loops, like acroplanes about to stall. In the mangrove swamps long-legged lily trotters ran along rafts of huge yellow and white blossoms that covered great stretches of the river. It was there, as I watched them, that I also saw my one and only crocodile disappearing beneath the vegetation. A bird I learnt to dread was the guinea fowl, a showy but alarmist creature who bustled about in large flocks croaking loud cacophonous warnings of my presence to everything within earshot. When these busybodies were around I had to give up hope of seeing anything else.

The topography of the park varied widely, depending on the presence of water. In some of the valleys tall trees hung with creepers formed a high canopy, underneath which was a dim green-lit world of winding water courses with the odd puddle not yet dried up. Between the valleys, the low hills appeared at first to be all bare, sun-baked laterite, but there was always a sprinkling of tough stunted acacia and low dry grass-like plants, all viciously barbed. The broad belt of land through which the Niger flowed is marked in the atlas as dry savannah, thousands of square miles of vulnerable marginal land, prone to erosion and lacking adequate water conservation for the crops of maize and millet that were needed to feed the population. Even though that population was one of the sparsest in the world, numbering only between five and twenty five to the square mile, it was already more than the land could support, and was growing all the time. I knew that I could expect to find wide areas of erosion, and the further north I travelled, the more that would be the case, as the climate grew steadily hotter and drier.

The park had given me the opportunity of a glimpse of the Sahel where nature, left to herself seemed able to manage her slender resources of water. The trees gave shelter to the lower brush, and this in turn protected the earth, bound it together and prevented erosion. It was a tough environment, but one with a sense of harmony in itself, and able to sustain and support life. But that life did not include man, and only by excluding him, like Adam and Eve being thrust from the Garden, had this small part of the Sahel been preserved in something like its natural state.

Now it was now time to move on, and see something of how the people of Southern Niger lived in their dry rolling savannah. Emily had supplied me with a few introductions to aid workers along the way, and I planned a roundabout route back to Niamey to round off this first part of the journey. One thing was certain, travelling at the speed of a bicycle I was bound to see considerably more than the occasional glimpse of trees from inside a cloud of dust, which had been my lot on the way down.

# 4

# Excursions through the Bush

I SET OFF AT AN early hour, in the hope of reaching the night's stopping place before the worst heat of the day. There was no abrupt change in the landscape as I left the W Park behind, except for huge termite nests that were often as much as ten feet high and stood like ungainly bollards set at irregular intervals beside the road. On either side, as far as the eye could see, were acacias, quite large for the most part and about twenty or thirty feet apart, with a thin mat of dry spiky grass and thorny bushes beneath them. The road climbed long hills every so often and from the top of these the acacia-covered plains spread out into the far blue distances. Close to, the well-spaced trees looked very bare with their tiny leaves that presented the minimum surface to the desiccating sun and so conserved their precious moisture. In the great wide vistas, however, it looked as though the land was covered in an unbroken forest. There were no people at all to be seen.

On the dirt road with a wind at my heels I found that I could bowl along at between eight and fourteen miles an hour until I hit a patch of dreaded corrugations, when I had to slow down rapidly to prevent being shaken to bits. The further I went the worse the surface became, and still there was no one about. The emptiness didn't matter in the least as I was so taken up with the exhilaration of being underway. I was also unconsciously listening to the cogs spinning round, and to the many small sounds that a bicycle makes, which tell the rider that all is well. A strange new country was unfolding all around me, and every tree, every bird was a bonus and something to be marvelled over.

After about three hours, when the dust and the heat were beginning to sap my energy and somewhat to dim this unalloyed pleasure in the day, I stopped in a patch of rare shade provided by a broader-leaved tree, to make tea and to eat the bag of dough balls I had bought from an old lady in the village before I left that morning. There was only minimal nourishment in these small pieces of greasy batter sprinkled with a little sugar, but they provided a bit of energy. The ritual of lighting the small petrol stove and organizing my limited kitchen was also satisfying, though not at all easy, as there was nowhere to sit on the thorn-strewn gravelly ground, and I had to squat on my heels, a position in which my leg muscles soon suffer from cramps. I inadvertently kicked over the first kettleful of boiling water, and had to start again, a serious loss as every drop was precious when I didn't know where I could get more. I could have drunk pints of tea, for the water I carried had soon become unpleasantly warm. I made myself take a drink of it every half hour to replace the fluid I was losing, but it did little to quench my thirst. The low humidity combined with the heat meant that sweat dried instantly and helped to keep the body cool, but it also made it easy for me to become dehydrated without realising it.

Early in the afternoon, I crossed the River Dyamongou, another tributary of the Niger which was about twenty-five miles to the west at this point and running parallel to my route. Across the bridge was the turn off to the small town of Tamou, and close by was the place I had been heading for, a green oasis in the dry scrub called 'Projet des Aveugles'.

'Monsieur Paul' or 'le patron', as he was known, was at first sight that specimen of Englishman that carries the race with him wherever he goes. A plump unmemorable figure in long shapeless shorts, and with the sort of bright pink perspiring complexion that would never become smoothly brown no matter how long he remained in the tropics, Paul made it easy to see why 'red ears' was the nickname given to white men by the black races of West Africa. His enthusiasm, energy and dedication also made it easy to understand why he was held in such affection by the people among whom he had come to work.

From Paul I learnt why the countryside I had been riding through all morning appeared so empty. Much of Niger's arable river land has been depopulated over the last thirty years because of river blindness, a condition spread by the simulium fly. Once the parasites have done their damage there is no cure because the backs of the victims' eyes have literally been eaten away. Sometimes the population of whole villages were blinded, and everyone died because they could no longer see to carry out basic tasks. Even if one or two were left sighted, a village could not survive. Life in the Sahel was such a hand-to-mouth struggle at the best of times that it could not be sustained without a corporate effort, and those people who remained whole had fled the area. River blindness has not been eradicated, but cures exist now if the condition is diagnosed early enough, and the spraying of the surface of the rivers helps to keep the fly in check.

Paul worked for a project to help the blind by re-establishing villages, particularly those which contained people who had lost their sight and whose prospects of any meaningful life without aid were very slim. Funded by a German Protestant organization, it sought to improve agricultural methods, by example and by direct teaching. It was the sort of role that in medieval England and Europe the monasteries had undertaken – religious conversion going hand in hand with dramatic improvements in land management. Paul's brief, as far as I could see, included no element of religious conversion, but like the monasteries, the centre of his operations was the farm that he had built in the wilderness. In the five years he had been there he had established something so similar to an English fifteenth century manor farm that it was like walking into a time warp. Everything was so self-contained, so organized and neat, yet essentially so attractive too, in a way that is seldom the case now in the West with modern farming methods. This was partly because here efficiency was combined with low-cost low-technology, in order that everything could be copied easily, using materials available within the environment. This resulted in every building harmonizing with its surroundings, which although incidental to the purpose was, I thought, a very real bonus. Even the rabbits had been provided with an ingeniously ordered complex of housing under the shade of a towering mahogany tree. It was in the style of local round thatched mud huts, a cluster of them built to rabbit scale, and interconnecting, so that does and bucks and family groups could be moved about as necessary. I never saw such fat, contented-looking rabbits. All the farm was like that: well-planned shelters for herds of healthy sheep, goats and cattle, and neat, sensible storage for grain, hay and straw, everything built with local materials. There were walled vegetable gardens, even a herb garden, and a dovecote; and everywhere were great shady trees and flowering shrubs under which chickens scratched industriously, and fat muscovy ducks waddled, their tummies almost touching the ground. It was particularly good to see so many different varieties of trees after the ubiquitous acacias. Although Paul had planted many new trees, he said his choice of site had been dictated by the presence of the established specimens.

A huge hump-backed bull was kept for the sole purpose of raising water from a tremendously deep well, to supply the needs of the farm and the various houses on it. It was an entertaining feature of the early evening to sit on the porch and watch this magnificent animal, whom no one but its handler could approach, being docilely led up and down the drive, its harness attached to the end of a rope several hundred yards long. By this means a fifty-gallon drum was slowly hauled up to the top of the tall tower to the point where a tripping mechanism caused the bottom of the drum to open and deposit its contents into the tank with a satisfying whoosh.

A smaller version of this simple but ingenious water system was used in the newly-established vegetable gardens around the local small town of Tamou, in which blind people worked. Here the ascending bucket, hauled up by a rope and pulley, was automatically tripped to deposit its contents into whichever one of four channels the user selected. The water then ran down into a small concrete pond from which watering cans could be filled. The vegetables, potatoes, carrots, onions and greens, with water melon and papayas, were grown in small beds, each with a raised edge of earth along which the foot of the blind person could feel to enable him to direct the water with accuracy along the rows. The old blind man who was doing the hauling was eager to demonstrate his expertise and independence; he presented a marked contrast to the sad resignation of the many blind people I had already seen in Niger holding onto one end of a stick by which a little boy led them about to beg.

A young blind gardener who had at some time received a mission school education, and who spoke English of a singular nature, seized the opportunity of my visit to down tools and practise his linguistic skill. For the best part of an hour I was made to listen to the story of his life which began: 'When in the year 1972 the Lord graciously revealed my Saviour Jesus Christ to me...', and which went on so interminably in this rambling high ecclesiastical style, that I lost the thread. But it seemed to be less about Jesus than about dark happenings of spells and witchcraft that had brought him to his present state. When I asked Paul about this conversation he said that he thought the Christian tone was just a gloss picked up by rote, Africans being such able linguists. Although Niger was nominally Moslem, animism was still very much the religion of the countryside. This was particularly true, Paul said, of the scattered primitive villages here in the south of Niger, where no affliction, not even death, was seen as the result of natural causes, but always of evil spells and sorcery. Every village had its shaman, and it was normal practice for him to go into a trance before the commencement of each day's activities. During this trance he would make marks on the earth in front of him with a stick, which he would interpret on awakening, and on the basis of which the every-day life of the village was directed.

The blind boy was employed by 'Le Vieux', an 'ancien combattant', one of the many Nigeriens who had served with the French army. He had lost a leg in the last war, and now his tiny war pension made him quite rich by local standards, while his title afforded him respect and distinction in his community, just as it does in France. Periodically he is trundled off to Paris at the charge of the French government to be fitted with a new artificial limb, a jaunt he looks forward to very much as he knows his way around the capital now, and enjoys the cosmopolitan life, he told me, proudly displaying the beautifully made artificial limb, carefully coloured to tone in with his own skin. Paul was keen to find out what happened to the discarded ones, since he was sure they could be adapted for another less fortunate one-legged person.

When Paul first showed me over the farm, I wondered how he would ever be able to leave it, since he so obviously delighted in every aspect, and in every single animal and bird and tree on it. He had, after all, carved it out of the wilderness himself. It therefore came as a shock when he said casually and with no hint of regret that he would be moving on in a couple of years or so. That was the first intimation I had of the extent of his dedication to the work, and his motivation in being in Africa. Over the two days I spent in his company I came to realize more and more what an unusually impressive person lurked beneath the amiable easy-going exterior.

He had had no particular leanings towards voluntary work overseas. The son of a farm labourer in the Midlands, he had turned out to be brighter than average, the only boy at his village school ever to go to university. A first in engineering at London was intended to lead on to a Ph.D, and the grant for this had already been awarded when Paul had an experience that was to change his life. He had been spending what he described as a pleasant Sunday morning with friends demonstrating in Trafalgar Square against the war in Vietnam. When they had boarded the train to return to their lodgings in South London, still carrying their placards and still rather full of themselves, an old woman had apparently poured scorn on them, telling them they were like all students, just talk and no action. Within a month of that seemingly innocuous but decisive encounter, Paul was a volunteer worker in Ghana, learning to exist as many Africans had to do on £12 a month. For several years he lived like that, queuing up with other needy people for the UN free handouts of dried fish and meal, and suffering several bouts of bilharzia and malaria, all experiences which he feels are no bad start for those who want to help the people of Africa. He began work as a teacher in a technical school, became headmaster, and gradually

41

got interested in projects for the blind. Now he has a Ghanaian wife and three young children, and says he would never be able to afford to return to England even if he wanted to. His plan is to retire one day to a farm of his own in Ghana.

The model farm of the Projet des Aveugles was the centre for training able and enthusiastic young Africans to work in the newly-established bush villages. There were a couple of these apprentices there when I visited, living as family, so that meal times with everyone gathered around the large table were also reminiscent of an English farmhouse scene of a bygone age. When his training was complete, each young man would live in the bush, responsible for five or six villages. He would have his permanent home in one, and make the rounds of the others by bicycle during the week, gradually introducing the improved methods he had learnt, and helping the villagers to acquire new skills. The area covered by the project was enormous, and the villages so scattered that for each worker to get around even six of them in a week was hard work. Many of them had only recently sprung up, as people had drifted into the area looking for new land on which to scrape a living. Life in these parts was still in a state of flux; some previous settlers were returning, and many people were in the process of making the transition from a nomadic to a settled existence, while others were somewhere in between. Paul was taking the apprentices around some of the nearer villages by truck in the morning, and he invited me to stay over and come too, an offer I accepted with alacrity.

We started very early, riding out in the back of the open truck as the sun began to flood the scene and the brief freshness of dawn was still in the air. There were no roads at all through the vast surrounding tracts of bush, only the small tracks made by human feet and the very occasional pack animal. The tracks vanished altogether in places or split into a bewildering jumble of choices. The truck heaved and canted and bucked over the uneven broken ground which was criss-crossed by numerous stream beds, dry now but creating impassable barriers, I was told, in the three months of the wet season, between June and October, when the whole area was totally cut off. Our cargo of live goats bleated and shifted their footing, their sharp little hooves digging into our feet which were spread wide for balance as we clung tightly to the rail.

Away from the dirt road, there were areas where the landscape had, curiously, something of the appearance of an English country park on a vast scale. I think this impression was given by the splendid well-spaced trees and the gentle rolling nature of the landscape with its covering of grass that, coarse as it was, nevertheless seemed very lush compared with the other areas of sand or laterite. Some trees like mahogany and deodar I recognized, but there were many shapely giants whose names I did not know but which were familiar from visits to Kew Gardens. But there were also exotic birds that were never seen in English parks, like red-throated bee eaters and the gorgeous birds of paradise which have black and white bodies the size of a sparrow coupled to a marvellous tail almost a yard long. Like the hornbill's enormous beak, these tails seemed far too heavy for flight, and indeed, the birds of paradise were always plummeting suddenly and heart-stoppingly out of sight.

The villages, separated by huge tracts of uninhabited bush, were nearly all only recently established, and were primitive and very small – just collections of tiny thatched huts in clearings among newly harvested millet fields. The people were mainly Gomanche, I was told, though they could equally well have been Djerma, Fulani or Peul, since these, and other tribes were all present in the area. The differences between them however were very slight and not immediately discernible to a traveller like myself who was just passing through and to whom everything seemed so novel. For centuries the pattern of the cultivators in these areas had been to move on every few years and sow fresh ground, a pattern that suits such marginal land, giving it the opportunity to recover. With a fast-expanding population such a practice becomes less and less possible and these particular people were slowly adapting to a less nomadic style of life. With the help of Paul's project they now had reliable wells and were beginning to plant vegetable gardens and to improve their livestock, but even so, their settlements still looked more like temporary camps than permanent villages.

Calabash vines tumbled over some of the grass roofs of the huts;

an important crop, for the gourds, dried and cut in half became hard like wood, and the larger ones served as excellent bowls, while the smaller ones with a long neck became capacious ladles and mouth-stretching spoons. Together with tall clay water jars, they were the only vessels the people owned. Inside the huts, blackened by the smoke of cooking fires, were just a few low woven beds.

The new wells, lined with a special type of locally made mud brick developed by the project, were quite rough but still startlingly modern in that setting. They had become the centre of village life and were surrounded by laughing, chattering women and girls drawing water. It was difficult to see how any settled life could have been sustained without the wells, since there was seldom any other sign of water. Even though each village was near a water course, these tributaries of the Niger were all dry now. There would be no more water in them until the next rains, still seven or eight months away. The water table is very deep, and locally made unlined wells had a habit of caving in, I was told, especially in the wet season. The project hoped that the efficient low-technology wells would be copied by other villages.

Strong lightweight donkey carts were being sold to the villagers by the project to encourage them to bring any surplus produce into Tamou to sell, and so obtain a little cash for medicine, clothing and the like. It was thought to be important not to encourage an over-dependence on handouts, so the carts were paid for with young goats and millet. The goats were then used to improve stocks in other villages. All morning bewildered bleating animals were being loaded into our truck in one village, and unloaded in another. Sometimes they were so frightened by the experience they wound their halters into inextricable knots, nearly throttling one another, and having to be cut free in a hurry. Fortunately we managed to unship them all before the long ride back, finishing up instead with more manageable sacks of millet, and two huge water melons to sell for their owners in Tamou.

In all the villages the background noise to our visit was the thump thump of pestles in the tall wooden mortars, as bare-breasted women went about their eternal task of pounding millet. As many as three of four women could be swinging their long round-ended poles up and down into a single mortar, never losing a beat and taking full advantage of the slight recoil. The youngest of them was often no more than eight years old. Any woman over twenty had hands already deformed from the hard relentless task which was every female's lot for several hours a day. Close to the villages were many of the strange baobab trees which at first sight look as though they are growing upside down, their roots reaching up towards the sky. In contrast to all the other green trees their branches were completely bare, as they had just been harvested. Baobab leaves, made into a sticky, slimy sauce and eaten with the pounded, boiled millet, is the staple diet of the people of the Sahel, a dish which to my shame I was never able to get down.

Poor as these villages were, some of them were hosts to Fulani nomads, who were camped beside them. These people, as distinct from their more settled relatives, still wandered in a great yearly circle with their flocks and herds. They cultivated no land themselves, but villages like these welcomed the nomads' animals onto their newly harvested fields to manure the ground while they ate up the stalks. The villagers paid the nomads in millet for this service, and when they stopped paying, the herds were moved on. The Fulani are a more slender people than the Gomanche, finer featured, and lighter skinned, and their women move with a willowy stateliness. Apart from their flocks, their possessions appeared even sparser than those I was carrying – a few calabashes for milk, a plaited line or two along which the young animals were tethered while their mothers grazed the fields, and tents which were no more than beds raised off the ground, with a sparse canopy to cover them. Though life teetered on the very brink of survival for everyone here, that of the Fulani had an air of romance about it. It was substantially the life lived by the patriarchs of Old Testament times, and after surviving for so many centuries the very idea that it might soon come to an end because of the pressures of the twentieth century gave it great poignancy. There was an air about the Fulani difficult to describe, but lordly was the word that came to mind. It was as though the very tenuousness of their lives gave them some quality of freedom, some kinship with the earth that most of mankind has lost.

# 5

# Mud Huts and Millet Fields

IT WAS A MUCH harder road that took me on towards the town of Say the following day, stony and sandy by turn, and sometimes both together, with ferocious corrugations to add to the problems. I could seldom get Evans even up to eight miles an hour, and was often going far slower. Moreover the first part of the ride was all uphill until I came to the dry Goroubi River, where a shallow downhill stretch was followed by a massive climb, at the top of which I gave up and made tea and wrote up my notes.

Going over the past days' events made me think again about the bush villages I had visited, and the boys and young men in their patchwork rags of modern garments examining the truck, eyeing our clothes. They had no possibility of an education, no likelihood of improving their lot, and yet such is communication in these times that even there, deep in the bush, ideas about the rest of the world filtered through to them. Their lives in consequence must have appeared to many of them as a hopeless trap. In this context it was not difficult to understand the escalating urban drift that was happening all over Africa, and the squalor of shanty towns did not seem quite so dreadful compared with the poverty of life in those small villages.

Say, however, an ancient seat of Islamic learning, was not a town that I would choose to drift to, I thought, as I tried to track down my contact among the dusty rubbish-strewn streets, only to succeed in becoming ever more enmeshed in a cluster of boys demanding '*cadeaux*'. The only restaurant was closed, and since it was not market day, there was no food for sale in the streets. I decided I had better move on to my next contact, in a place called Guéladio, twenty-five miles away. As it was already 3.30 p.m. I had every need to hurry, so I turned my back on my anticipated reunion with the Niger, which touches the eastern edge of Say, and set off westward along the valley of the Goroubi, which I had crossed a little earlier.

It was a much more beautiful route than the one I had followed so far that day, and more populated; an area of gently undulating hills, with villages every two or three miles, and lots of people working in the fields or walking beside the road. The brightly dressed women, bedecked with beads, coins and cowrie shells, often had a large old silver coin hung dead centre on the forehead. It seemed a shame to be rushing through, especially as the people seemed so friendly and called out to me as I passed, but I knew I wouldn't make it to Guéladio before nightfall unless I kept going, and I had no lights on the bicycle. Even so I was able to pick up the local greeting from hearing it so often, and instead of '*Bonjour*' could soon call back the Djerma greeting of '*Fo fo*' or '*Ng Gwiya*' which sounded altogether more satisfactorily African.

The first and only truck I met was driven by my prospective host, an elderly American Peace Corps volunteer named Aaron. He had been summoned to the prefecture at Say in order to have his vehicle 'borrowed' for the forthcoming elections at the weekend, a 'courtesy' extracted from all Westerners in the area unless they could find a way out of it. Seeing a strange Western woman bicycling towards him, Aaron stopped, realizing that I must be coming to visit him, and he kindly passed me the key to his hut and told me to make myself at home. At that point I still had fifteen miles to go and the sun was visibly sinking. Fortunately the surface was not too bad and with the wind behind me I sped on, reaching Guéladio at 6 p.m. very tired, very dirty and starving hungry, but glad to have arrived before dark.

It is never easy to orientate oneself in a strange house, but when that house is a thatched round mud hut made of clay spread over a timber frame, and is in the centre of a dark compound, with little that one would recognize as modern conveniences, it has grave inherent problems. A stiff tot of my precious store of whisky was necessary to get me started, after which I located the hurricane lamps and the calor gas and had both lit in no time. Half a packet of chicken noodle soup and a tin of Moroccan sardines was not exactly a sumptuous spread, but with some stale bread Aaron had said I might have, it certainly filled a hole that had been growing steadily larger since daybreak.

By wandering around the edge of the large compound I tracked down the bathing arrangements, which consisted of a jug and a bucket of water housed behind a mud brick wall in a corner, adjacent to a cunningly constructed lavatory seat, poised over a deep pit. As I took my bath under the stars, pouring the welcome water carefully so that it trickled slowly down from the crown of my head to my ankles, washing away the accumulated sweat and the red streaked dust, I could hear the sounds of the village all around – the pounding of pestles, the bleating of animals penned for the night, conversation, laughter and drumming. The flames of cooking fires made pools of flickering light in the darkness, and the high-pitched voices of children running from one patch of light to another reflected their excitement at the descent of the African night. It made me remember my own childhood, and playing out after dark when there were no street lights to veil the magic.

My host appeared at around 9 p.m., having managed to keep his vehicle from the clutches of the governor's electioneering. The gas had just run out, the paraffin in the lamps was failing, and I could barely keep my eyes open for exhaustion. Aaron insisted that I should take the only bed while he shacked down on a camping mat on the floor, and I was much too tired to protest.

It wasn't until the morning light began to filter in that I was able to appreciate to the full the unusual nature of my accommodation. From the outside the little thatched hut was no different from all the others surrounding it in the small township. Inside was a wholly different matter. Printed calico curtains and pelmets framed rude glassless window holes. College pennants, posters, and printed homilies about the needs of the Third World hid the mud walls. There were doilies on the crates and packing cases that did service as furniture, and rag mats on the bare earth floor. Ornaments, framed photographs, and knick-knacks were displayed on every available surface, so that it was difficult to move about without knocking things over. In spite of the dust that drifted in ceaselessly, and spread in a gritty film over everything, Aaron had created a fussy little suburban interior, exotic in the extreme in a place where every other home contained nothing whatever that was not strictly functional, and precious little of that. I was not surprised to learn that Aaron found it difficult to enjoy any privacy. His neighbours were always wandering in, ostensibly for a chat, but all the time their eyes were darting round and round the room, resting with incredulity upon all these riches, while they spat reflectively and repeatedly on the floor. Understandably, one of Aaron's priorities was the building of a loggia in his compound at some distance from the house, where all these guests could congregate and spit away to their heart's content, but I didn't think the idea would find much favour with his neighbours.

Aaron was on the point of departing to Niamey for a conference, so I had only a short time to enjoy his company and to learn what had brought him out to Africa at an age when most of his contemporaries were enjoying retirement. He had been a gardener in Maine, he told me, when President Kennedy had started the Peace Corps, and he and his wife had been so inspired by its aims and ideals that they had decided they would both apply to join after their children had grown up. Sadly his wife had died before that time, and Aaron was doing his stint alone, trying to set up vegetable gardens, to promote better standards of hygiene, and generally fostering understanding between the two cultures. I don't know how far he was succeeding in any of these activities – change is a slow process in Africa – but judging from the way many of the people of Guéladio came to the hut after he had left to ask when he was returning, and to express their fears that I might have been sent to replace him, he seemed to be valued, where other, younger volunteers were often merely tolerated. His age was certainly a help in a country where grey hairs are honoured, but I think his success sprang from the fact that he was a deeply religious man, in a simple and functional way. He was motivated not only by a desire to help those less fortunate than himself, but also by a genuine belief in the equality and worth of all men, a belief which I was coming to realize was a good deal rarer than might be supposed in this sort of work.

Aaron offered me the use of his hut until his return, in order that I could see more of the area. I was also to have the services of Bouba, his right-hand man, a youth who would not have lasted long, I felt, with anyone less tolerant, for he was far more interested in establishing his position as privileged confidante than in getting on with what he was paid to do – like watering the plants, and chasing the marauding goats out of the compound before they ate the last few sorry stumps of the newly planted trees. But in one respect he was the ideal companion for me because he had a great passion for riding Aaron's mountain bike, and knew all the paths through the bush. He seized happily on Aaron's idea of escorting me to the neighbouring town of Torodi for market day and we set off on one of the most exhilarating rides I was to have in the Sahel.

Relieved of the luggage, Evans showed his paces, and made me almost a match for the strong young Bouba mounted on the lesser machine. We rode in single file along narrow paths that twisted and turned between fields and in and out of trees, plunging into shallow rocky ravines and around the sides of little hills. Only where the paths had degenerated into deep, soft sand did Bouba gain a decided advantage on his wider tyres, but I was quite content to ride behind where I could spare more attention for the scenery. It was essentially the same dry landscape as I had been riding through for days, a symphony of ochreous shades, with sudden bursts of colour where a man walked through the fields in a bright robe or a red shirt. Millet fields stretched away on every side, all harvested, and some-times with goats and cattle browsing on the stalks. Villages appeared far more frequently than in the area I had seen with Paul, and appeared to be marginally more prosperous. The most noticeable difference was the more intensive cultivation, and the erosion it was bringing in its wake, the soil in many places turning into fine sand.

The closer we came to Torodi the more thronged the paths

became, with people converging on the market from all sides. Soon we were forced to dismount and become part of a procession that had all the richness of a medieval pageant. Another bicycle was being wheeled alongside, great bunches of bright guinea fowl hanging head down from the handlebars, all alive and squawking. On the other side a young man, one of many cutting a dash in a western suit of unusual flamboyance, led a single goat on a string, picking up its hooves as daintily as a poodle in a Parisian park. A donkey came nudging along behind, with the round-eyed children of nomads riding in baskets strapped to its sides. Little boys in ragged earth-coloured tunics kept well to the periphery, balancing large sections of woven fencing on their heads, their eyes swivelling in all directions to take in the scene, without moving a muscle that would unship their cumbersome loads.

The wealth of colour concentrated in the market was dazzling. No matter how poorly dressed the children might be – or naked as often as not – the women all wore gorgeous patterned robes or long wrap-round skirts and tops in strong contrasting colours, with matching cloths tied in extravagant shapes around their heads. Most of the older men had crocheted cotton caps or pill box hats, and long plain-coloured gowns, though a few wore robes as vibrantly patterned and coloured as those of their womenfolk. The vendors sat so closely packed on mats on the ground with their few items of sale spread out before them that it was difficult to find a path through. Above them were other mats, raised on poles, to protect them and their goods from the sun.

Although there seemed to be a wide variety of things for sale, from car tyres, pots of vaseline and brylcreem, to tiny little piles of bright red peppers and bunches of dried herbs, there was curiously little that I could find to buy. I had almost exhausted the small supply of food I had set out with, and would have been glad of almost any kind of fruit and vegetables, but even though these were so plentifully available in Niamey, only forty miles away, here they were unobtainable. Most of the food was sold either live on the hoof or the wing, or else it took the form of grain, or the 'condiments' – all sorts of leaves, powders, berries, spices and peppers to accompany the unending diet of millet. My sole purchases were a kilo of groundnuts which I reckoned was likely to become my staple fare in the Sahel, a few tiny onions, and four shrivelled limes.

The long trek through the bush to Torodi and back had proved exhausting, and I planned to spend the following morning sitting by the hut door, writing up my notes and browsing through Aaron's few books. This plan was foiled by importunate small boys and bold young women who studied me over the compound fence, jumping up and down and lifting each other up the better to see. It was impossible to ignore them, because they went on shouting until I answered their '*Fo fo's*', and then, delighted by my response, they started shouting again to elicit another. It was too hot to retire inside the hut so, seeing I couldn't win, I attempted some sort of conversation, but the girls had no French and were interested only in my few bits of jewellery. They would have had my wedding ring off my finger in a trice, together with the gold cross and chain from around my neck, had I let them. Since it was impossible to work I wandered around the town with the little boys who were far less predatory.

Guéladio was a collection of 'concessions', dirt compounds in various states of decrepitude, roughly fenced with matting walls, and intersected by narrow rubbish-strewn alleyways. Some concessions were large and contained several huts, some were so small they were not even fenced, just a bit of open ground with some sort of rough shelter that was home for as many as a dozen people. What really improved the look of any concession was the number of trees growing in it, in the shade of which the daily tasks could be carried out. In towns, just as in the bush, life was essentially an outdoor existence, and, apart from the wet season, huts were used only for storage and for sleeping in. There were no 'services' of any kind, not even standpipes for water; that had to be carried in from the remaining pools in the river, or from a number of rather suspect wells on the outskirts of town. Very few of the children attended the tiny school, about one in thirty it was reckoned, and none of them girls. The only sign of progress was the newly-built co-operative, a huge modern shed with just a dozen sacks of millet in it, and a boutique attached, stocked with six pairs of plastic flip flops, a few boxes of matches, some pens, and nothing else that I could see.

Near the centre of town was a small fenced space which I gathered was the mosque. However, I do not think there can have been many practising Moslems in Guéladio, for not only was I spared any 4 a.m. call to prayer, but Bouba told me that the chief had thirty wives, and that the other men had as many as they could afford, whereas Moslems are strictly limited to a maximum of four.

Most of the adults were away from the town during the daylight hours, tending their fields and their animals, gathering firewood, fetching water and attending to the hundred and one things that keep a self-sufficient people busy. Bouba's friends, however, seemed to enjoy unlimited leisure. They flocked into the hut, endlessly making cups of coffee, and picking up any item that caught their fancy, even if it happened to be the book I was reading. Again I gave up the struggle, and went out in the hottest part of the afternoon and walked for a few miles through an unpeopled land-scape until I found a place to rest, in the shelter of a band of thin trees, on the edge of extensive millet fields.

The dry stony ground was sprinkled with hard black dung and there was scarcely a stalk left to tempt even goats. But in spite of these signs of cultivation, it seemed in no way a domestic landscape. From where I sat the land stretched out vast and alien, a seemingly-endless arid savannah, with considerably fewer trees than I had seen on the first day's ride. Over it all blew a strong dry searing wind from the north, a harmattan that comes from the Sahara Desert. It was well over a hundred in the shade, but the sun was not fierce enough to need dark glasses, and the shadows lacked any hard edge because of the quantities of dust in the air. I could almost feel the moisture being drawn not only out of my body, but out of the land itself.

The agronomists and land conservationists I had met in Niamey had nearly all expressed the opinion that Niger was in a desperate state, that man and nature had finally combined to destroy these marginal lands beyond all hope of recovery. The last decades had brought drought so severe to the Sahel that for the first time in its history the River Niger had for a while ceased to flow. Natural disaster had combined with a population explosion that made it necessary to plant every available acre, and to keep planting, without any respite for the exhausted land. The inevitable erosion that followed such destructive husbandry could only be halted by a complete change of policy, but the desperate needs of increasing numbers of hungry bellies made nonsense of attempts to introduce such revolutionary ideas as contour ploughing, fallow fields and the like. Few of the experts could see any possible long-term future for a country in which the erosion was already so widespread. The spectre they raised was one of wholesale migration.

I was to hear these doom-laden prognostications about Niger's future again and again, both from foreigners and from Nigeriens themselves. One urbane ex-minister said quite seriously 'This country is finished, they will have to find us some other place to go'. And there, it seemed, was the nub of the problem. In earlier times when periods of drought had destroyed pastures and dried up the wells, people had been able to move on and find other areas for their herds to graze, other places to cultivate. The land left to itself before it had been totally exhausted was then able to lie fallow until the cycle of drought was ended, and was able to renew its fertility. But now the population has grown to the point where there isn't anywhere else to go, and the delicate balance between cultivators, nomads and the land itself has been irrevocably broken. In the desperate and losing battle to feed the rapidly increasing numbers more and more of the marginal land of the Sahel has come under cultivation. The empty rolling scrubland that has pastured the flocks and herds of the nomads for generations beyond reckoning is being swallowed up at a galloping rate. As the trees are cut down and the bushes are grubbed out, as repeated ploughing causes the topsoil to slide down the hillsides and be washed away in the rains, the fierce drying wind blows through what is left and completes the process. The newly-coined and dreaded word *desertification* exactly describes the process – the land is being changed into a desert from within.

While I sat there mulling over these dark prophecies the late afternoon began that sharp acceleration that occurs only in the tropics, bringing a sudden change in temperature, the biblical 'cool of the evening' before night finally falls, and I could feel my heart lifting in response. Suddenly through the empty landscape strings of people were appearing from nowhere, wending their way towards shelters of woven grass that were dotted inconspicuously about the edges of the fields. I wondered if these were perhaps temporary dwellings, like the summer sheilings the Highlanders of Scotland had once used. Women with silver bangles on their arms and ankles, towering stacks of vessels balanced upon their heads, and children at their heels were approaching me along the ribbon-like paths. I found myself slipping a coin into a woman's hand for no reason other than that it seemed suddenly so wonderful that life did still exist in this dry place. It was out of happiness, not pity that I gave, and the small gift was accepted with a brief gesture of thanks, palms pressed together. The women clustered around me, but without the boisterousness of the girls in the town. It was as though the small gift had ended that side of things; no one expected anything further from me, or I from them for that matter. We could just stand there quite naturally, satisfying our curiosity about each other, simply enjoying the meeting. Without any common language they ascertained that I had come from Guéladio and was on my way back there, before they drifted on.

The whole exchange had taken only minutes, and yet for the first time I felt I had made some genuine contact with the people of the country, and my sense of happiness expanded. Inevitably a traveller is cast in the role of the stranger, someone on the outside looking in. Occasions like this, when for a brief moment the barriers and divisions are down, and one is accepted simply as another human being, are rare and very special.

The last thing I saw as I wandered back was a father bathing his young son beside an isolated hut, carefully pouring the water over the small gleaming body. Goodness knows how far that water had been carried, in a day that could have provided little leisure, and now it was being poured over the child like a libation. It was a scene that symbolized for me the extraordinary strength of the human

family to endure against formidable odds, and it added immeasur-
ably to my newly realized happiness, so that I was suddenly conscious
again, as I had been when I first saw the Niger, of how glad I was
to be in Africa.

# 6

# Taking to the River

WITH THE AID OF A tarmac road and a great desire to make up for many missed meals, I rode the forty-five miles from Guéladio in fine style, and was back in Niamey in time for a late buffet lunch at the Grand Hotel. I felt it was appropriate to celebrate the fact that nothing had gone wrong on this first excursion through the bush, but in any case, if you were really hungry the buffet at the Grand was one of the best bargains in town, as you could have as much and as many helpings as you liked. It was quite a while before I felt that all my hollows had been adequately filled.

I had a further ten days to spend in Niamey before I set off on my next trip, which was to be in the Aïr Massif, in the far north-east of the country. Four-fifths of Niger are part of the Sahara, and among the vast sandy wastes are several mountain ranges whose oases continue to serve the same purpose for travellers and nomads as islands do for voyagers on the high seas. The Aïr Massif is one of these great islands among the drifting dunes, home for some of the last of Niger's Tuareg nomads who are still clinging to their traditional way of life after the disastrous droughts of the seventies destroyed the majority of their herds, and, incidentally, created an army of night watchmen to guard the homes of the aid workers who had come to help in the wake of the catastrophe. Together with the Ténéré Desert, which lies beyond it, the Aïr Massif is reputedly among the most beautiful areas of the world. I longed to see it, but it was very far from the route I would be following to

Timbuktu, so again I would need to make a separate excursion there from Niamey, and I had been puzzling about how I could do this in the time I had available.

The difficulty was resolved unexpectedly while I was having tea on the terrace with my friend Abou one morning, and a friend of hers who organized tours to the Aïr happened to pass by. Mano Dayak is himself a Tuareg and proud of the nomadic traditions of his people, which was perhaps why he was intrigued by my bicycle travels through his country, and he promptly invited me to join a tour of the Aïr which he was arranging for friends. An offer from another of Abou's friends in Air Niger, of an air lift for the 700 mile journey to Agadez, from where the tour would start solved the problem of how to get there and back.

There was no worry about where to leave Evans while I was away, because I was now staying at the residence of the American Ambassador, having very kindly been invited to come and make use of the library and enjoy a little luxury before the rigours of the onward journey. The air conditioning, and the high security bars, floodlights and armed guards might have made me nostalgic for the simplicity of the Catholic Mission at times, but it was an ideal stronghold for a vulnerable bicycle.

Life on the plateau, where the French had originally built their colonial capital of wide tree-lined boulevards, gave me quite a different view of Niamey. Here I was rubbing shoulders with those for whom Niger, one of the poorest countries in the world, was a land of opportunity – largely people from the upper echelons of the many different international agencies that dispensed aid to Niger. Many were Americans, former Peace Corps people who had found their way into lucrative posts by being in the right place at the right time, but nearly all western nationalities were present in some capacity. There were also the foreign businessmen and contractors, mostly French, and the staff of the various embassies and consulates, among which Britain was not represented, but Libya was. Libya, in fact, was in the process of building a very splendid ambassadorial complex in close proximity to the American Embassy.

Compared with the standard of living enjoyed by foreigners,

Nigeriens of a similar status – government ministers and the like – existed at a far lower level, in meaner houses on narrower, unpaved streets. It was much the same in the foreign businesses, where there was a marked disparity between the salaries of indigenous employees and those of expatriates in equivalent positions. There appeared to be a limit set in these companies, above which no Nigerien could rise. More than once it was pointed out to me that colonial exploitation was not a thing of the past, but was continuing under another guise. On the other side, I was constantly hearing that the problems of the country were caused by the Nigeriens' inherent lack of organisation, and by their craving for the material advantages of the West without working for them. I rode my daily round now between several different worlds, invited to tea here, lunch there, a beer on the river, meeting a wide variety of people, and listening to contrasting opinions about the country I had come to see.

Even with so many new friends, and with the Ambassador's excellent books about the Sahel to peruse, I wasn't content to wait in Niamey until it was time to leave for the Aïr Mountains. From my bedroom window at the Residence, beyond the floodlights and the permanently watered lawns, I could see the Niger spread out below, huge, brown and inviting. I had not yet been out on it, or even dabbled a foot in it, but the more I saw of it the more I longed to do both, and I wondered if I could stretch my funds to the extent of hiring one of the slender native dugouts known as a pirogue for a few days, and make a journey downstream. The Ambassador's wife, Jackie, sounded out the man who normally took her guests out for short trips, but he proved much too expensive, and it was once again while I sat drinking tea with Abou that coincidence took a hand.

Among the many young men who plagued the customers to buy their wares on this particular day was a young Hausa who handed us a scrap of paper on which was a message in rather crude English to the effect that the bearer owned a pirogue, and was willing to take people out for trips on the river. Someone else had written it for him, as he himself had no English, but with Abou in charge of the bargaining he soon agreed a price of about £75 for a four-day voyage down to the W bend and back. This seemed an inordinately high payment in a country where the yearly income of an average family was reckoned to be well below £200, but even so it was still appreciably less than the usual tourist price.

At Abou's insistence we went off to make sure that the boat at least existed – something I would not have thought of. Neither Abou nor I were at all reassured about the young man's trust-worthiness, even after being shown a small, rather battered pirogue, but as I wasn't paying him anything in advance I didn't think I had much to lose. It was arranged that he would provision the boat, provide something for me to sit on, and be ready with his partner to set off early in the morning in two days time. Having made the decision, I stopped worrying about all the things that could go wrong, and instead began to look forward to a restful pleasant jaunt, being punted silently down river in the wake of Mungo Park, though hopefully avoiding that intrepid explorer's final watery demise.

The gear I needed for the river trip was transported to the landing place by Sarah, an American aid worker friend who had herself made a long trip downriver not long before. The young Hausa, Amadou, was clearly glad to see us arrive: he had not trusted me any more than I had trusted him. The difference was that I had worked on the principle of getting everything ready just in case, whereas he had done nothing in the way of preparation.

The small pirogue, about eighteen feet long and three feet wide, was like a cross between a punt and a dugout canoe, and lay bleached and leaking, among the reeds in a small muddy creek. It was quite bare of anything except a broken paddle and a long bent pole. Just give him half an hour, Amadou assured us, and everything would be ready. Unconvinced, Sarah took a hand, going over the same ground as Abou had done when the arrangements were first made – 'Did he know the river? Did he really think he could make the fifty miles down to the W bend and back in four days? Surely that was impossible?' But questions like these were useless with Amadou, and only made him sullen. Of far more help was her organization of the boat, something she certainly seemed to know more about than he did. The 'partner', a nice-looking Malian youth named Omarou, who was waiting shyly in the background, was sent for a load of grass to place on the flat floor of the pirogue amidships, and the mat which Sarah had thoughtfully brought along was placed on top of this for me to sit on. Most of my camping gear was in a rucksack which she had also lent me, and with this behind my back, lodged up against a thwart, and with her wide-brimmed straw hat in place of the missing awning, she thought I should be reasonably comfortable for the fourteen or so hours I could expect to be afloat each day – not that she was convinced that the trip would last as long as a day. Her estimation of Amadou as a 'nasty little jerk' who knew next to nothing about boats or the river, showed a fine degree of perspicacity, but she was reckoning without my great longing to be on the Niger, which would have enabled me put up with far worse than Amadou.

It was the lack of provisions that I found worrying. The ambassador's wife had very kindly organized my food supplies, providing a large basket of American-style 'goodies' which even included paper plates, plastic knives and forks and napkins, all of which gave promise of elegant little picnics, in charming contrast to the general rough nature of the trip. But I was only the passenger; it was the crew that would need adequate sustenance for the hard work ahead, and as yet they had assembled none of the promised stores and had nothing except two sleeping mats, a couple of cotton cloths, and a change of clothing. Amadou said they could buy food on the way, something I had severe doubts about after my experiences in the bush, and Sarah confirmed that there was nothing at all to be had in the riverside villages. In the initial bargaining, Amadou had demanded a sum of money for their food in addition to the price for the trip, and I now offered to pay this in advance, in case it was lack of funds that prevented them stocking up here in Niamey where everything was available at the cheapest prices, but to my surprise the offer was refused; he was not short of money, he asserted arrogantly.

In what was to prove the pattern of the trip, Omarou was again sent running; this time to the nearest street market, to return in half

an hour covered in sweat but carrying very little except a small bag
of flour and a packet of cigarettes. We then set off immediately,
with the perspiring Omarou wielding the long bent pole from the
platform at the rear of the little pirogue, while Amadou sprawled
in the front, doing nothing at all, and earning a last incredulous gasp
of disbelief and censure from Sarah who stood there, growing
rapidly smaller as the flood carried us away downstream.

It soon transpired that, except for a little bailing, Amadou had
no intention of working at all on this voyage. He was, he said, a
businessman who had hired both the pirogue and the services of
Omarou. Now all that was arranged, it was his job to sit back like
a tourist, and to keep me company. My protest that the agreement
had been for the services of two boatmen, and that both were needed
if we were to arrive at our objective, earned only the promise that
he would help on the return journey against the current, when I
would see what a fine boatman he was, and in preparation for this
effort he must rest now.

Very soon he launched into an account of his sexual prowess with
older white women, at the same time attempting to appropriate the
map, the binoculars and the bird book, all with the greatest show
of familiarity. There was no question of him pretending to be
attracted to me, he was simply letting me know that he had no
objection to playing the gigolo should I wish. Having finally been
persuaded that it was a boat trip and not a young black lover that
I wanted, and that his approaches would lead nowhere – not an easy
matter as he had a fine regard for his own worth – he changed tack
and began a lengthy discourse on why I should pay double the
amount already agreed for the journey, a subject to which he would
return several times a day.

In a land where chances for young men are so pitifully few, and
where disaster is ever ready to pounce, it was impossible totally to
condemn his buoyant optimism and his determination to succeed –
but only in retrospect. At the time I found him unpleasant and
irritating in the extreme, especially as it was not only gain that
motivated him, but an insatiable need to dominate every situation.
He was a young man who had cut himself off from his own culture

in order to embrace Western values and attitudes of which he had only the vaguest understanding, and that from a purely material point of view. He had put himself in a situation in which he could not win, since the role he had chosen only made him look ridiculous.

When he became impossibly impertinent or annoying I found the only way to shut him up was to threaten to abandon the trip immediately without paying anything, and to start packing up my gear to show that I meant it. This would bring on a spell of sullen non-communication, and give me some welcome peace to enjoy the scenes of the river. But his natural resilience meant that these silences never lasted quite long enough.

We headed downstream, mostly hugging the east bank of the river out of the main flow. Fishing hawks, black-headed ibis, herons and cattle egrets were busy in their various territories. Scores of black and white kingfishers were hovering mid air in their marvellous fishing posture: bodies arched almost in two, with touchingly disproportionate beaks pointing down towards the surface of the water and wings in rapid motion above them, until, like an arrow, they were onto a fish and up with it and away in a flash. The river itself was immensely wide, golden-brown, and not sparkling exactly but holding the light richly, like thick bottle glass lit from behind. A low rocky escarpment on the west bank swept down to the river in steep striated cliffs, while on our side were flat green fields of coarse grass and large spreading trees.

We stopped under one of these trees at midday, and again it was Omarou who did all the work of tying up, spreading out the mats and unloading the things to make lunch. He and Amadou sat some distance away and the sharp-eyed Amadou, who had already made himself familiar with just about everything I had with me, begged a cardboard plate so that he could mix up the flour Omarou had bought that morning with some water scooped up in their hands from the river. The resulting porridge looked unappetizing, but Omarou had poled for hours and he wolfed down what Amadou left for him and then stretched out and fell asleep.

After lunch the supply of cigarettes which the young men had been puffing away at the whole morning was exhausted, so we stopped at a small village to get more. A small boy was peremptorily summoned and sent running on this errand, and we stayed in the boat among a sudden plague of flies that seethed over the dark smelly mud of the landing place. Women up to their knees in the water thumped their washing on stones, and small skinny girls scoured pots among a flotilla of ducks who hung about hoping for scraps. The little girls chatted like old gossips as they scrubbed, without for a moment interrupting the flow of their work. Some of the pans were aluminium replicas of the three-legged pot-bellied iron cauldrons traditionally associated with the boiling of missionaries. They were deeply blackened by the fire but the competent little girls, some no more than eight or nine, restored them to a state of gleaming cleanliness with handfuls of grit and mud from the river bank. When they had finished their scouring, they waded further out to rinse the pots in cleaner water, and then filled them to the brim, and with the help of another child raised the heavy load onto their heads, stiffening their slender necks to take the strain, before walking away straight-backed, the water overflowing and splashing them as they went.

By late afternoon we had reached Kolo, a large village only half way to Say. It was clear now that there was no possibility of getting down to the W bend and back in four days; in fact, at this rate we would be lucky to cover half that distance. When I put this to Amadou he seemed unmoved by his perfidy, and announced calmly that Kolo was where he had intended to stop for the night, as he had a girlfriend there. We could stay at her house, and then he could bring her with us for the rest of the trip – no doubt to give him something to do.

Another of my attempts at being very angry in French got us past Kolo and the girlfriend, at which point all our energies were directed at changing course as the wind had started to make things uncomfortable on the east bank. For the first time that day Amadou wielded the broken paddle as we made diagonally across the fast-flowing choppy river, the wind piling up the water into steep waves that had me furiously bailing to keep pace with it pouring in through the spaces between the gunwale and the slab sides. We passed a fishing village on an island half way across, and could relax for a welcome respite in its shelter. Women with babies tied on their backs were flailing grain with sticks, three of them keeping time and changing hands in mid stroke. The babies' heads were turned sideways, flopping backwards and forwards with each stroke.

The second leg of the crossing had us all liberally soaked by the spray, so that whatever else the journey brought, I felt I had now been thoroughly asperged by the waters of the Niger. Had both boys been working the pirogue, taking it in turns to rest, and with an adequate amount of food inside them, we could have continued until about 9 p.m., which was the usual practice of the Niger boatmen. But Omarou was already very tired. I had developed great confidence in him during the day, for young as he was he knew a great deal about pirogues, as was clear from the skill with which he had caulked the worst leaks in our miserable little craft with a handful of grass, and from the way he moved the boat through the water with a lovely economy of effort, swinging the pole up and down, and following through with the weight of his body, all in one flowing movement, maintaining his balance effortlessly. Later I learnt that he had been involved with pirogues since childhood and had worked on them in Mali until, for some reason, he had drifted to Niamey to look for better opportunities, and had fallen in with Amadou. Before this trip it had been some time since he had wielded a pole and his shoulder muscles were hurting badly. He told me these things later when he had overcome his shyness and had remembered enough French to communicate. He also said how much he wanted to go home, and when the trip ended I was happy to give him the money that would get him a lift back on a truck, instead of giving it as a tip to Amadou.

A further problem surfaced once we had made the crossing. It had been agreed that we were to camp at night, the boatmen in the pirogue, and I in my tent. But as evening began to draw on it became clear that my two young men believed that the bush teemed with malignant spirits, and they were scared witless at the notion of sleeping away from human habitation. Amadou confessed ingenuously that he had only agreed to sleep out in order to clinch the deal, and had hoped I would change my mind once we were underway. But in any case they did not have enough with them to be self sufficient, and I had already realized that we would have to find some sort of village where they could be fed and found a shelter to sleep in.

Such a place appeared right at the water's edge at around 6 p.m., when we were all feeling a little subdued and in need of refreshment. It was a small hamlet of four square mud brick houses, with about fifteen adults, a few children and assorted animals. It all looked very charming in the fast-gathering dusk, with the women setting about preparing the evening meal at their open-air fires, the smaller children gathering round in happy anticipation, while the older ones tethered the animals in their places for the night. An old man welcomed me with upraised hands in patriarchal blessing; '*Bon arrivée, bon arrivée.*' His house was my house.

While guinea fowl bumbled clumsily up into the dense-leaved trees overhanging the river, preparing to roost for the night with the maximum of squawking and fuss, I pitched my tent, making sure it was well clear of the heavily limed ground beneath them. It was up in a jiffy, its entrance towards the water across which the rising sun would throw its first beams in the morning, and I sat there in the entrance of the taut little blue nylon dome with the guinea fowl still fussing overhead, delighted to enjoy for a while my own inviolate space. Then I lit the petrol stove and heated up some soup, and the smell of it brought Amadou and Omarou round to help me drink it. Before they could quite finish it all they were called over to one of the cooking fires to eat millet dough with gombo sauce, and I was able to have the rest of my meal in peace.

Not until I had zipped myself into the tent to escape the mosquitos did I quite appreciate how very excellent a shelter it was going to make for this journey. I had chosen it because it looked light and airy with its large expanses of mosquito netting, and because its hooped shape made it freestanding, so that there was no need of pegs, except to stop it being blown away. I hadn't realized that if I used only the inner tent as I was now doing, the mosquito netting would also allow me to see virtually the whole of the night sky, as well as what was going on around. Also, as the netting was black, it acted like a veil, and people couldn't see in except in bright sunlight. Once dusk fell I was almost invisible, and could observe the life of the village without people feeling inhibited by my presence.

I did little watching of anything that night, however, being tired out with sitting all day in the sun, and with the emotional strain of coping with the perfidious Amadou. He and Omarou had gone off on their perpetual quest for cigarettes, which they seemed to be able to buy only in twos and threes. The families sat on around their fires talking and laughing softly. Somewhere there was singing, and a drum was beating, as seems always to be the case in Africa, and I fell asleep with that thought in my mind, and with the huge panorama of brilliant stars throbbing in harmony with the beat.

It was a sleep punctated by minor interruptions of scratchings and scurryings, as little creatures like frogs and mice went about their nocturnal business. Each time I surfaced, I was conscious of how glad I was to have exchanged the air-conditioning, the bars and the floodlights of the Residence for starlight, the smell of the river, and these little visitors. Once I was assured that none of them were actually finding their way into the tent, I could pull the sleeping bag up closer around my ears to counter the faint chill in the air, and go to sleep again, feeling all the more snug and content. When I opened my eyes to the day, it was before the sun had quite risen above the opposite bank; a magical morning, the river flat calm, the air cool and fresh like a perfect May day in England.

My hopes of getting breakfast over before the boys arrived were not realized. Amadou was there begging for the 'rest of your coffee to give us strength' before I had even taken the first sip. By 7.30 we were under way, with every stump or rock that offered a perch bearing its solitary heron or little knot of egrets, each poised with concentrated purpose above its fishing ground. Slender wading birds with long delicate bills stalked the shallows, one backward-bent angular leg always hesitating in the middle of each deliberate, elongated stride. By 8.45 the wind was blowing from the north-east, fluffing up the surface into a jumble of little waves. A variety of hawks and kites were now quartering the skies, and the little birds had grown wary. There was a sudden commotion as a fishing eagle grabbed something from the water that looked like an eel or a small snake. He dropped it again almost immediately, and then plunged back after it, joined now by a scrum of other predators.

We stopped at ten at a horrible landing place full of rubbish, where there was no protection from the fierce off-shore wind blowing grit continuously over the boat. Amadou and Omarou went off to look for supplies, and I forgot the discomfort of the situation in watching what seemed to be a school of children at their ablutions. They rubbed the river water around their faces in a circular motion, like a cat washes its face, and finished off by squeezing the last drops from their noses between thumb and fore-finger. Afterwards they carried water in heavy galvanized pails to some distant gardens, rakes and hoes in one hand, while the other supported the pail.

My companions reappeared after forty-five minutes with a Nescafé tin of oil which they said was to mix with flour, a packet of biscuits, and a greasy paper of dough balls. It was their first food of the day apart from the American popcorn and bits and pieces I had been giving them, and they fell upon the dough balls ravenously. But it was cigarettes they really craved, and of these they could never seem to find enough. We stopped at village after village where small boys were ordered off on the search, and as often returned empty-handed, at which Amadou grew increasingly morose and unpleasant.

By now I was quite resigned to not reaching the W bend. The river itself and the life upon, above and around it was all so fascinating that it was sufficient just to be there, going nowhere in particular. By lunchtime we were at Say, the town I had passed through without much pleasure on my way back to Niamey. Here the waterfront was especially colourful, for we had arrived at a time of day when a wider spectrum of the life lived on the river's fringes had come to bathe, to wash something, or just to drink. Strings of oxen were threading their way between the beached pirogues, their hooves stirring up the mud; some were already standing ruminating knee-deep, with gently swishing tails. Donkeys drank cautiously at the edge, reluctant, it seemed, to get their hooves wet. Foraging ducks rooted about upside down inside porridge-encrusted cauldrons that had been placed in the shallows to soak. Fat babies covered in soapy suds were being dipped beneath the surface again and again to rinse them off, no one taking the slightest notice of their heartbreaking howls. Solitary men bathing in the deeper water squeezed their genitals modestly between their thighs as they rose gleaming and squirting out water between their teeth like so many fountains. Everywhere were young girls who, I was now convinced, conducted the whole of their complicated social exchanges standing in the river, the ones nearest me showing off a little for my benefit until restored to propriety by a sharp word from the women. Small poke-shaped plastic bags of blue detergent were adding their quota to the soupy mixture around the flat laundry stones, where women who were not washing babies and toddlers were pounding clothes. For the women too, it seemed that the time spent in the Niger was the high spot of their day. Apart from the few adult men bathers and very small boys, the river's edge was a predominately female world.

Mutiny broke out in the afternoon in direct proportion to the distance we put between ourselves and Say. Possibly Amadou had another girlfriend there, but in any case, both young men clearly preferred the town to the bush, and hoped to persuade me to stay close enough so that they could spend the evening there. For my part I wanted to get as far as possible downriver before we turned back, and I certainly didn't want to camp in the outskirts of Say, so I did my best to resist these latest attempts to manipulate the voyage to their advantage. We did go on, but it was slow, tiring work, with frequent stops for lengthy calls of nature. For the first time on the journey they also decided to heed the inner call to afternoon prayer, and went ashore to make a few perfunctory genuflections. Eventually, when my energy to resist was exhausted, we found an indifferent village in which to camp, and Amadou and Omarou, suddenly full of renewed vigour, disappeared to walk back to Say.

Returning upriver was quite a different experience, because we made our way largely through channels in the reed beds which stretched out from the banks for as much as a hundred yards in places. Here the current was almost non-existent and the going much easier. Some of these marshy places grew a sort of rice, with which most of the pirogues we met were loaded high, like floating haystacks. Omarou found his way through hidden channels by following these boats, or by getting shouted instructions from the men cutting on the banks. Every so often we found ourselves in the middle of a spread of huge blue waxen water lilies. It was all as beautiful as could be imagined, and in extraordinary contrast to the complaints of Amadou which grew in volume and extent after he was forced to take up his oar to assist Omarou for the more taxing passages of the return journey. I had given them more than half the food to keep them going, but I had no cigarettes.

Amadou's craving became so acute that before we had found somewhere to stay for the last night, he had withdrawn completely into a sullen shell, communicating with neither of us, and refusing to do anything. I took over his oar to assist the exhausted Omarou, and together we brought the pirogue to a spot where some reed cutters said a track led up to a village. Still Amadou refused to help, so we were obliged to carry all the gear up the escarpment unaided. Many of the villages were built on high ground to be free of the mosquitoes and other winged nuisances that bred on the water. The place we were directed to was hardly a village, just a number of scattered unfenced homesteads set among poor fields on a dry sandy plain. The headman's homestead, where we were to stay, had three grass huts, and one of them, a store-place, was swept out, after which I was urged to go in and inspect it. When I explained that the boys would have the hut and I would pitch my tent, wife number three, a very young pretty girl, was instructed to sweep the ground where I proposed to pitch it. She went over the space backwards, bent double, making neat fan-shaped patterns in the sand with a handful of twigs. Her elderly husband watched closely and only after her third attempt was he satisfied with the result.

As always the transformation of the small limp bundle of nylon into a taut little dome was an occasion that brought everyone from round about running to exclaim with wonder over it. All of them, except for some old cronies, were soon chased off by my host, who had been waiting, it appeared, to practice his English which he had learned on some distant occasion when he had gone to find work in Nigeria. He was delighted to have attracted a suitable audience for what must have been a rare display of his accomplishment. 'You sin,' he said to me, beaming all over his face, and as the look of puzzlement must have crossed my face, he repeated more urgently 'You sin, you sin,' pointing to the descending sun and then to my forearm, by which I realized with relief that he meant only that I was very brown. He continued with his mercifully small repertoire, making every remembered word earn recognition through mime and gesture, and fortunately it covered up the embarrassment over the arrival of Amadou who greeted no one, but rudely pushed straight into the hut.

As darkness fell, and I lay in my tent watching the little family lit by the flickering fire, the scene had a quality of timeless beauty that was almost holy. Behind them a double-trunked palm tree was black against the growing canopy of stars, and a huge white cow that had just wandered into the circle of firelight to be milked loomed above the seated figures, its wide horns curving upwards and inwards so that they almost met in a perfect halo. The three wives and the five small children, who seemed to belong to all of them equally, generated a spirit of quiet contentment and a whole-hearted acceptance of the harsh conditions of their lives, as they prepared the evening meal together, laughing with shared delight when the small baby, whom the patriarch was nursing, shat on his lap, and he clearly didn't know how to cope with the situation.

# 7

# The Aïr Mountains

I CANNOT PRETEND that I did not relish being back in the Residence again after my river excursion, nor enjoy the brief respite from the rigours of Africa. Just to be able to speak my thoughts lucidly, without recourse to circumlocution and mime, was the greatest luxury. But a few days with all the paraphernalia of security and I was again quite ready to exchange all the comforts for a bed under the stars.

The time had now arrived to leave for the Aïr Mountains, and I was waiting only for confirmation of the departure time of the Air Niger flight to Agadez. I felt sure that the trip would be plain sailing compared with the hassles I had experienced on the river, though what inspired this confidence I cannot think, since I had only the vaguest idea about arrangements, and no idea at all about the other members of the party I was to join. But Mano Dayak had struck me as a very capable organizer, and travellers are by their nature optimists. What I had totally left out of consideration was the 'Africa factor' – the law which ensures that anything that can go wrong with arrangements will be certain to do so, particularly when those arrangements concern Westerners full of notions about being in control of their own destiny. Nevertheless, for an airline to go bust on the very day it had been going to fly me up to Agadez did seem a little extreme! The only solution was to go by car – a horrible 700 mile journey on a straight narrow tarmac road, with a heat mirage trembling perpetually on the horizon. This rare sealed highway owed its existence to the discovery of uranium at Arlit, 150 miles beyond Agadez, and the source of Niger's brief spell of prosperity.

Had I been on a bicycle I would doubtless have found some interest and diversity in the journey, but at a constant ninety miles an hour I was aware of nothing but endless featureless scrub, and my hands clutching nervously at the edges of my seat. Halfway there we hit a donkey with a small frantic child on its back, attempting, with flailing feet, to get the creature to move out of the middle of the road. Solid though the shock of the impact felt, it could only have been a glancing blow on the animal's rump, for when I could bring myself to look back I saw that the child was still on the donkey's back, and the small shaggy creature still stood there, immovable, in the middle of the road. What shocked me deeply was that the driver hadn't even attempted to slow down, and his only concern seemed to be that his wing mirror was bent. Later I learnt that if there had been a serious accident, the donkey's owner would have been held responsible, which seemed to be standing reason on its head.

In Agadez, after a few hours' sleep in a claustrophobic, windowless cell in a fly-blown hotel, I was taken to Mano's centre of operations, Temet Tours, a large courtyard packed with desert trucks and littered with items of camping equipment. Around the walls were robed and turbaned men squatting in the dust, patiently making tea while they waited to be employed.

Mano was still in Niamey, but a small voluble Frenchman was in charge and was expecting me. The party I was due to join was now a day and a half ahead, so there was no time to lose, he said, ushering me into the front of a pick-up truck. There was no opportunity to put the many questions I wanted to ask. I had no idea about the route, or where I was supposed to meet up with the others, or even who the others were. All I knew with any degree of certainty was that the two men I was squashed in between were called Ali and Bomba, the driver and the cook, and that neither spoke any tongue with which I was familiar.

We drove off north-eastwards, through the bleak outskirts of Agadez with their tented slums of dispossessed nomads and their malodorous rubbish heaps, and almost immediately found ourselves in the powerful beauty of the Aïr Massif. After that I didn't mind what happened, or where, or with whom I was supposed to be, because once again I was quite content to be exactly where I was. Dark volcanic hills of fantastically jumbled blocks of stone, totally devoid of the smallest scrap of vegetation enclosed flat, bowl-shaped expanses, dividing the pure desert from areas of comparative fertility where scattered acacias held the thin soil, and where herds of camels and goats grazed on tough herbage that would have defeated more selective feeders. Every so often we crossed a dry wadi lined with trees, where a single Tuareg family was encamped, the flies buzzing thickly around their tents. Occasionally I caught glimpses of larger oases, with little tented villages clustered around them.

At noon we stopped in the shade of a tree-hung wadi, and the men quickly collected some of the bone-dry wood which littered the ground, and got a fire going. Bomba unloaded a tin trunk full of cooking things and prepared a meal of macaroni with sardines and tomatoes. He made such vast quantities that there was enough left over to give a large enamel bowlful to a ragged Tuareg child who had been hovering at a respectful distance. Tinned pineapple followed, and as I was already defeated, I gave my share to three children who had been sitting behind a tree taking it in turns to lick out the tin. They were scrupulously fair in the sharing of this unexpected bounty, even offering the occasional lick to the dog they had with them. Afterwards they paid for the treat by cleaning out the cooking pots for Bomba. The meal ended with Tuareg tea, the preparation of which is a lengthy process, enjoyed as much for its own sake as for the small quantity of tea produced. It is brewed in a very small enamel teapot over a tiny charcoal brazier, using finely chopped Chinese leaves, and served in liqueur-sized glasses. The liquid is poured back and forth many times between glass and teapot from a great height, adding sugar, and then heated up again and again, until the degree of strength and sweetness is judged to be right. The ritual is repeated three times, the tea getting weaker with every brewing; traditionally the first bitter glass is for the men, the second for the women, and the third, often with added mint, for the children. Tuaregs can brew tea anywhere, even on the backs of their camels while on the move.

While the men rested and smoked, I wandered over to the tent a little way down the wadi, where the child had taken the remains of our lunch. A young woman was outside, weaving lengths of matting, which seemed to be the main building material for the tents and windbreaks. The tent was held together with rope made from the long spiky leaves of a cactus-like plant, which the woman first cut into thin strips, and then soaked in water before plaiting. The toddlers hanging around her skirts screamed with terror when they saw me coming, but a sugar lump from the store that I had in my pocket soon had them smiling. The woman was light-skinned and rather beautiful, with small even features and a slim body which was shown to advantage in the tight-bodiced dress. She wore quantities of silver jewellery around her neck and arms, and brought more pieces out of the hut, together with the traditional daggers and heavy ornate Agadez crosses. The medieval-style silver crosses are a feature of the region and each of the seven cities of the Tuareg is said to have a slightly different one. I was not pressed to buy anything, and the woman was just as interested in inspecting my far more modest rings, and my plain gold cross and chain.

All afternoon the truck plunged and bucked its way onwards over the tortuous tracks which ran up rocky winding precipices and through deep soft sand by turn. By mid-afternoon the heat was cruel, though it was still only winter, and our sweat mingled, jammed together as we were in the cab. The close contact had the advantage of preventing us from being thrown about too much as the vehicle lurched and twisted. In spite of the rope lashings, Bomba's tin trunk was bounced off the back, and the cooking things spilled all over the track, sugar lumps and macaroni disappearing into the sand. One of the petrol drums sprung a leak and saturated my borrowed rucksack, but fortunately the habit formed through a lifetime with English weather of packing everything in double plastic bags saved my clothes and sleeping bag from ruin. Neither discomfort nor near disaster mattered much, however, compared to the delight and the novelty of everything; there was in one sense little to see, but the extraordinary sense of space gave beauty and significance to every bent and twisted tree, a beauty heightened by the marvellous clarity of the desert air.

The few figures that moved through this stark bright landscape were robed in dark blue, and stood out sharply from the surrounding rock and sand. On their tall camels, with their flocks about them, they were like manifestations of an archaic past – the seed of Abraham spread far from their ancestral lands. Actually, the thought of Abraham was not so inappropriate, because the light-skinned Tuareg people have their origins in the East rather than in Africa. It is assumed that they are of Berber stock, but no one knows their precise origins. There was a time when they were thought to be descendants of a lost army of Crusaders, because of the medieval cut of their robes and weapons, their silver crosses, their war-like demeanour and their notions of chivalry. They were the Lords of the Desert, the much-feared pirates of the Sahara, preying upon the caravan routes that traversed the desert to and from the great trading centres like Timbuktu.

Although the Tuareg were converted to Islam, they have remained very different to other Moslem peoples. Theirs is a matrilineal society, where the women traditionally write poetry and enjoy considerable freedom, even to the extent of sexual relationships before marriage, and the right to divorce their husbands. And unlike any other Moslem people, it is the men who go about with their faces veiled, not the women. Only the eyes are left free of the yards of rich indigo cloth that swathes their heads, adding considerably to the air of romantic mystery that distinguishes Tuareg men. This prized indigo cotton is very dark in appearance, almost black in fact, but the dye is not fast and it leaves a permanent blue stain on faces and hands that has earned for the Tuareg the title of the Blue Men of the Desert. Swathing the head in the Tuareg manner is a very practical protection from the terrible sun and the winds of the Sahara, and many Western desert travellers copy it, but then the effect tends towards the comical, especially when combined with shorts or jeans.

When, centuries ago, the Tuareg moved south into the Sahara,

they enslaved a race of black people, the Bella, who adopted many
of the Tuareg customs, and who continued to till their fields and to
do most of their menial work until the French colonizers attempted
forcibly to free them in the early twentieth century. Many Bella
however found the security of serfdom preferable to the uncer-
tainties of freedom, and continued voluntarily to serve their former
masters for decades after their manumission. In the tragedy that
overtook the Tuaregs in the terrible droughts of the last decades,
the Bella did all they could to aid their former masters. Nothing
however could prevent the wholesale destruction of the great herds
and flocks of the Tuareg, and without their animals they were
doomed. No accurate census has ever been made, but it is reckoned
that after the droughts only the tiniest proportion of the Tuareg
people have been able to continue their traditional way of life. The
rest are scattered throughout the Sahel and beyond, either in refugee
camps or eking out some other sort of subsistence living. To be a
night watchman is a favourite job in the cities because it fits in with
Tuareg notions of bravery, and of what is fitting employment for
a man. There are not nearly enough rich foreigners however to
employ all who join the urban drift, and the rest try to survive by
selling their souvenirs, until it becomes too hopeless and they either
go mad, or end their lives broken-hearted in the refugee camps. It
is an immense tragedy of which the rest of the world remains almost
totally unaware.

A poem written in one of the rare resettlement projects in the
Sahel gives some idea of how the Tuareg see their future:

### The Poem of Tidarmène

If you want me to give you news,
Then we must join hands here
And stop scattering among foreign countries.
We see our comrades leaving, to travel aimlessly,
Leaving sisters and brothers here at the mercy of famine.
I am afraid we will all end our lives like that
On a journey of poverty.
Such a voyage is a bad departure,

And those who leave are like the traveller
Making for Tamanrasset with no sense of direction.
Accompanied by neither friend nor guide,
He embarks on the Sahara without water or food,
And he will find none on the way.
He presses into the desert until his camel
Breaks loose with all the baggage.
At this moment a fierce wind squalls,
The traveller looses all control; helplessly
Crouching to cover his head with a corner of his robe,
He closes his eyes but continues to think:
'What will be become of me? Will I die alone?'

Of the two men accompanying me Bomba, the cook, was Bella, and very dark; Ali, the driver, was a Tuareg and lighter skinned. Both dressed exactly alike in robes, and wore a long length of cloth wound around their heads in the form of a turban, with a fold left loose to cover their mouths and noses when they were not either smoking or eating. Both appeared contented with their work, and I felt very contented to be with them in the undemanding silence, and the sense of companionship that was communicated by a smile (when they were not veiled) or by the wordless pointing out of things of interest.

We drove on through the spacious land until the sun was near to setting. As it sank it flooded the sand in a sea of red, and the dark stone of the hills flamed as though on fire, lemon and red clouds gathering above them. At the same time the green of the foliage cooled and darkened, and the shadows ran swiftly through a myriad of changes between mauve and purple, and it was all over before I could take in the smallest part of it. A lifetime would be far too short for the sunsets of the Aïr.

Before the last shreds of colour had quite disappeared from the sky, we turned off the track into a stand of acacias in a small shallow sandy bowl backed by low hills, and there we made camp. While Ali and Bomba busied themselves with the fire, I took the foam mattress they gave me and found a spot for it some way off under a tree, and suspended the mosquito net over the bed, securing it to a branch. I did not expect to encounter mosquitoes in the desert, but if there were sand flies about I didn't want to wake to find them crawling over my face. Apart from these few arrangements I wasn't allowed to do a thing, but sat on a blanket spread for me by the fire, while Bomba skilfully manipulated the heat under his various pots by pushing the sticks further in or pulling them out, preparing another huge meal, this time of couscous. Girls from a nearby encampment drifted through the firelight like wraiths, with camel's milk to sell, a thin, faintly astringent drink poured in a graceful classical movement from earthenware pitchers.

The night was very cold, the silence punctuated suddenly by the sharp cracks of the fuel drums contracting. The men slept close to the fire wrapped in their blankets, stirring from time to time to put on more wood. I lay awake watching shooting stars falling all around, and it was so bright I could see my breath condensing. I hardly seemed to have slept at all before we were up again, the chill not yet off the day. Bomba stirred the ashes of the fire into life to boil water for me to wash, and then made coffee, serving it with bread and processed cheese and jam – luxury camping indeed.

The sun flooded the desert as we moved off, so that the immensely long shadows of hills and trees shortened visibly as we drove towards them. Out of one such shadow there suddenly erupted a flock of about forty ostriches, huge amazing creatures that raced away towards a rocky corrie at tremendous speed, looking less like birds than some species left over from a previous age. I was lucky to see them in such numbers for they are not plentiful, and though protected by law, the local people rob the nests when they can in order to sell the huge eggs to tourists. Gazelles appeared too from time to time, lovely delicate creatures that exploded into great springing leaps, bounding into the distance on legs that seem far too fragile for their habitat; but clearly they thrive, because I came across their tracks everywhere. Of the far rarer antelope, the adax, for which the area is famous, I saw nothing.

As soon as the sun topped the highest range of hills, the day instantly became very hot. We stopped at the ancient ruins of Asodé, once a famous city and the capital of a great empire, though I didn't learn that until several days later. At the time I was more concerned about a boy of eleven or so who came limping along after me as I wandered among the low square stone-built walls and fallen wooden rafters. He was thin and clad only in a pair of ragged trousers, but he had the partially shaven head and the long plaited braids of a Tuareg noble that I had read about but never seen, since the men's heads were always covered. In his thigh was a deep suppurating hole which he patently was hoping I could heal. All I had with me in the way of first aid was iodine, and I applied some of that and covered the hole to keep the flies out of it, but I cannot think that it helped the poor child much.

Soon afterwards I began to suspect that we were catching up with the group I was to join, because we kept stopping to talk to Tuaregs, who then pointed towards the far horizon. Each Tuareg moved within his own dense cloud of flies that covered his shoulders and buzzed thickly about his head. Crowds of them detached themselves and came through the car window to inspect us, only departing when we drove off at speed. This was a less romantic aspect of the nomadic life, and it bothered me a lot more than it did the others. The ability of even quite small Tuaregs to remain seemingly totally unaware of flies crawling all over them, including their faces, I had only seen equalled by Egyptian children, whose mothers prevent their offspring from brushing the flies away, in the belief that all life must be respected.

At lunch time we caught up with my party, and I had to bid farewell to Bomba and Ali and to the undemanding companionship I had enjoyed with them. The party turned out to be a pleasant French couple of around my own age, Jean and Marie France and their son, Pascal, together with a guide, two drivers and a cook. Some of the excellent French wine and food I was to have the pleasure of sharing had come from France with Jean and Marie-France who were keen to make their trip in the Aïr as memorable an occasion as possible. But the main success was due to the young Tuareg cook who worked wonders, getting up long before dawn to bake delicious fresh bread with only the most rudimentary of equipment, and toiling on far into the night to prepare various delicacies for the next day.

Everything needed for the week we were to spend in the desert, including fuel and water, had to be carried in or on top of the two vehicles. With seven people and their luggage, as well as the cook's table, tools and stores, it meant packing and unpacking several times a day, and both drivers and the cook worked extremely hard to make sure we enjoyed ourselves. Every night one of the drivers reported in to Agadez by radio to assure the agency that all was well, for we were off any beaten track and could easily vanish without trace. There were strict regulations governing all movement in the area, and no tourist was allowed to travel without an approved guide. This was important not only for reasons of safety, but also for protecting the Aïr itself and its wildlife. It is an area the size of Switzerland, with enormous potential for tourism, which in turn could provide much needed employment and additional income for the people, but it could so easily and speedily be ruined by indiscriminate exploitation. Even the firewood that we found so readily each day would soon be exhausted if many parties such as ours burnt it, and then the living trees would begin to be used, and in no time at all it would all become pure desert.

At one time all the Sahara had enjoyed the same sort of warm humid conditions that are now found in Central Africa. Vast river complexes and lakes watered it, herds of elephants and other creatures which have since shifted their ground far to the South grazed its plains and roamed about its mountains and valleys. There was still abundant life of this sort in the Sahara even after the wheel had been invented, and chariots regularly crossed it in both directions. We know these things not only from the geological evidence – such as dried-up water courses, but, more dramatically, from the marvellous rock paintings and engravings that prehistoric people left behind them in a pictorial record of their times. The paintings were executed in great abundance in several sites around the Sahara, mostly in places which became so remote in the increasing dry fastnesses as to remain undiscovered until the Frenchman, Henri Lhote, stumbled upon one particularly prolific site in the remote

82

Tassili region of southern Algeria, and in 1954 revealed the results of his ten years work there to an astonished world.

There were several such sites on the Aïr Massif, some of which we visited. One was an isolated hillock of sandstone blocks and boulders that had been deposited on a flat plain in some distant geological age. The carvings spanned many centuries, the earliest of them probably being five thousand years old. The majority had been dated to around 1000 BC, and these were the most beautiful, and consisted entirely of deeply incised giraffe, very detailed, even to the patterning of the hide. There were wide-horned cattle, and elephants, and stick people too, but all these had been executed at an earlier period, which suggests that by 1000 BC, many of the species had already migrated south. Giraffe still roam the the remoter stretches of the Niger, their long necks enabling them to browse on trees and find food where all other herbivores, even goats, would be defeated, and they are still hunted and eaten. That they once formed a very significant part of the diet of the people of the region was evidenced by the prolific carvings: elaborate giraffe of all sizes, some very large and perfectly proportioned, were carved on every available surface, even in places which seemed impossible to reach. It was the setting of ancient ritual and worship, when the world was a very different place, and although I found the area so extra-ordinarily beautiful, the impoverishment that had overtaken it since the time this evidence of plenty had been carved here was a sobering thought.

Every moment spent out of the vehicles was unadulterated delight, especially sunset and sunrise, and the best of these came on Christmas Day, when I awoke really early, just as the false dawn was breaking. The air was very cold in the shadow of the mountain, and as I began the climb I had planned the previous night, a thin bank of cloud was beginning rapidly to fill the sky, obscuring the last of the stars. The peak was not high, but it was composed of jagged tumbled slabs of blue marble from which the softer surrounding stone had been eroded aeons ago. It looked ghostly in the faint light, but the edges were as sharp as knives, and the spaces between the blocks were filled with blown sand, so that it required all my concentration to climb. When I topped the ridge, and could at last look about me, it was upon a scene of quite astonishing beauty. The Eastern sky was the palest most lucent blue imaginable, and filled with feathery roseate clouds, each of them outlined in bands of gleaming gold. The sun was still just below the rim of further jagged ranges which were also thinly rimmed with gold. Below me, the next narrow valley was in shadow, a dark chaos of fantastically riven rocks and chasms. The contrast of all this harsh stony wilderness with the tender sky overhead, growing minute by minute more marvellously blue, and with the golden rosy clouds thinning and reforming constantly, made it seem more like the dawn of a new creation than a mere sunrise.

Another morning, after a night spent watching falling stars, I awoke late in my little sandy hollow to see two veiled and blue-robed Tuaregs leading a string of camels silently up the valley towards our camp. To my great joy, for I knew nothing of the arrangement, I discovered they were to be ours for the day, and it was on them that we swayed sedately out of the Aïr and down into the fringes of the Ténéré Desert, traversing a new country of steep-sided sand dunes, scoured constantly by the desert winds to a sharp-edged pristine perfection − nature's own amazing pyramids, as breath-taking as anything the Pharaohs built. With our backs to the rock walls of the Aïr, huge panoramas of this fantastic wind-sculptured sand opened up all around, and it indeed felt as though we had departed from the safety of an island, and set sail on a vast ocean.

That day was our last before we turned back towards Agadez, and we pitched camp among the dunes of the Ténéré in a place called Temet, after which Mano Dayak had named his tour company, because, as he told me when we first met, 'In all of the desert, it is the most beautiful place'. Each day in the Aïr I had seen locations that I could have described in the same way, but I had to agree that this spot was very special. An isolated outcrop of the Aïr called Adrhar Chiriet, the place of secrets, was across to the south, a great horseshoe of towering jagged bare stone; otherwise there was nothing but these exquisite endless dunes beneath a vault of brilliant flawless blue. It was at once a harsh and marvellous landscape, one with an infinity of variety that was, nonetheless, endlessly the same.

Some thousand miles to the west lay Timbuktu, and a further two thousand miles eastward, across the uncharted sands, was the Valley of the Nile, where, in 1324, the great emperor of ancient Mali, Mansa Musa, passed on his pilgrimage to Mecca. He had left Timbuktu with a huge entourage of wives, camels and slaves; and most of all, with gold. So much gold had he brought that even the rich land of Egypt had been staggered by it, and rumours of the fabulous wealth of Timbuktu had begun circulating in the wider world. It was a satisfying link in my own journey to muse on the thought that Mansa Musa's exotic caravan could not have passed far from this austere and lovely place.

# 8

# Agadez

FROM THE HOTEL ROOF in Agadez, in the early morning, I watched long lines of men running through the dusty, littered streets from the abattoir, with basins on their heads in which the bloody quarters of freshly slaughtered meat bounced up and down, spattering blood everywhere. The contrast with the clean empty desert I had so recently left was jarring, and Agadez did not seem an attractive town. Nor at first could I find much pleasure in wandering through those same wind-swept crowded streets and alleys, as I was the focus for the hundreds of itinerant hawkers who mobbed me wherever I went, like wasps around a jam jar.

Being the Christmas break and the height of the tourist season, Agadez was full. What few dark airless hotel rooms the town offered were already taken, and there was no choice but this elevated and, for me, preferable perch on the roof of the three-storey Aïr Hotel – the highest building in Agadez, and once a sultan's palace. Below in the dining room was a beam, enthusiastically pointed out to all new arrivals, where the Tuareg leaders of the 1916 revolt against the French had been hanged. The roof terrace was probably the hotel's biggest money-spinner because, although the charge was modest, the mattresses were laid as close together as it was possible to get them. I shared the companionable space with travellers from several European countries. Many of them had just crossed the desert with battered vehicles to sell in Niger, so there was the sort of atmosphere that was in keeping with a town that had always been at the crossroads of trade routes. These other guests, being new to the Sahel, were far more disoriented and bewildered than I was by the predatory hawkers, and many were too intimidated to make more than one sortie into the streets, preferring to gaze down upon the colourful crowds from behind the safety of the parapet. But immunity was not guaranteed even on the roof, as some souvenir sellers were able to bribe the hotel staff to turn a blind eye while they quickly nipped up the stairs with their stock in trade and their high-pressure salesmanship.

I preferred to run the gauntlet of the streets, rather than to sit endlessly on the roof, and this had distinct advantages, as did going about solo rather than in what was seen as a potentially more profitable group. After a couple of days, all the vendors had tried to get me to buy whatever it was they had for sale, and knew that they need no longer waste their time on me. Subsequent approaches were made then for interest's sake alone, to satisfy curiosity, or simply to be friendly, at which stage it was possible to really begin to appreciate this frontier town.

Agadez possessed no memorable building, except for the Great Mosque opposite the hotel. This was only about a hundred years old, as it had been rebuilt several times since the original went up in the sixteenth century, and was in the traditional style of the Sahel. The problem of constructing a tall Islamic minaret out of *banco* – the ubiquitous building material of northern Africa, which is no more than river clay mixed with a little straw – was first solved, it was said, by a Spanish architect brought over by Mansa Musa. It was achieved by constructing a simple wooden scaffolding from branches of trees, around which the clay could be moulded, work usually done by hand, which gives a characteristic rustic finish. Beams of this rough scaffolding are left sticking out all over the lofty blunt tapering spike, for ease in applying future coats, a job which needs to be done after every season of rain. The low square structure that surrounds this central spire is of the same hand-smoothed *banco*, and enlivened with a few freely-executed decorative pinnacles. The total effect of the tall bristling edifice is extraordinarily lively in its monochrome setting.

Behind the mosque is the oldest quarter where the traditional craftsmen and small traders live in square houses with blank faces backing onto narrow shadowed lanes. For the rest, the town is a perfectly level expanse of desert with drab flat-topped *banco* buildings lining wide littered sandy streets. Rickety shacks and stalls cluster together to form markets, and spill over wherever there is space. On other empty sites between buildings, the tents of nomads are set up for the short duration of the tourist season. The whole effect, apart from the mosque, is one of impermanence, a temporary resting place, a bustling market for a desert-dwelling people who are here today and gone tomorrow, and as such, once I had the eye to appreciate it, I found it had the exciting atmosphere of a long continuing tradition. In a curious way, it was faintly reminiscent of a Hollywood film set for a Western movie.

All the colour and the interest lay in the people themselves, and while it is a Tuareg town, and the people are mostly of that race, the differences between the various tribes are wide, and did, for once, show themselves in details of dress, hairstyles, ways of wearing the turban, and in facial features; though one would need a Tuareg guide to put names to the differences. There were many other tribes present too, not related to the Tuareg, so that a record of the costumes and diversity of racial types could have filled several sketch books. Some stood out more than others; the Wodabé men for instance, a part the Peul nation of nomads, were unmistakable – very tall and slender, with braided hair and coolie-shaped hats trimmed with ostrich feathers. In spite of their great height and their reputation as warriors, the Wodabé also place an emphasis on male beauty akin to that of the ancient Greeks. At their annual gathering where they assemble from all over Niger, the young men, beautifully painted and adorned, dance before the women, who then select their favourites on such points as whiteness and evenness of teeth, and grace of movement. Not surprisingly, every visitor wants to photograph the Wodabé, myself included, and the six-foot-six Ismael who reluctantly posed for me, hand on hip, as elegant as any model, complained bitterly that 'Everyone want photo, but no one want buy'. His job was to entice tourists back to the family's market stall where they could be pressed to buy Wodabé hats and jewellery. I drank several glasses of tea in the market with Ismael, and gave him my spare pen as a souvenir. He told me how frustrating he found the months spent in Agadez, trying to sell the year's accumulation of trinkets before the short tourist season ended. He much preferred the life he lived in the desert for the rest of the year, he said, but the family had to have money.

This seemed to be the pattern for most people I met in Agadez; everyone was part of a large family, some of whom remained with their animals in the desert, while the rest spent the few short months of winter, the tourist season, in town, trying to sell the jewellery, hats, weapons, slippers, leather work and anything else that they had made during the rest of the year. The trouble was that there were far too many people selling the same merchandise, and far too few tourists to buy it. There were the traditional merchants too, town dwellers whose families had lived there for centuries, dealing in the hundred-and-one different commodities, from incense and magic potions, spices and condiments, to grain and cloth, that the nomads had come to town to buy when they traded their animals. How they and the traditional silversmiths and blacksmiths coped with the competition from the nomad hawkers was hard to see.

I also drank tea among the tents of the Kel Awiyé, a tribe of the Tuareg, where the women were carrying on with their lives in the centre of Agadez exactly as they would have done in any of their stopping places. They sat in groups among the tents, either on mats or very low stools, some cutting leather into thin strips and plaiting it into camel whips, others stirring cooking pots or combing their children's hair, all in a very relaxed atmosphere of conversation and banter. They paid rent to the town for the space on which they pitched their ephemeral shelters of mats spread over a framework of light boughs. There was little in these tents other than a low wooden bed, and perhaps a few bolts of cloth, or sacks of whatever was their stock in trade. The few items of equipment for preparing food clustered on the ground outside were not much more extensive than I would use for a camping trip, though somewhat heavier. It would not take long for them to up-sticks and away I thought, and this gave me a feeling of kinship with them. The young men toured the streets to find potential customers who would be invited in and given tea, the better to soften them up for a sale. But a sense of ancient hospitality was there even in these exchanges; they did not seem to me to have become totally cynical. Even in tourist-centred Agadez, their culture seemed very much alive, with values of mutual dependency still intact. But of course these were just the few who still had their flocks to tend and their age-old routes to follow for the rest of the year.

In the centre of the enormous camel market on the outskirts of town, I was fortunate in being spotted by the older black-veiled menfolk of the Kel Awiyé, and invited to sit with them on mats under a little awning they had erected to keep off the fierce afternoon sun. This gave me an excellent viewpoint in the centre of the proceedings, protected from the jostling crowds. Nothing at all was expected of me, as the men were not selling anything, just sitting making tea and watching the goings on in an area of their world that interested them most. The camel is by far the most prized possession of the Tuareg; together with his weapons and his veil, it is an essential part of his identity. Tuareg poems and legends are full of the courageous exploits of the warrior and his camel and, according to one French general active in the campaign to subdue them in the early part of the twentieth century, if they could have combined their bravery, and fought with some degree of co-operation, they would have been extremely difficult to defeat.

As with horses, camels come in many varieties, from the strong pack animals to beautiful thoroughbreds, and the finer points of them can be mulled over endlessly, as the Kel Awiyé men were doing. The white camel I had ridden in the Aïr had seemed a very classy creature at the time, but having the real aristocrats pointed out to me here, I could see now that in spite of its haughty expression, its silk-covered saddle and rich accoutrements, it had, in fact, been only run of the mill. The finest camels seldom change hands, I was told, as no Tuareg would ever sell a favourite mount or allow a stranger on its back.

I had never seen so many camels in one place: they were mostly in small groups of five or six, some so young that their coats were soft and woolly and they were still suckling their dams. Together with hundreds of small bunches of goats and sheep, they were all being kept on their feet by attendants who quickly checked any attempt on their part to lie down, trying to make sure they were alert and ready for inspection by the hawk-faced desert men drifting around, pretending to show only cursory interest. The huge dusty space was full of tension – heads tossing, hooves stamping, snorts and cries of bewilderment. Arresting tableaux, constantly shifting a little and re-grouping, were played out against a vivid blue desert sky, full of white wind-clouds pulled out in long straight strands. Here was the real heart of Agadez, and I spent most of my stay there, until finally the huge UTA plane on its delayed weekly passage from Paris to Niamey, flew in low overhead, and it was time to make for the airport.

Half way into the flight back to Niamey a strange change came over the sky. Instead of the clear hard blue of the Aïr, or the dust-filled skies I'd grown used to further south, it grew darker and greyer with what could only be rain clouds. Nigeriens in the plane began to look distinctly worried, as though rain was unwelcome in this drought-plagued land. The man sitting next to me, who was from Niamey, explained the reason. It was unnatural, he said, it never rained in the middle of the dry season, it meant something serious was amiss with the natural order of things. Rain at this time would do no good for anyone; it meant that the gods were angry. In fading light, the plane landed at Niamey just as a few fat wet drops fell from the swollen clouds and plopped into the dust. As my taxi drove through the town, people were gathered in the streets with drums, dancing to placate their angry gods.

Once again, travel-stained, and without an identifying bicycle, I was dropped off before the gates of the Residence. This time I was recognized straight away, but the air of satisfaction at being able to confound the plans of 'Les Blancs' was very apparent when the guards informed me there was no one there, and the Residence was all locked up. I knew that my hosts were spending Christmas in neighbouring Nigeria, and since it had been assumed that I might well be back before them, the Embassy had been informed that if I arrived in their absence I was at liberty to stay. 'No one there', however, was meant literally; the staff had gone home, and the house was in darkness, and locked. I would need to go and seek for a key at the US Embassy across the road.

Across the road is a relative term: there were two long driveways and a quarter of a mile of wide empty avenue to trudge along before I came to the Embassy building, surrounded by its Fort Knox-style security, and its close-circuit TV screens. The only compensation was that the rain was still holding off. After being up all the previous night waiting for a flight that had been delayed for fifteen hours, I was tired and sticky and longing for a bath.

There was the usual hassle of getting past the native guards, and then through a remotely-controlled electric turnstile. The front door was also operated by remote control, and the armed marine sat facing it behind a system of railings and bullet proof glass. It was all most impressive, including the pale earnest crew-cut young man, who quite properly regarded me with the deepest suspicion. I took care to explain slowly and patiently who I was, and why I wanted the key to the Residence, and when he had the general picture, he phoned his duty officer. After a while the reply came back that yes, there was a message in the book about a Bettina Selby being let into the Residence, and sure, go ahead, give her the key. On the wall behind the guard was a glass-fronted case with neatly labelled bunches of keys; it looked as if there would be no further problem and I began to anticipate a long restorative soak in a hot bath. The Marine, however, regarded these keys with the same sort of suspicion he had fixed on me, and then said 'I guess these things need reorganising, I don't think they do what it says they should. Why don't I just give you a whole bunch, and you go try 'em'.

The long trudge back to the Residence was bad enough, the unproductive tour around the house in the cold and inefficient glare of the floodlights was worse. None of the keys fitted any of the quite astonishing number of doors I tried them in. I became so demoralized, that had I not promised the marine I would return the keys the moment I had located the right one, I would have taken out my sleeping bag there and then, and curled up on the lawn.

I will gloss over the second attempt at entering the Residence - it was no more than a sad repetition of the first – but how the marine, quite unmoved by my growing despair, got me to repeat the whole ridiculous procedure for a third time, with yet more inaccurately labelled bundles of keys, I have no idea. Once through the last of the electronic defences and into the vestibule of the Embassy for the fourth time, I collapsed onto the sofa saying that I could go not a step further that night; I had, quite definitely, had it. It was now up to him. 'Ma'am, staying there on that sofa is against regulations, and absolutely not allowed,' he informed me. I suggested he phoned the duty officer for a better idea. While we waited for this person to arrive, the marine put on a tape of 'Brush up your Spanish' which, quite apart from the bizarre timing, seemed to be an odd choice of language to be studying in a French-speaking country. But the marine said 'Not at all', he didn't like French, and the main purpose of language anyway was not necessarily communication. I never did find out what he thought language was for, because just at the point where I had begun to think that fatigue really had got the better of me, a plump little colonel arrived. A veritable angel he appeared to me by that time, telling me to relax and not to worry; he would go off with the keys and attempt entry, and if all else failed, there was a guest room available, and we could sort everything else out in the morning.

Clearly his training had equipped him for success, and he returned very shortly, having effected entry via the kitchen. He whisked me back there in his car, waiting until I was safely inside behind locked doors before he departed. The final denouement that the day had in store was the wrecked kitchen of the Residence. A new cooker and refrigerator were to be installed while the Ambassador and his family were away, work that had been expected to take a couple of days at most. Clearly things had not gone according to plan, and an effect had been produced akin to a small bomb having been exploded. The whole of the kitchen wing was in chaos, everything disconnected, doors off, cupboards gaping away from walls, and all the crockery, glasses and cooking equipment under dustsheets in the dining room. I couldn't even have boiled a kettle for a cup of tea. As it was I was too exhausted to want to, and pausing only to check that Evans was still intact in the cellar, I stumbled off to bed.

Before I drifted off to sleep, it occurred to me that in spite of all the sophisticated military security in the Embassy, and the poster in the vestibule reminding marines that 'SECURITY DEPENDS ON YOU', no one had taken the basic precaution of asking me for proof of identity. It also occurred to me that the 'Africa factor' had once again proved a lot more powerful than I had allowed for.

There was nothing further to keep me in Niamey. After a night's sleep my energy was restored, and I was eager to get under way and begin the long haul towards Timbuktu. There was little I needed to do in the way of preparations, other than to re-pack Evans, and buy a few supplies for the journey. I spent one last day riding around town, saying a final goodbye to the friends I had made there, and visiting all the places I wished to remember, especially the river as I had first seen it from the terrace of the Grand Hotel.

When I had first planned the journey, the idea of following the course of a great river conjured up charming visions of idyllic camp sites with lots of refreshing swimming, and perhaps a little fishing too, but after some detailed study of maps I realized that the reality would not be like that. Roads and tracks are seldom able to run close beside a river like the Niger that experiences such tremendous seasonal flooding. Rain falling on the jungle-clad mountains of Guinea during the wet season, from May to October, provides the majority of the annual flood, while the rainy season in the south of Mali and Niger adds to the flow. The river bed is shallow, and as the level rises, a vast area is inundated. There are also hundreds of lesser rivers and streams draining an area several times the size of Britain, and all these eventually empty into the Niger. So although in the main the area I would be travelling through was not a very mountainous one, it would be rugged and broken, with many dry river beds to cross at this time of year. Although our ways would frequently converge, the Niger would often be out of sight and inaccessible, sometimes for days at a time.

I sat for a long time over my drink on the terrace. The thick grey cloud cover over Niamey had not yet dispersed, and the light was flat, so there was no sparkle on the river's surface. But that robbed it of none of its aura; it remained, as always, an immensely powerful presence, and the thought that our paths would be running together throughout the journey ahead – even if it was often out of sight – was both comforting and exciting.

# 9

# North towards Mali

IT WAS NEW YEAR'S EVE, and a Sunday when I set out from the empty echoing Residence: an auspicious day, I thought, to be starting on the long haul to Timbuktu. The kind old cook, Joseph, surprised me by turning up at dawn, to make me breakfast in the wrecked kitchen, so there was someone to shake my hand and wish me '*Bon voyage*' before I rode off. The small pulses of anxiety that accompany the start of each new phase of a journey, and often spoil the previous night's sleep – small worries about what might have been forgotten, or what might go wrong – at this stage give way to relief at actually being on the move once more. To be on my bicycle, and dependent upon no one but myself, filled me with elation as I rode out of Niamey, past the half-built Libyan Embassy and the last of the shanty towns, and on into new territory.

The chilly start to the day soon brightened to more tropical African weather, as the sun climbed to its near vertical position, and the grey clouds were blown away by the dry wind from the desert. I was riding on a plateau with the river far below on my left, flowing through the bed it had cut for itself over the millennia. It was only visible occasionally, but its route was marked by the cliffs on its far side.

After a few miles the road was blocked with huge piles of rock and sand, and diversion signs pointed off towards a very wide meander into the bush. Often a cycle can get through where a vehicle cannot, so I edged around the obstacles and rode on along the tarmac. In about a mile I came to the reason for the diversion; a bridge across a wide tributary of the Niger had a neat gap of about twenty feet right in the middle of it, and the missing section was lying far below on the bed of the now dried-up river: it looked as though it had been like that for a long time. Rather than retrace my steps, I decided to find a way across the bottom of the chasm, a feat that would have proved impossible had not a couple of men immediately appeared from nowhere to help manhandle the heavily laden Evans through the deep sand and up the steep bank opposite.

Apart from the distant glimpses of the river, the landscape from the road was rather featureless scrub, with a few large trees in whose shade I sought refuge when I stopped to brew coffee, and later to make lunch with the bread and cheese and fruit I had brought from Niamey. There was little traffic and only a very few people about, young men mostly, walking along with a small bundle of possessions, hoping for a lift. It was hotter than I had at first realized, and I was getting through my supply of water fast. By three o'clock I was tired and finding the going hard. I had covered fifty-five miles against an energy-sapping head wind, and although Tillabéry, the town where I had intended to spend the first night, was still at least an hour's journey away, I thought it was high time to stop.

I was at the junction of a minor road, where a few people sat patiently waiting for bush taxis, and someone was selling snacks and cigarettes. I went over to ask if there was anywhere to stay round-about and a man told me there was a 'bon village, un village de projet' called Sona, just down the track. He seemed keen that I should visit it, and I thought I would go and see if there was somewhere there, and if not, then I could perhaps find a place to pitch camp beside the river.

As soon as I'd bumped and slithered down the stony sandy path to the village perimeter, a very tall man appeared, and asked me what I was looking for. When I told him 'le chef' he took over Evans and led me through a maze of higgledy piggledy little dirt alleyways, liberally be-spattered with animal droppings, and bounded by mud brick walls, over which I could see into various compounds. There could have been no doubt that the man who rose from his seat to shake my hand and murmur a formal welcome was the chief, for he was a splendid looking personage, even taller than my guide, and immensely dignified. Another *ancien combattant*, he had fought with the French in Indo-China, he told me, and I am sure that with his great height he must have proved a tremendous asset. When he took over Evans to lead me through further alleyways to the compound where I was to be entertained, it looked like a little boy's toy in his enormous hands.

This new compound seemed more prosperous and less littered than the others I'd glimpsed on the way there. A chair was brought for me to sit on, and water to drink, and while several men and boys hovered around, a child was sent running to bring back a young man who spoke excellent French, and was, it transpired, studying agronomy at Niamey University. Unlike the rest of the villagers who were all Djerma, the young man, Dan Tani, was Hausa. His father, who was away at present, was in charge of a large irrigation project for growing rice, which was centred on the village, and in his absence Dan offered to show me around. He didn't explain that it meant an exhausting six-mile hike, which perhaps was just as well as, tired as I was, I might have declined, and missed seeing a different side of Niger.

It was a very large project, and a lot of government money had gone into the construction of the extensive series of sluices, dykes and pumping houses that allowed a large tract of land to be flooded with river water to create rice paddies. Teams of oxen for ploughing and for transportation had been provided too, rather than tractors. Roads, dykes, fields, pumping houses all looked well constructed, but suitably 'low-tech'. It was altogether different from the scenes of desertification and poverty I'd witnessed further south, and the people certainly seemed a little more prosperous. Dan told me that the village was run as a co-operative, and that the money that had been put into the scheme was a loan that had to be paid back gradually to a central fund. The fund then helped other villages to start similar projects. I had no idea, of course, how well it all worked, but what I particularly liked about it was the fact that there were no foreign aid agencies involved, not even any Peace Corps volunteers; all the impetus came from the people themselves working out their own solutions.

Before it grew dark the chief came to take me to meet the elders who were all reclining like Romans at a banquet, chewing kola nuts under an open-sided corrugated roof in the main square. Many of these old men had worked in Nigeria or Ghana, and had picked up a little English there, which gave me my first opportunity to go through the whole lovely sequence of traditional greetings in my own language – 'How are you? How is your health? How is your family? The work goes well?' and so on with each person in turn. Where there was less English, what was remembered came out all in one breath and on a single note – 'Goo'night Master goo'bye goo'morning my name is Kano', delivered with as much delight and the same happy toothless grins as were the other exchanges. They found it all such fun that it was impossible not to share the merriment. I was also required to make a formal tour of the huge storage shed that led off the square, and which had a little office in one corner for the 'secretary' who would one day occupy it. Every stick of furniture, every piece of apparatus, and every sack of harvested rice was pointed out and appropriately admired. I became so dazed by the end of it that I needed to be reminded to take a proper formal departure of the old men, still reclining and spitting kola juices into the dust of the square.

The chief returned to the compound a little later, followed by a servant carrying a speckled hen upside down. First the hen was shown to me, then given to one of the men for immediate decapitation, at which point I realised it was destined for my supper. I was now left to sit quietly in a corner where I could watch the women of two separate households, who shared the compound, beginning the preparations for the evening meal. There were a good few visitors and relatives milling around, and half a dozen children, pretty as pictures, sat on the ground playing a sort of game that required nothing more than a handful of small stones or sun-hardened goat droppings, while another drew in the dirt with a stick. One tiny naked cherub had the most dreadful burns all down one side of his body where he had fallen into a cooking fire;

fortunately his face had been spared, and the damage was healing well, but he would be left with extensive scars. They all looked healthier than the average Nigerien children, and the only obvious common complaint seemed to be sore eyes, which I thought was probably caused by wind-blown dust, aggravated by the attention of flies. In fact there were not as many flies as usual, as great efforts had been made to improve the sanitation and the cleanliness of the village, Dan told me. Because mud was readily available so close to the river, the small huts, like the compound walls, were made of *banco* rather than grass, which helped, and pit lavatories were dug in almost all the compounds. The pit in this compound was not a particularly commodious loo by Western standards, just a very small hole in the ground, in a corner, behind one of the huts, and after dark it had the distinct disadvantage of disgorging quantities of large cockroaches.

Taking my bucket bath alongside this pit I was invisible to the folk in the compound, but the walls were so low that I was in plain view from the waist up to all passers by. Although in every other compound people were taking baths in similar states of exposure, my white skin was creating a lot of interest, so I became inhibited and made do with a quick wipe over instead. After my ablutions, attempts were made to install me in the *maison etrangers* which most large villages provide for visitors. This was a windowless cell of dark unpainted *banco* bricks, with a platform of the same material for sleeping on. With my incipient claustrophobia, I find it difficult even to enter such places, let alone to entertain the idea of spending the night in one, and I explained that I had my tent with me. So back we went again to the compound, where to the great delight of everyone, especially the children, I set it up in a free corner among the scratching hens. The men were worried that it wouldn't provide adequate protection from mosquitoes, but they were reassured as well as impressed when they realized that the tent had a built-in ground sheet. All the children took turns to listen to the sound of the air being sucked into the self-inflating mattress, and crowed and chortled as it slowly took shape, writhing and uncurling. They were so fascinated by the details of my little camp that they were reluctant to be sent off to watch one of the three battery-operated televisions in the village.

When it was quite dark, my dinner was brought to me where I was seated in honour on one of the worst modern inventions to have hit this part of the world – a chair made of plastic cord wrapped around a metal frame. Even when new the thin plastic strands cut into the flesh, leaving deep narrow weals. In time the plastic begins to break and gets retied, the strands becoming ever fewer and further apart, and the agony of sitting on them ever more acute. Dinner however was regal, even though I had only starlight and my torch to eat it by, the only source of illumination in the compound being the cooking fires. On a low table in front of me was placed the entire chicken, roasted and jointed, together with rice and baobab sauce served separately. There was a tin of milk in case I would prefer to mix this with my rice, and in case I couldn't manage any of these things (for as my host explained he didn't know what Europeans ate) there was a loaf of bread, clearly obtained especially for me. I was deeply touched by so much solicitude and hope I repaid their efforts by eating heartily. But before I left the following morning, I had trouble in getting my host to accept a modest sum to cover the cost of feeding me, something I had no problem with anywhere else in the Sahel. Not to insist that they accept it was unthinkable in a country as poor as this, so I said it was for buying presents for the children.

The two families had their meal on the other side of the courtyard, also, to my surprise, using electric torches to find the food. While they were still eating, a young teen-aged boy came into the compound with two huge white hump-backed oxen, which were bedded down by the midden after adding their large droppings to the sand. I was invited to join the men after dinner for a glass of Nescafé, while the women were putting the small children to bed. The scarred cherub was sitting on a plastic potty in the light of a torch held by his mother. Goats were tethered all around him, and he kept pushing away their inquisitive heads as they nuzzled him. Everyone retired to bed by nine o'clock, which suited me as I could no longer keep my eyes open. I fell asleep almost as soon as I had crawled into the tent, but not before I became aware that the night chorus was different from usual; instead of cicadas, millions of frogs were pouring out their song from the flooded paddy fields.

Tillabéry was further than I had thought it would be, and uphill all the way, and when I reached it I found the Niger roaring along at a great rate, a totally different river it seemed from the broad calm flood I'd left at Niamey. The town itself proved a disappointment, just a short stretch of run-down buildings behind crumbling walls, a police post at which I got the necessary stamp in my passport, and a tourist restaurant which had a menu of impressive length, but with not a single item on it available, except for cold beer. There were no tourists, only local men drinking beer in the shaded garden overlooking the river. The management offered to make me spaghetti, which was not on the menu, and which proved to be barely edible and ruinously expensive. While I attempted to get this down (it never seems wise to reject food in Africa where the next meal can be a long way off) some of the men took over my labours with the filter pump which had become so stiff I could hardly manage it. It required the combined efforts of six of them to produce the three litres of purified water necessary to see me through the afternoon.

The tarmac road ceased abruptly after Tillabéry, and I had a most pernicious surface of mixed sand and gravel to contend with. At its deepest, I seemed to be wading through it rather than walking, and at its best I could ride only with difficulty, and at no more than five or six miles an hour. The desert was closing in on the last remaining miles of scrubland. The day was unrelentingly hot, with the usual awful head wind blowing sand into every crevice. I did not feel at all well: my throat felt on fire, my lips were cracking, my knee hurt and my head throbbed. Evans fell over when I stopped to have a drink, and sustained its first injury, breaking the mirror that enabled me to see what was coming from behind. Since there was hardly any traffic this didn't really matter, but I actually found the mirror's greatest use was when brushing my hair and cleaning my teeth, and the unnecessary breakage further depressed me.

I began to wonder where I could spend the night. The next town,

Ayorou, was said to have a Sofitel hotel, whose comforts would have been most welcome just then, but it was seventy-five miles from Tillabéry and there was no possibility of doing anything like that distance on this atrocious surface. There were very poor-looking villages flanking the road every few miles, none of them in the least inviting. I still had a tin of sardines, a packet of fish soup, peanuts, some wedges of processed cheese, dried fruit and a little bread that was hard as biscuit after two days, but edible. I would happily have camped if I could have found water to wash off the sweat and dust, but streams did not exist in these parts, and the map showed the river to be some distance off.

By six o'clock, when I had been eleven hours on the road, moving at an average speed of a little over four miles an hour, I decided there was nothing for it but to try and find somewhere to bed down in the next village. This turned out to be quite a substantial settlement, but with such an air of resigned hopelessness hanging over it that my heart sank. Unsmiling people sat about apathetically, and the two small stores were both bare of everything except paraffin. As I stood there undecided what to do next, a car pulled up beside me. It was from the Sofitel Hotel at Ayorou, and the two men in it seemed concerned to find me there. They told me I could not possibly make Ayorou that night, and offered to take both Evans and me there in the car. For some reason, possibly because I was too tired to think straight, I refused, and said that I would cycle in the next day. They then asked if I would like some ice, and thinking they meant ice-cream, and that it was a joke, I said I would, very much indeed. An enormous vacuum flask was produced, full of balls of ice giving off clouds of smoke in the hot air. I hastily passed them my plastic pint mug, which they filled to the brim, and drove off, leaving me holding the cycle with one hand, and the mug of already melting ice in the other. There seemed nothing for it but to lay Evans down in the squalid street, get out the coffee powder and make iced coffee. It was a great pick me up, giving me the energy to find a well and sweat away with the pump, refilling all the empty water bottles. Once that was done I knew I could manage for the night, whatever transpired.

After a few more miles of alternately pushing and riding Evans, I came to a track leading off in the direction of the river. I had no great hope of finding a camping place beside the water, as the map showed there to be extensive marshlands around it at this point. But I didn't even catch a glimpse of it, because the next village I came to was even more off-putting than the last. Several horrible decomposing corpses of dogs and donkeys lay on the waste ground around its perimeter, and fly-infested children in filthy rags peered out from the decaying squalid cabins. It was all more than I could cope with in my present state, and I turned around and fled back to the road.

I waited for darkness to fall, so that no hidden watcher would see where I pitched camp. Then, by the light of the stars, I made off across some harvested maize fields where a few isolated acacia trees stood blackly against the midnight blue sky. These trees offer welcome shade to cattle and goats whose hooves help to keep the earth beneath them clear of the tough burrs and thorns that grow everywhere, making it so difficult to find any place to sit and rest in these parts. I chose a tree at a suitable distance from the road, scraped a space clear of droppings and debris with my boot, and, blessing the ease of erecting my little shelter, I was soon sitting in its entrance, sipping a restorative whisky, while the stove purred quietly under the kettle. Replacing the quantities of body fluid I had lost was my first priority. Even though I was careful to drink at frequent intervals, in the two short days since leaving Niamey I had become somewhat dehydrated, and it was this, I decided, coupled with the unrelenting hard work and the tough conditions that was making me feel so unwell. With the extremely low humidity, the heat and the drying wind it was almost impossible not to dehydrate, for I sweated constantly, though without being aware of it as the moisture dried instantly on my skin.

I had Earl Grey tea first with slices of lime in it, and it was delicious. The fish soup which followed was not so good, but I got it down by concentrating on the lovely sliver of the new moon rising among the bright stars. But even with this ploy, I wasn't able to eat anything, except the slices of lime that had been in the tea. I sacrificed enough water to clean my teeth and to wet a flannel to remove some of the salt from my skin, which seemed only slightly less urgent than drinking. I remembered that Moslems, when far from water and needing to perform their ablutions before prayers, use sand instead, and I thought I might try that another time. My clothes too felt stiff with sweat, and when I got them off I discovered to my surprise that my body was covered with mosquito bites, the result of sitting outside after dark the previous night. It was strange that I had not felt them biting, but West African mosquitoes are small and subtle, though virulent for all that, and it was the malaria they carry that had killed off most of the early Niger explorers and traders. I took anti-malaria tablets daily, but the best prevention was to avoid getting bitten. Now that I had discovered the bites and rubbed them over with a flannel, they began to itch like mad.

In spite of my extreme fatigue I did not sleep well. There were so many noises – animals in the distance, traffic on the road (one vehicle every hour) bits of detritus falling from the tree onto the taut nylon, and the little tin in which I carried petrol for the stove making sharp cracking sounds as the temperature dropped. More worrying were the unidentified rustles and creaks that I couldn't put a name to, and it was these which kept me wakeful, so that morning came as a relief.

Dawn was particularly beautiful, with flights of white egrets passing overhead, their undersides catching the rays of a sun not yet risen above the horizon, so that they seemed like fabulous birds of gold against the pale blue sky. I made coffee and ate some bread with a processed cheese wedge and a few dried apricots, but I still didn't really want food, and had to force it down.

From the moment I set out I was plagued by a raging thirst that dominated all my thoughts. I kept one pint of water for emergencies and not to drink it required a good deal of willpower. No villages appeared, and the road surface was, if anything, even worse than the previous day. Only very short stretches were rideable, and I was becoming exhausted simply from getting off and on the bicycle constantly, so that sometimes it seemed less effort just to keep pushing when I could have ridden. Ten miles took me nearly three

105

hours. I kept going by telling myself that the road must improve soon, and by thinking about the fleshpots of Ayorou.

The first people I saw were a black family whose car was halted under a tree with the bonnet up, the man busy beneath it. They gave me two litres of water from their hundred-litre tank, and I drank it all in one go. A couple of Italians who were full of the euphoria of a recent desert crossing pulled up in their jeep a little later, and came straight over with their water bottle without waiting to be asked. They gave me the unwelcome information that the road grew steadily worse all the way to Gao. At this I acknowledged defeat, and hailed the first vehicle going in my direction. It was a pick-up, with two burly black men and a heavily made-up black woman inside, who I realised later were probably under the influence of drugs. The thuggish driver took off at breakneck speed, bouncing and thudding sickeningly into the potholes, slewing through the deep drifts of sand, and generally showing off to the danger of us all. The other two affected nonchalance at the lunatic progress. They kept up a game of uncapping bottles of mineral water, offering them to me, and then withdrawing them if I reached out to take one. I was too angry to be frightened, and told them I would pay them nothing at all if my bicycle was damaged by the driver's stupidity. He slowed down a little at that, but they all kept up a heavy banter on the subject of 'Les Blancs timides'. I was only grateful that Ayorou was so close.

After this unattractive trio, even the hordes of Ayorou boys descending with their shouts of 'Donne moi un cadeau' were a welcome relief. One of them came and hung onto the saddle, announcing proudly that his name was Ibrahim (there seemed to be few males in this part of Africa, where the tide of Islam has swept through so thoroughly, who are not called either Ibrahim, or Mohammed, or some variation of the two). I told him I didn't need a guide, and certainly not one who demanded cadeaux, at which Ibrahim said virtuously 'Je ne demande pas un cadeau Madame. J'escorte vous à l'hôtel', which quite restored my faith in the intrinsic goodness of small boys.

Ayorou was another one-horse town, but with a famous market.

This was not the day for it however, which was just as well, as it would have been wasted on me. All I wanted was water; water to wallow in, water to soak the sweat out of my stiff clothes, and endless quantities of it to pour down my throat, and all this I could find without stirring a foot from the hotel. My room even overlooked the Niger, so I could also gaze my fill on its wide expanse. I had been welcomed at the hotel with an unusual degree of enthusiasm, for it was the manager who had given me the ice cubes the previous day, and he was very relieved that I had finally arrived. Nothing was too good for me. I was given my pick of the rooms, and lots and lots of cold bottled water. Since both Evans and I were so thickly coated in dust, it seemed sensible to get under the shower together, with the luggage and my stiff sticky clothes as well.

Several soakings, a few beers, and a short respite from the sun proved to be all that was needed to restore me. I spent the afternoon hanging out washing, and changing Evans' tyres, in the hope that the pair of 'Extreme Terrains' I was carrying would be able to cope a little better with the sand. While I was doing my chores the hotel staff were keeping me company, trying to restore the lights and the fan, and sort out the plumbing which worked in sudden gushes of dark brown water. Repairs were effected by vandalising other rooms for spare parts, and when science failed Allah was invoked, often with better results, no doubt because faith was stronger than skill. The hotel was quite new but already a little tatty around the edges, and beginning to crumble in places. Even so it seemed very grand and luxurious to me, so quickly are one's standards altered by even a few days travelling through Niger's bush.

There was a famous hippo pool not far down river, and I was urged to take a trip in a pirogue in the cool of the evening to see it. The Niger wore a different guise at Ayorou, its great width broken by many rounded boulders and great numbers of grassy islands. The hippos, who emerge at night to feed on the grass, were just coming up from the river bed. There were about five of them popping their heads out one by one, snorting and bellowing with tremendous volume. Hippos can be the most dangerous of animals, fearless and very fast, both on land and in the water. I had once camped in Uganda where scores of them had come out of the lake and grazed around my tent all night without showing any animosity towards me. But here on the Niger I had already learnt that they were greatly feared; perhaps they behaved differently in its shallow waters.

The ancient pirogier kept a very respectful distance, but cackled wildly each time a pair of huge piggy ears and domed eyes broke surface, '*Regardez, regardez,*' he screamed digging me in the ribs, although my glasses were already firmly fixed on the spot. He seemed to think he had stage-managed the whole thing, and demanded a large tip on top of the price of the hire. All the way back to the hotel he kept up a chant in rhythm with his paddle – '*Un cadeau, un grand cadeau pour moi, parce que c'est beaucoup, trop, trop beaucoup des hippos.*' But the modest tip he received was accepted with a quite angelic smile.

# 10

# Through the Desert to Gao

LITTLE IBRAHIM MET ME the moment I wheeled my bike out of the hotel the next morning. He and a friend (Mohammed, of course) proudly pushed the newly washed and gleaming Evans through the sandy streets, so I was able to pay him legitimately for a service, rather than giving him a *cadeau*. I had slept well, and was filled with renewed energy and optimism. There had been a great deal of discussion among the hotel staff about the possibility of a bike getting through to Gao, and it was generally reckoned that I might make it to the Malian border, about twenty miles away, but after that the sand would defeat me. They thought I was mad, but valued me none the less for that, and did all they could to help me on my way by filling all my water bottles with ice-cold water, and giving me fresh bread; they could do no more, I thought.

Once I had been processed at the police post and was back onto the strip of churned-up ground that was the northern highway, Evans came into his own once more, the new tyres coping far better than the previous ones, which were now relegated to spares. A quite wonderful eight miles followed in which I fairly sped along close beside the Niger for once – a pretty riverside scene of birds and trees and sparkling water. This was my idea of real bicycling, and I enjoyed it to the full, dispelling from my mind the association of the lovely jade-colour of the water with the presence of increasingly large tracts of pure sand – the transition from scrubland into desert.

I was cushioned from the first harsh jolt of reality by the hotel's car, which overtook me at the point where the rough track had suffered a calamity. An area of land, about two miles square had subsided or been washed away in floods, and what was left looked like a giant sandpit which had been bombed repeatedly and then used for tank practice. I cannot think how even a four-wheel-drive vehicle was able to find a route through, but that the hotel manager had clearly followed me in order to offer assistance moved me deeply. I was put down at the other side and told that I would be alright now as far as the border.

The frontier presented no problem. On the Nigerien side a friendly soldier helped me to fill in the usual lengthy form, and then took me in to shake hands with the officer in charge who murmured something about '*bon courage*' as he filled another entire page of my passport with the exit stamp. I then sped on into a dreary area of no-man's land, a vast flat treeless gravel plain, rideable with the new tyres, but decidedly tacky. Far in the distance now the great Niger provided a strange sparkling contrast to the lifeless monochrome land. By the time I had covered the ten miles to the frontier post of Mali my lovely cold water was almost hot enough to make tea, and the day, once again, had become a battle with heat, dust and exhaustion.

The Malian border guards were sheltering from the heat in a grass hovel, their ragged uniforms creating the impression that I was entering an even poorer country than Niger. Keeping relatively cool under some wet sacks were bottles of soft drinks which they must have brought from miles away, and which they were selling at just half the price the Sofitel charged. They were very solicitous to me, begging me not to continue by bicycle but to wait there until they could find me a lift on a truck, and it was difficult to persuade them that I needed to go on and see how things were for myself. Only when I promised to return if I found the road as impossible as they claimed it to be did they let me continue on to the customs post. Here there were several vehicles, all being subjected to heavy scrutiny from the guards, who were taking a fancy to many of their contents which would, I could see, necessitate a judicious giving of *cadeaux*. I escaped all such attention and was quickly waved on, a humble bicyclist clearly being judged as unlikely to have anything worth rooting through.

There was another little hovel at this isolated frontier post where an enterprising old man, assisted by a skinny half-naked six-year-old girl who hauled water for him, served up an oily stew of brown beans. The bubbling brown mess neither looked nor smelt in the least appetizing but I persevered with a plateful of it, and bought a kettle of boiling water to make tea to wash it down. A cyclist, like any engine, needs fuel to run on, and this particular stoking worked wonders, carrying me onwards for a further twelve almost impossible miles. After the first few, there was no question of even thinking about riding. This was the true desert, and I was now fighting sand that was feet deep in places, with occasional patches of a peculiarly soft consistency – notorious stuff known as 'fesh-fesh' into which it seemed possible to disappear without trace.

At the end of those twelve miles I decided I was an ex-cyclist until conditions returned to something approaching the reasonable. That settled, and with little more than an hour of daylight left, I sat in the sandy wilderness at the side of what passed for a road, waiting for whatever help my guardian angel decided to send me. Only about five minutes elapsed before a Mercedes land cruiser drove up, its roof piled high with a stack of spare tyres, water and fuel tanks, and metal ladders and spades for digging vehicles out of sand. Inside were two stout Germans, and an exotic-looking black youth perched on quantities of luggage in the back. They didn't think they had room for the bicycle and me as well, but said there were Italians following closely behind with a large caravan that could easily accommodate us. While we waited they gave me a melon which I tried not to wolf down in too unseemly a fashion, and we swopped stories of what we were doing there. They were librarians, they told me, who had spent their month's annual holiday for the past eight years crossing the Sahara Desert for the fun of it. They had come, as always, via Algeria and Tamanrasset – a route which is, they said, becoming a veritable highway now, and littered with the vehicles that don't survive. They had provisionally sold their land cruiser in Niamey to the father of the black youth, but wanted to make a brief tour of Niger and Mali before they surrendered it and flew home.

The youth who was about fifteen, and kitted-out in the most beautifully cut denims and expensive trappings, was like some gilded catamite from another age – Alexander's Persian boy perhaps. His air of decadence and amorality, combined with the boyish good looks, was disconcerting and fascinating at the same time. I was to see quite a lot of him over the next few days, but I never grew to like him. He had the sort of knowing, over-familiar manner that alienated most people, both black and white alike. He reminded me of the perfidious Amadou of my river trip; I felt that, like him, this boy too had been ruined by the wrong sort of contact with an alien culture.

The Italian camping van soon appeared, a very expensive vehicle on which much love and care had clearly been lavished. Carlo, a middle-aged Sicilian with flashing brown eyes, and Adra, his pale bespectacled Finnish girlfriend, young enough to be his daughter were, understandably, not keen to mess it up, even with as uncommon a bicycle as mine. It was decided that poor Evans must endure the dust and sand lashed to the spare tyres on top of the Germans' truck, while I rode in luxury in the camper. Adra spoke English reasonably well, but Carlo knew only Italian and a little French. I thanked them for taking me on board their fine desert vehicle, and when my remarks were translated for Carlo it was clear I had said the right thing. '*Molto bene*' he said, lovingly slapping the top of the dashboard. I responded with '*Tuo Bambino*' which was about the extent of my Italian, but quite enough to ingratiate me with Carlo, who endorsed the assessment with delighted nods of agreement and a few more loving slaps on the dashboard.

At nightfall we came to a splendid campsite by the river at Fafa, and while Carlo wanted to drive on through the cool of the night to Gao, the Germans wanted to stop there and drink cold beer. Had I been asked, I too would have voted to stay, but the Germans won anyway by driving in and parking under a thorn tree and getting their top load, including Evans, firmly stuck among the vicious spikes. It was decided that morning would be a better time to

112

extricate it. The site was unpretentious; just a few round huts which served as a dining room, a bar and a kitchen, and a few others ingeniously and simply furnished as bedrooms. The whole complex, however, stood in a pretty garden full of flowers and trees that seemed amazing after the desert, but it was the river running right alongside that made it magical. Frayed and desiccated by the heat and dust as we all were, water in such noble quantities was like a vision of Eden. I waited only long enough to down a cold beer, and to change into a borrowed swimming costume, before stepping into the Niger's welcoming embrace.

Beyond the pool of light from the hotel the water was quite dark, and nobody had thought to tell me there was a six-knot current running. Afterwards I couldn't imagine how I had been unaware of the great tumult of the Labbezenga rapids, which were only a little way upstream, and which should have warned me to exercise extreme caution. The first that I was aware of anything being wrong was when I noticed a boat coming straight towards me at great speed, and had to swim out fast to avoid it. It was in fact a moored raft which held the pump for the campsite's water supply. Had I got into its turbine blades, it would have been the end of my journey. I now realised that it was I who was on the move, being carried down river like a piece of flotsam at what seemed like the speed of an express train, and that I needed to do something about it fast if I was not to return to Niamey rather quicker than I had come. It was when I tried to turn back and felt the full force of the current that the first cold fingers of fear clutched at my heart. This was the domain of the 'strong brown god' of which Eliot had also written – 'sullen, untamed, intractable ... destroyer' and it was in the role of destroyer that I now saw it. I had to make a conscious effort to fight down the rising tide of panic, and decide fast on what I should do. There was no possibility of making any headway against such a force. The only course was to swim directly towards the shore and hope that I could gradually work towards it as the river continued to carry me down stream. I needed all my concentration to get the maximum out of each stroke, and that kept the panic at bay; but the thought that I was hurtling down towards those wide-mouthed hippos who could cut a pirogue in half was difficult to dispel entirely.

To my great relief, and much sooner than I had expected it, I felt soft ground beneath me, and lay there for a while letting my breathing return to normal. I could see the lights of the campsite some way upstream, and thought I could edge my way back there, wading along through the shallows. But I rejoiced too soon – the river had not finished with me yet. I was in fact nowhere near the bank, but had fetched up on an isolated sandbar midstream. Within seconds of making a move I was in deep water again, in the grip of the current, and this time it was much harder to smother the surge of fear. My strength was ebbing fast, and I knew now that I couldn't hope to make the river bank. I also knew I should try to summon help. I had known this almost from the first, but strange though it seemed in retrospect, and not withstanding the fear and nascent panic, I had the greatest reluctance to reveal my predicament to the world at large. Balanced against the stark reality of drowning was the equally strong fear of appearing ridiculous. I was alone among strangers, clad in someone else's scanty bathing dress, and altogether too old to have got myself into such a pickle. For a while it seemed touch and go which would win. It was only when I felt one of my sandals being torn from my foot by the current that reason gained the upper hand, and I made a conscious decision to call for help. Even then it felt absurdly theatrical, as I piped up with an *'Aidez moi !'*, and then, having cast the die, with several louder cries (I had forgotten the more dramatic *sauver*, and the *au secours* of distant school lessons). *'Aidez moi! Je suis dans le fleuve'* was good enough however. Rash bathers were swept away several times a week from the campsite, I learnt later, and local people were used to responding to their various *cris de coeur*. The reassuring shouts of rescuers came almost immediately, and I continued to call so they could locate me. Very soon there was a swirl of water against a hull, and invisible hands were reaching out and hauling me aboard over the rough planking of a pirogue, but I felt nothing because my flesh was numb. I could barely make out more than the shape of my rescuers, but there were at least two of them, one at the paddle, another sitting

114

behind me rubbing warmth back into my arms and shoulders, as I worked on my legs. From where we landed there was a half mile to walk back, and I was clad only in the costume and a single sandal, but that was nothing against the realization of how very good it felt to be alive.

No one at the hotel was aware that I had been away, let alone almost drowned, for which I was most relieved. I was back in time to join the others for spaghetti cooked by Adra in the cunningly contrived kitchen of the camper van. They were entirely self-contained in every single thing, even to Carlo's home-brewed Chianti, which was soon flowing in true Roman banquet style, and in due time induced a deep dreamless sleep, mercifully free of struggles in dark rushing water.

The following morning witnessed the whole international gathering of desert hoppers – Sicilian, Finnish, German, Nigerien and British – having a late breakfast of aspirin and coffee beside a benign-looking sunlit Niger, above which the kingfishers hovered, and around whose margins laundry was already being spread. Adra was the only one not suffering, as she hadn't drunk any of Carlo's Chianti, being from past experience well aware of its lethal nature.

While the others prepared for departure, the Germans were hard at work hammering and levering tyres off rims to get at punctures acquired from driving into the acacia tree the previous evening. I wandered off among the few hovels that made up the village of Fafa, trying to find the pirogier who had pulled me from the river. His grandson found me first, an earnest boy of about eleven who spoke excellent French, having had the opportunity of staying with relatives in Ayorou and attending school there for a while. He said life in the village was terrible, everybody was so poor, and when they got ill there wasn't any medicine. When he grew up he wanted to be a doctor, he said. At that point his grandfather appeared and I thanked him and gave him a small reward for his efforts the previous evening. He took it willingly but would really have preferred medicine for his cough. Everyone coughed here; it had a lot to do with the dramatic change in climate from the hot dry season with the desiccating winds from the desert, to the high-humidity wet season when everything turns green with mildew, as Mungo Park had noted on his first journey. Unfortunately I had nothing that would help.

As I was going, the old man called me back and offered me the boy. He fetched an older youth out of a cabin to translate and make sure I understood. I was to have the boy to take back to my country because they could see that I liked him. He would have a better chance in my country; he was a good boy and would look after my house well. It was not the first time I had been made such an offer. They were not selling the child, or giving him away, but were looking to his future. As they saw it he belonged to the tribe, and nothing could change that. He would return to his people from whatever new world he went to, and the knowledge and skills he had acquired there would then be at the disposal of them all. My feelings didn't really come into it; I was from the wealthy West, and could provide what was necessary, and the boy was old enough to repay the cost of his keep with work; it was as simple as that. I told the boy that I did not think he would like my cold wet country, but he knew otherwise, and was sad that I would not take him. To give an able child the chance of a good education would have been a just and proper reward for the grandfather's action, and I am sure the arrangement would have benefited everyone. I was equally sure that it would prove impossible to organize, for the West isn't able to live by such simple logic any longer, although once we too had thought it good to send our sons to be educated in another's household.

I got back to find Adra and Carlo impatient to leave. The gilded youth, who had exasperated even the tolerant Germans by his feeble efforts with the pump, was hanging around the Fiat to the outrage of Adra who couldn't bear him. I had my own troubles; the Germans' entanglement with the tree looked as though it had scratched Evans' paintwork rather badly, and until I could get it down I couldn't see what other damage it might have sustained. I was secretly worried too in case the two vehicles might lose contact permanently, but once again I was only a passenger, and no longer in charge of my own destiny. The Fiat pulled out with me aboard, leaving the Germans to follow later with Evans.

Watching Carlo as he drove along the tortured desert track to Gao was to see how apt my earlier remark had been: the Fiat was indeed his baby, and he loved it with a single-minded passion. Like the Germans, he too was an inveterate desert-crosser, making the yearly trek through the Sahara by the same route each time, not because he was captivated by the scenery or the people but because it was a challenge. It had to do with man's technical expertise pitted against the forces of nature, and was something he shared with the Germans, and with all the other addicted desert-crossers I had met in Niger. For some of them, like the Germans, selling their vehicle at the end of the trip and making a profit was also important, but not for Carlo and Adra. Everything that they had with them – tools, cameras, clothes, kitchen equipment – was the most expensive of its kind, and they treasured it. I served a useful role in being a fresh pair of eyes to admire it all. They were both engaged on a search for ultimate material perfection, as elusive as the crock of gold at the end of the rainbow, and needed constant reassurance that they were enjoying the best of everything. During the time I spent with them I never saw either express any delight in the scenes of Africa all around them, or do anything that did not centre upon the vehicle. Wherever we stopped that day, usually to wait for the Germans who continued to suffer tyre problems all the way to Gao, there was no question of them sight-seeing. Carlo, his brown torso bared to the waist, would take the opportunity to get under the truck to effect some minor repair, or plan some new modification. Adra would assist him, somewhat nervously, for he had a quick temper and would turn on her in an instant if she handed him the wrong tool, at which she would stand there saying 'Scusa scusa' hopelessly over and over, until he stopped shouting. Or else both would be cleaning the small interior – the kitchen-bathroom-bedroom – battling with the unremitting gritty dust that found its way inside in spite of all the measures taken to keep it out. The importunate Malians who invariably appeared at such times to watch and comment irritated them unbearably, especially with their endless demands for *cadeaux* and the familiar *Ça va?* with which the

117

requests were prefaced. 'Why you say "*Ça va*" to me?' Carlo would demand angrily in his terrible French of some startled African. 'You don't know me, so why you greet me? Huh?' Or it might be, '*Cadeau?*' on an ascending note of rage. 'Do I ask you for *cadeau*? Huh?', and the poor man, or boy, terrified more by the anger than the words, would flee.

Adra's role of helpmeet to Carlo was plainly of the greatest importance to her, and she would frequently point out to me how he couldn't manage without her. 'I do everything for him while he drive. I light the cigarette, hold the water bottle, watch for the kilometres and the *fesh-fesh*. He do nothing, only concentrating on the road. It is so difficult, so tiring for him.' It did seem fiendishly difficult, a question of constant split-second decision-making, choosing between one vile set of tyre tracks in the sand and another, or a diversion onto virgin ground instead, wrenching the wheel round at the last moment and keeping the wheels turning no matter what. The ruts were often as deep as the axles, and it was important to maintain the right speed and the revs because to lose either was to stick fast, maybe in a patch of *fesh-fesh*, which would take an age to dig out of again. The effect of such driving was mesmeric; the eyes were glued permanently on the patch of road ahead, and the heart lurched constantly as the truck canted over at precarious angles. Adra and I were for ever clutching at one another in sudden alarm, and there certainly was no time to take in details of the surroundings. Carlo said they always preferred to team up with another vehicle, and proceed in convoy, which was why they were travelling with the Germans as far as Gao. It was all taken so seriously, with such an air of desperate endeavour, that I had to keep reminding myself that it was essentially a game and one which had no world-shattering outcome; that we were not in fact bringing 'the good news from Ghent to Aix'.

**South of Niamey**

1. (*top left*) A village in the bush
2. (*top right*) A vegetable garden newly planted in virgin bush
3. (*above*) Village women

4. In the Aïr mountains

5. Bomba the cook

6. Tuareg camel guide

7. Pirogue under sail with Boubacar, Madame and Evans

8. The village chief of Sona

9. The Red Dunes north of Gao

10. Mopti from the terrace of the Bar Bozo

11. Small town market near Mopti

12. A mosque in Timbuktu

13. Sori, my Bozo friend in Djenné

14. Djenné

**Dogon Country**
15. (*above*) Towers of the vanished Tellem
16. (*below*) Granaries at Yabatalou

17. The sorcerer with his 'fizzy'

18. Yabatalou

19. A headman's door with carved ancestor figures

20. The Niger at Segou
21. Sunset on the Niger

# 11

# Boats and Benefactors

HEINRICH BARTH, the German explorer whom the Royal Geographical Society had employed in the mid-nineteenth century to uncover the many questions left unanswered by his intrepid predecessors, had been consumed with excitement on nearing Gao. He had expected marvels of this ancient centre of the Songhay empire, of whose splendours and riches the travellers Ibn Battuta and Leo Africanus had written so enthusiastically in the fourteenth and sixteenth centuries. 'The fourth part of Africa is the land of the Negroes where there is a great plenty of corn and cattle, milk and butter.' 'Salt changes hands for a great quantity of gold. European cloth sells for up to forty times its European value and horses for five times, thus a horse fetches fifty ducats and a young slave six.' '. . . and there was a nugget of gold so large the king could tether his horse to it.' Barth was expecting something very special: 'As soon as I made out that Gogo (Gao) was the place which for centuries had been the capital of a strong and mighty empire, from whence powerful princes had spread their conquests', he wrote, 'I felt a most ardent desire to visit it.'

Gao was already flourishing on the North African trade by the eleventh century, but the Songhay, having no great military force of their own at that time, were under the hegemony of the empire of Mali to the west of them. In 1325, the entourage of the Malian emperor Mansa Musa passed through Gao on its return from the famous pilgrimage to Mecca. Before taking ship for Timbuktu

119

Mansa Musa ordered the building of a great mosque in Gao; an act that was afterwards seen as strangely symbolic, for it marked the end of Malian domination. The empire, having reached its apogee, rapidly declined, and within a decade of Mansa Musa's royal progress the Songhay had expelled the Malian garrison from Gao and begun their own rise to prominence. By the mid-fifteenth century most of the rich influential trading cities along the huge bend of the Niger were under Songhay control. Djenné, the last of them, fell to Sunni Ali Ber in 1473, at which point the Songhay ruled over a territory which stretched from the Aïr Massif in the north-east to Segou in the west, and from the Sahara southwards to the borders of present day Nigeria. Under their rule a centralized administration was established that marked the highest achievement of the empires of the Sahel.

This golden period came to an abrupt end in 1591, when the Moroccan armies of El Mansur poured out of the Sahara, and, having the advantage of musketry, scattered the armies of the Songhay, and captured Gao and Timbuktu. Brief though the period of invasion was, the effect was catastrophic, as the Arab chronicler El Sadi recorded: 'They found one of God's most favoured countries in prosperity and security and made it a place of danger, misery and calamity.' The Moors had little interest in anything other than quick profit, preferably in gold, and under them the empire fragmented, trade declined and the administration collapsed. For the next 250 years the Sahel was cut off from the rest of the world.

Gao had long sunk to the status of a small provincial town by the time Heinrich Barth approached it. Mulling over such heady passages as 'The great town of Gogo (Gao) is without walls, but there is a passing rich palace in its midst', he was bound to be deeply disappointed, and he declared it 'a miserable place'.

I too was initially disappointed in my expectations, for although, unlike Barth, I had not anticipated a splendid city, I had now reached the port where I intended to embark upon a steamer to take the royal road to Timbuktu. Gao marks the beginning of a long stretch of the Niger that is free from rapids and navigable for some 900 miles upstream, almost as far as Bamako, the modern capital of

Mali. The depth of the Niger however is sufficient for passenger steamers to operate only for about four months of the year, and because of the paucity of the previous year's rains, these boats had already stopped by the time I arrived in Gao.

No sooner had our vehicles pulled in to the caravanserai on the outskirts of the town where it was decided we should camp, than we were besieged by numbers of young men who worked in some slight capacity at the site, but whose main source of income was what they could make out of tourists. It took them very little time to discover everyone's business, though they very narrowly escaped injury when they asked Carlo how he was related to Adra; 'For you are an old man and she is young'. They offered every service from the washing of clothes to the finding of a prostitute, but the standard of their laundry was pretty poor, and the bold prostitutes of Gao were quite capable of finding their own clients. I was a godsend to them, for once I knew that the boats had ceased to run I was only too pleased to hire the assistance of two of them, both called Musa, to help me find substitute river transport to Timbuktu. They claimed that there was a *pinasse*, a very large motorized pirogue, just about to leave, and hurried me off to the port right away to negotiate a price.

And there my experience and that of Heinrich Barth parted company, for I found the port of Gao quite wonderful. Sharp-beaked black pirogues of all sizes and conditions were moored side by side in enormous numbers. Others were plying to and fro, people spilling out of them, their robes hitched up as they waded gingerly ashore, flip flops in one hand to toss just clear of the water so that they could step straight into them and not get their feet muddy. Women stood ankle deep gutting fish into the rich potpourri of mud and filth that swilled around the margins, rinsing the fish in it before tossing them to other women who were grilling them on braziers, or stringing them up on long lines to dry in the sun. The pervading smell of roasting fish hung over a host of other scents, both fair and foul. Stacks of firewood, bales and bundles, leaning towers of baskets and clay jars, tethered hens and goats, and a vast miscellany of goods and chattels were piled in glorious profusion

121

on the rough unpaved waterfront, among the colourfully gowned and turbanned throng. Boys raced to and fro dodging the various hazards and jumping from pirogue to pirogue. Vendors wandered in and out of the crowds, baskets on their heads from which they sold nuts and fruit and little bags of fried dough balls.

In the shade of the row of dilapidated warehouses that backed this vibrant and exciting waterfront sat the merchants and the pirogue owners conducting their business in the totally unhurried style of Africa, and it was to them that we made our way. I had already seen the *pinasse*, looking vast and impressive beside the smaller more shapely pirogues. Although, like them, it was essentially a flat-bottomed slab-sided canoe, sharply attenuated at both ends, it was driven by an engine, and was further distinguished by a canopy covering most of its length, spread over hooped bamboo poles. It looked an exciting alternative to a steamer, but unfortunately it wasn't going to Timbuktu. Desperate not to lose a client the two Musas rushed around the waterfront questioning all the pirogiers they could find, and eventually returned in triumph. They had found a large pirogue which had recently brought a load of wood down from Diré and would be going back there shortly, passing Timbuktu on the way. The owner said he had planned to wait until he had sold his wood before returning up river, but if I paid his price he would leave as soon as I wished. I wasn't keen on the idea; 270 miles with only poles for propulsion would take an age, I thought. No, no I was told through the Musas, there would be four pirogiers to pole the boat, day and night, and we would reach Timbuktu in five days, the same length of time as a *pinasse* took, and only twice as long as the steamer.

After what was undoubtedly far too short a bargaining period, I agreed on what the two Musas assured me was a reasonable price, but which was probably at least ten times as much as a local would have paid. The Musas, I suspected, were getting their fees from both sides, but then I doubted they were making a bigger percentage than a Western travel company would, and were working far harder for it. The fare was no more than first class on the steamer would be, although five days in an open boat didn't exactly seem like luxury. Altogether I was relieved to have got the arrangements made with so little trouble. We would depart in four days' time *Insh'Allah* (God willing).

Disaster almost struck again before I could leave Gao, though this time it was my money rather than my life. I had taken out the large stack of currency which was hidden in a secret pocket of my bag, in order to replenish the small supply I kept handy in my purse, when something had distracted me and instead of replacing the notes in the pocket I had walked away leaving my entire funds for the journey in a transparent plastic envelope on a restaurant table in the camping site. Rapacious local youths and boys for whom such a find would have been a fortune were all over the place, as were quite a few of the rougher type of western traveller. Why the *patron*, who normally never graced the site, should choose that precise moment to visit was one of those things that have to be put down either to the very long arm of coincidence, or as I prefer, to my watchful guardian angel. I was as shocked as the owner was by my carelessness, and listened with unaccustomed meekness to his scolding. After that he took a kindly interest in my welfare, and made one of the cabins at the site available to me at no charge; even though I still preferred to sleep in my airy little tent, he thought that Evans and the rest of my gear would be better locked up.

He also invited me to dinner one night, and sent his man around with his beautiful new Alfa Romeo to drive me the short way across the sand to his house. Expecting an establishment in keeping with the car, which certainly wasn't one that had arrived via the Sahara, I was shown into a large room, unattractively furnished with western plush furniture and mattresses on the floor, and a large refrigerator in pride of place. Dinner was food from the camping site kitchen – unidentified meat and very dead chips reheated in a greasy frying pan on a primus stove in the porch, by the man who had driven me there. While we struggled with this quite awful meal, we were entertained to a painfully inane French comedy on the video, whose sole merit was that it provided the distraction for me to slip the majority of my portion into my handkerchief to dispose of later, just as I had done so often at school, years before.

123

After such kindness I couldn't dream of moving to the convenience of Gao's solitary and rackety hotel, which together with a few other decaying old colonial buildings graced the centre of the unpretentious little town. The French had rebuilt Gao in the early part of the century, laying out the wide streets in an orderly grid pattern with neat drains down either side. But it was Africanised now and rather ramshackle, with large colourful markets and low *banco* houses whose courtyards throbbed with life, and I found it full of charm.

The caravanserai on the other hand, although by general consensus the cleanest place to stay had definite drawbacks; like the lengthy hike into town across the soft sand, the minimal showers and horrid loos, and the awful food which was, I discovered, cooked by kitchen *totos* of around nine years of age. Far worse than all these, however, was awaking each morning to find the walled sandy courtyard swarming with beggars who had managed to bribe the gateman to let them in. Some of them were pitiful – paraplegics shuffling around on their haunches, lepers, blind men led about by children – others were simply part of the multitude of the poor of Africa. All were perfectly good-natured, even cheerful; it was the travellers who experienced difficulty, for we didn't share the beggars' patience, nor their acceptance of the evils of life, their notions of fate, and of the will of Allah. Trying to eat breakfast with a dozen pairs of eyes boring into my back from just a few feet away was not something with which I learnt to cope. But it wasn't only alms that they wanted. We were also their entertainment, their glimpse into another world. They loved our clothes, our machines and our gadgets for their own sakes, as part of that world which they, unlike the gilded youth, did not yet aspire to, and so were free to wonder at without the pain of desiring it. I gained some notoriety among this fraternity because of Evans, which a crippled boy came each day to see. He would persuade me to ride it round the compound, changing the gears, and everyone would watch closely and exclaim in astonishment as the chain leapt from cog to cog. It made me feel like a circus performer.

The diversity of peoples in Gao seemed even greater than in

Niamey, possibly because here Berber blood had mixed so thoroughly with Negro. All were black, but of a wide variety of shades, and features ranged from the aquiline to the purely Negro. The totally distinctive costumes and the intricate ways of braiding the hair which would tell someone knowledgeable in these matters the difference between tribes is also lost now in most cases. Many people wore a mixture of ethnic and western garments, and experimented with different hair styles. It was quite common to see girls with a wrapround native cloth skirt topped by a T-shirt, or vest with some slogan like Coca-Cola across the bosom. Some of the older women wore western-style dresses of forty years ago, but always covering the ankles. Many of the younger men had adopted trousers with shirts worn loose over them. Children were often dressed completely in western dress. I gathered that these were usually second-hand clothes donated to charities overseas, which somehow fetched up in the markets of Africa where they were sold much more cheaply than the price of cloth.

One day a couple of Swiss desert-crossers called Jean Claude and Laurence who were also staying at the caravanserai, invited me to eat with them in a small restaurant that served capitaine, the huge delicious Niger pike. The dark interior, welcome after the blinding light, hid the grosser imperfections and the worst of the grime, and the gloom was relieved by glimpses through the open doorway into a sunbaked courtyard. Like most restaurants it had its complement of prostitutes; middle-aged, shapeless and raddled, their faces powdered with what appeared to be white flour, and dressed in pathetically youthful and out-moded western fashion, that, shockingly for Moslems, revealed the legs almost as far as the knees. Since it was only lunchtime no one was importuning particularly hard, and the most outrageously dressed of the women came over to talk French with us, and to tell us, in a little-girl voice, about how she had worked in Paris. At this, one of a group of men chipped in and said that it was all nonsense and lies; she had only wasted her money on a trip there. Everyone's dream was to get to Paris, he told us disparagingly, just to say they had been there. People saved for years, he said, just to get a flight there and turn straight round and come back again. It was the first time I had heard of this but the Swiss were well aware of it; they said Paris had more pull than Mecca, and that when French Airlines had a slack period they ran special cheap flights to accommodate these pilgrimages.

The prostitute was hurt by having her story ruined, and began to annoy the man and his friends, behaving in an even more childlike way, demanding beer, pouting and throwing remarks around in a language I couldn't understand, but which were clearly taunts. Finally, exasperated, he rounded on her and said cruelly in French, 'You were never a pretty girl anyway'.

Jean Claude and Laurence seemed more concerned over my forthcoming boat trip than I was. Jean Claude was not at all sure that I had given the necessary consideration to all the things that might go wrong. He was probably right but, as I explained, if I did so, I would probably never get up the nerve to go anywhere. Laurence's worries over washing and toilet arrangements I didn't share, as these were common needs and I was sure they would present no problems. But over food I thought she might have a point, and I agreed that I would buy nuts and fruit to take with me.

They came to the port to see me off, and to give me a parcel of food, supplies for their desert trip, which they had brought with them from Switzerland, and which they said they didn't want to take back again. By the old reckoning of the value that goods accrued after crossing the Sahara, they were handing me the equivalent of a king's ransom. How glad I was to be of it I had as yet no idea. To everyone's relief, especially the two Musas who had come in with me and were waiting to collect their fee, the pirogue was actually there and waiting. The man who had baited the prostitute in the restaurant the previous day was also there, together with a stout, respectable-looking woman surrounded by bundles. He explained that she was a relation of his who was also going on my pirogue as she had missed the last steamer back to her husband in Niafounké, after a protracted visit to her family in Gao. From his profuse thanks for my taking her, and from her stern and unsmiling demeanour, I gathered he was glad of this opportunity of shipping her off. She was introduced to me as Madame, and during the time I was to spend in her close company, she was never referred to by any other name, and I never once saw her smile.

The ship-owner told the Musas that I should buy a mattress for the journey. At first I demurred, thinking I had paid out quite enough, but when I was shown the row of rough uneven logs swilling about in the inch of mud and water in the space which I was to occupy for the next five days, I too thought a bit of padding would not come amiss. We went off to market and bought a thick straw-stuffed mattress for about five pounds, which I learnt afterwards was only twice what it should have cost. As soon as it was spread on top of the logs, Madame scrambled aboard and made a dive for it, but was ejected by the ship owner and made to sit between the next two thwarts on a pile of sacks of rice. Evans had already been carried aboard and tied against a thwart alongside my mattress, and no sooner had I taken my place than two young men sprang aboard, and we were off; the two Musas, Laurence and Jean Claude rapidly disappearing into the bustle of the water front.

I couldn't believe we had actually started, for where were the promised four pirogiers who were to pole night and day? But we were heading straight out across the wide expanse of the Niger towards the beautiful rose-red dunes of the opposite bank, a single pirogier wielding his pole at the rear of the boat in the lovely fluid movement I remembered from my previous trip in Niger. 'What did my brother tell you about how long we would take to Timbuktu?' asked the other cheerful young pirogier, whose name I learnt was Boubacar. He had been busy stowing away various bundles, but now seemed inclined for a little conversation. When I told him I had been given to understand that the journey would take five days, he whistled increduously between his teeth, and continued in his sing-song French, 'That man he is one big liar. Five days! It cannot be done. Maybe ten is possible if everything goes very, very well'. 'Where are the four pirogiers I was promised?' I asked. 'There are never four,' said Boubacar, 'A pirogue is always for two men only, this one is for Mohammed and me.' 'And what about travelling night and day?' 'If the wind is right then we travel at night, if not, we sleep, *Voilà!*'

As the Swiss had tried to warn me, nothing is ever what it seems in West Africa. But so what? I thought, I was afloat on the majestic Niger again, this time with a black Madame and two young men who seemed both pleasant and competent. There were herons, black ibis and kingfishers overhead and rafts of pink water lilies floating past. This sort of travelling had nothing at all to do with times and schedules. Five days or ten, two pirogiers or four, what did it matter? It wasn't a mood that would continue unbroken until we reached Timbuktu – I was too conditioned by western attitudes for that – but while it lasted, it felt like being freed of a tremendous and quite unnecessary burden.

# 12

# Shaking down on a Pirogue

NOW THAT I HAD THE leisure to study it in detail, I could see that a
real working pirogue was a most ingenious craft, as different as
could be imagined from the simple dug-out canoes used in other
parts of Africa, and bearing only a superficial resemblance to the
small craft on which I had gone down river from Niamey. It was
about eighty feet long, flat bottomed, with the slab sides flaring
outwards and tapering towards stem and stern to end in long
attenuated platforms overhanging the water from which the two
pirogiers, Mohammed and Boubacar, plied their long poles. A beak
of wood, rather like the ram of a Roman galley, extended the prow
by another few feet, further enhancing the slender lines. The width
amidships, where I sat, was about six feet at the bottom and eight
at the top of the freeboard. Like all pirogues, it was literally sewn
together, through holes bored around the edges of the various planks
of which it was made. Wire rather than the usual rope had been
used to lace up this one, and long hand-made nails had also been
employed in the many repairs it had undergone during the sixty
years it had traded on the Niger. Eight thwarts provided the lateral
strength, and these too were lashed to the sides through holes bored
in their ends, and in the side planks, and could be moved from place
to place at need. Several of the thwarts had been broken and had
lengths of bamboo placed like splints across the fractures, odds and
ends of string holding them in place.

It was a very flexible craft, superbly adapted for its purpose. The

Niger is essentially a wide, shallow river that rapidly loses depth between the rains, producing a plethora of shifting sandbanks on which it is all too easy to run aground. Even heavily laden, the supple pirogues, with their ability to literally change shape, can be eased off again with little effort, where a stiffer vessel would be likely to damage itself or get stuck until the river rose again in the next rains. The shape, too, presents the least resistance to the water so that they can be poled relatively easily against the current.

Adjusting to life aboard took me a little while, partly because I did not really know what to expect. Only one of my three companions spoke anything other than Songhay, of which I knew not a word. By reasons of language, race and religion I was very much the odd one out, and rather in the position of a child who must 'wait and see'. In the boat's pecking order, however, it soon became clear that I was something more elevated than a mere passenger. The sum of nearly fifty pounds which I had paid for my passage apparently conferred upon me the rights of '*patron*', and this was my title when I was not addressed as '*Madame Blanc*'. If there was any question of choice about where we stopped, or for how long, my wishes were consulted and given preference. Had this not been the case, the voyage would have taken considerably longer than it did, for pirogiers, like sailors everywhere, are notorious for wanting to make protracted visits to their friends and relations ashore, and Mohammed and Boubacar proved to be no exception. This first day however everything – boat, companions and the shoreline – was delightfully novel, and I hardly knew where to direct my gaze.

When we had been underway for about an hour Boubacar laid down his pole and lit a wood fire in an ingenious clay bowl, the rim of which swept inwards, forming four prongs on which a cooking pot could be placed. A sack of rice was broached, and some of it was put on to boil. Thinking I should contribute, I passed up a tin of carrots, supplied by the Swiss, and these were boiled with the rice so that in the end nothing at all of them remained except a faint orange stain. Madame was handed the stick to stir the rice, while Boubacar made repairs, hammering caulking into a few of the more obvious leaks, and bailing out the boat.

We tied up to the bank while we ate, and afterwards everyone went ashore, taking their separate ways to attend to their bodily needs. Madame disappeared carrying a child's red plastic potty with a bar of soap and a pan scourer in it; this puzzled me, especially since she had no pans with her, these having already been rinsed in the river. The boys stripped off to their underpants and stood waist deep in the water, soaping and shampooing themselves, and this looked so inviting that I went some way off and followed suit. I swam in my shirt in the interests of modesty, but even so I received some dirty looks from Madame on her return, probably for exposing my legs. The boys made a few brief prostrations ashore, and Madame made slightly more protracted ones aboard, on the sacks of rice, and we continued on our way, visibly more relaxed, Madame belching and noisily cleaning out her sinuses, Boubacar playing his radio and making Tuareg tea in a little blue teapot, while I studied the herons poised like statues at the water's edge.

Where a bend in the river necessitated a change of course Mohammed laid down his pole and took up an enormous primitive oar, its broad-leafed blade lashed into a rough slit in the long shaft. He hung this in a rope sling fastened to the side of the pirogue and, leaning on it with all his weight, brought the boat with great ponderous strokes across the wide river. Once against the other bank, we were running along the edge of bare red sand hills which rose steeply from the water. Figures in flowing robes moved through the barren landscape, with donkeys, flop-eared sheep and little naked children. Scores of very primitive pirogues loaded high with rice were being poled across the river from the extensive marshes on the other side. Doubtless the villages were built on the sandy side for protection from the teeming mosquitoes breeding in those ancient paddies.

When there was nothing else requiring his attention Boubacar too wielded his pole, swinging along hour after hour in a tireless mesmeric rhythm. The eastern shore was still bright, while in the shadow of the western bank it was deliciously cool after the midday heat, and the water murmured softly against the hull. Then it was no longer cool but chill as the sun began the last of its rapid dip towards nightfall. The sky softened to pink and grey, and great skeins of egrets and black ibis crossed purposefully overhead, homeward bound, and still the boys swung their poles steadily in unison, plunging them down, lean and push and up again, as they had been doing for seven hours.

We pulled into land as dusk fell, at the foot of steep red sand dunes. Climbing them in the very last of the light, I saw beyond a sandy plain with figures moving about between scattered huts. There were a few flickering lights as cooking fires were started, and the thud and boom of a hundred pestles pounding into mortars. At the water's edge there was no one but ourselves. It was cold enough now to don several more layers of clothing, and to think of getting into my sleeping bag. Madame was already wrapped in several shawls and blankets. Earlier we had bought some small silver fish from a passing fisherman, and these were now cooked and served, eyes, entrails, everything, all mashed up together in rice. I could not cope with the bones, particularly in the dark, and after struggling for a while I surreptitiously slid my share into the helpful Niger.

My straw mattress on the crooked uneven logs was not very comfortable, and there were persistent attacks by mosquitoes coming right across the river in search of blood. Only after Boubacar had rigged a spar on which I could hang my net was sleep possible. He and Mohammed lay up near the bows, on another rough platform of logs, with no padding at all other than the sacks they were wrapped in. They were smoking and playing tapes of Malian pop songs. Madame was a rounded shape between us, snoring gently on the hard rice sacks, hemmed in by her many bales and bundles. All night, as I drifted in and out of sleep, I was aware of Orion making his great passage across the sky among the lesser constellations, and later, when the night was almost spent, the Plough appeared briefly, climbing up out of the north.

We were aground when dawn broke, and Madame, eager to be on her way home to her husband in Niafounké, woke the pirogiers with a gruff tirade. We got going quickly into the brief miracle of early morning, the colours very tender and the air warming deliciously. By half past seven we were passing villages where the day's work had already begun, men and women standing in circles, threshing piles of green rice with sticks, babies sleeping soundly on their mother's backs in spite of their heads flopping backwards and forwards with every movement.

By mid-morning the wind shifted south-westerly, and to my surprise and delight Boubacar began to rig a sail. Never have I seen such a Heath Robinson arrangement of sticks, wire and sacks, and unlike the admirable hull, it was difficult to believe that something infinitely better could not have been devised, although for ingenuity and absolute minimum cost, it was marvellous. The only spar that looked remotely fashioned, rather than found, was the mast, which was square-sectioned and had clearly done service as something else earlier in its life, before it had been broken in several places and abandoned. It was roughly mended in the usual Malian way with a few splints, and Boubacar now lashed it against the similarly repaired thwart, staying it to the sides of the boat with a couple of short pieces of bamboo, also lashed in place with odd bits of string. The sail was a simple lateen design made of old rice sacks sewn together, some of which bore the legend 'Free gift of the people of America. Not for Resale.' The many holes and tears in this tattered patchwork were of great benefit, allowing much of the wind to escape, and thus lessening the strain on the hotchpotch of perilous rigging. Even so we had to manoeuvre swiftly several times in the first hour for Boubacar to effect repairs after rotted string had parted, or a grossly inadequate spar had snapped or given way under the strain and the whole rig had come tumbling down about our ears. A wind from this quarter was so unusual that the others suspected that it was something I had organized, and Boubacar warned me sternly that if it blew any stronger he would take the sail down. I promised to try and moderate it.

The pirogue was steered by Mohammed hanging on to the huge oar in its rope sling, and because the sail, left to itself, could only pull when the wind was dead aft, which it seldom was, Boubacar had to spend most of his time keeping it in position with the aid of a long stick. Even so it gave the boys a welcome rest from poling, and we creamed along at between six and seven knots in the most exhilarating fashion. The water came inboard more swiftly with the faster passage, and Madame, whom Boubacar said had never before been in a pirogue, was kept busy with the bailer, so that I wondered if she was working her passage as a deck hand. Because my space was now invaded by Boubacar, and my view was blocked by the sail, I found a new and exciting perch on the front platform.

There were many small flotillas of pirogues, mostly less than half the size of ours, also making up river, going to market perhaps, or returning home. They travelled in threes and fours, each carrying a small family group and loaded with a few bales, sacks and bundles. We had passed and repassed some of them who, like us, had camped overnight. They were now all rigged in much the same crazy fashion, and it looked as though a number of Huckleberry Finns were having a lark on the river with tablecloths and sheets purloined from home. It lent the Niger an air of gaiety.

By eleven o'clock the wind had died and it was too desperately hot to do anything but keep still and try not to think as we poled mile after mile through channels in the rice paddies, with flies coming off them in droves to invade the boat. Following a little flotilla through one of these channels, our prow caught the man who was poling the last pirogue and knocked him into the water. We did not stop – I don't think we could have done so in that narrow channel. The man vaulted back onto his platform with hardly a pause, still in possession of his pole, his shoulder muscles looking immensely powerful through the wet cloth of his shirt. He took up his position behind, and no word of recrimination or apology, not even a look was exchanged between the two boats.

The midday stop for more mashed-up fish and rice was by a muddy bank where Madame could find nowhere suitable for her ablutions, but the rest of us swam from the boat. Tempers which had become somewhat strained by the heat, and by the flies which had plunged into our meal with frenzied abandon, were wonderfully restored in the cool brown water. Poor Madame, deprived of similar refreshment, was even more censorious of my swimming in my shirt and shorts than she had been the previous day. Not contenting herself this time with black looks, she let fly a torrent of words. I could understand nothing of her outburst but the import of what was said was clear, and Boubacar (called after Abu Bakr, the uncle of the prophet) came to my defence, saying how sensible it was to swim in this great heat, though what he said to Madame I have no idea. Boubacar had the sunniest of natures and a great capacity for enjoying life, qualities I valued tremendously after the previous boat journey. Even Madame was not proof against them, and was soon as close to smiling as she ever came, and I was chuckling to myself from the effect of his final triumphant '*Voila!*' which was how he ended all his conversations with me. It made me feel that our ages had been reversed, and that he was patiently explaining life to a small, not very bright child.

Both boys had pink painted fingernails, and a cockleshell fastened by a leather thong to the front of their throats. It did not signify anything special, said Boubacar, they just wanted to look alike because they were friends as well as being '*grand frères*' – the same father, but different mothers. Boubacar was slightly the younger, but he had been to school for a short time whereas Mohammed had not, a fact, together with speaking French, that might have had something to do with his being the natural leader of the two. Their one great luxury was the radio-tape machine on which they played the rather repetitive and lugubrious Malian pop music. They had saved up for years for the player, and could afford only one set of batteries every trip. Cooking the batteries in the embers of the fire to prolong their life became a thrice-daily feature of the journey, and even on the tenth day enough energy could be produced by this method to give a few minutes of music.

There was not a breath of breeze for the rest of the day, so nothing tempered the sun beating down upon us in the unshaded boat. The lovely hour of softening colours and cooling air had never felt more welcome. Herds of lowing cattle were winding homewards to some remote village along the eastern bank; dark herons and brilliant white egrets were wheeling low overhead. Boubacar raised no objection to my sleeping ashore, so I pitched my tent behind a little hummock and enjoyed a few hours of solitude, in far greater comfort than on the pirogue. The Swiss crackers, cheese and tinned

135

fruit which I ate instead of fish and rice were also a great treat.

Just before dawn the wind got up suddenly with such force that I had the utmost difficulty taking down the tent without it being torn from my grasp. We got going in a light as grey and flat as England in February, in a temperature practically as cold. By eight o'clock the wind had gone round first to the east, and then to its usual winter quarter of north-east. The boys were poling hard, being unable with the primitive lateen sail to make use of any wind that was forward of abeam, and our course was now roughly north-west. The adverse wind remained very strong, whipping up the shallow Niger into hard little white-topped waves, and we hugged the shelter of every small island and sand bar, many of which had nomads' tents on them; other tents and equipment lay in heaps along the shore waiting to be ferried out to other islands.

We creamed into Bourem at 2.45 p.m. on the third day out from Gao. Sixty miles in a little over two days was a record, said Boubacar, and entirely due to the freakish wind, which had gone round to the south several times, blowing great guns and threatening to tear our frail sail to pieces. We must have reached speeds of ten knots at times, only to have some part of the worn out gear break under the strain, throwing us broadside on to those steep little waves, with the Niger coming in solidly over the gunwale and Madame bailing for dear life. But even when the mast gave way with a great crack and Boubacar leapt forward crying *'Doucement, doucement'* no one else had let out as much as a squeak. It was now firmly established that *'Madame Blanc'* was in charge of the wind and Boubacar continued to deliver his little lecture about taking down the sail if I would not moderate the force of it, to which I, equally seriously, promised to do my best.

We had seen several large villages with a prickly-spired mosque rising from the middle of them, but Bourem was a sizeable town in comparison, and we stopped there for the boys to buy supplies. Madame and I, left sitting in the boat on the muddy shore, were soon besieged by extremely importunate children and teenagers who had caught sight of my white skin and come to demand largesse. They were very bold, and not above trying to snatch things out of the boat if they could distract our attention. There was little we could do except to hang onto things as best we could and hope for a speedy return of the crew, though Madame did seem to be giving them a sizeable piece of her mind.

I thought of Mungo Park making his voyage down the Niger and refusing to have any truck at all with the land; keeping centre stream and shooting at any craft that came too near. He has always been much criticized for adopting this course, and indeed it does seem a little extreme to consider that you have the right to shoot your way through someone else's country. But possibly Bourem's waterfront almost two hundred years later offered some understanding of his actions. Other white skins appeared some distance off at one point, and the predatory cries that the young people uttered as they rushed to intercept them was enough to make anyone's blood run cold.

The boys returned with a fresh supply of firewood, and borrowed an axe to hack it into pieces small enough for the fire pot. The axe was standard to these parts and hadn't changed in design since the Stone Age, except that a metal blade was now bound into the rounded wooden club, rather than a piece of worked flint. They had also bought a length of nylon cord to repair the halliard, parted now for the fifth time, and made up of more different pieces of string than I could count. It would have been an excellent idea to renew all the running rigging and the various spars, but I'm sure it would have to be in a far worse state before that happened. As soon as the new halliard was rigged, Boubacar hoisted our tattered sail and we sped out of Bourem like a train, heading due west now, for it was here that the river made its right-angled change of direction. With luck, we might be sailing down-wind all the way to Timbuktu.

# 13

# The Royal Road

AS THE NIGER SWUNG ever deeper into the fringes of the Sahara Desert, it seemed increasingly to me a miraculous thing, a thread of life in an otherwise completely dead land. Sometimes at night I would turn my back on the pirogue floating so peacefully above its mirror image, the taped Malian music coming softly from the bows, and walk out beyond any little settlement or minimal patch of pasture or cultivation there might be to where the formless sands stretched away into unimaginable distances beneath the enormous stars of Africa. All deserts are formidable, but none had ever struck me with the sense of dread that I experienced on these solitary forays. I am not sure whether it was because these wastelands seemed to possess none of the intrinsic beauty of the Aïr or the Ténéré, or whether it was something purely atavistic, a feeling that I was picking up from past travellers who had struggled against such terrible odds to cross these immeasurable trackless sands, and had so often perished almost within sight of safety.

It was from ports upon this stretch of the Niger that the camel caravans had set forth upon the terrible ocean of the Sahara, and it was to its shores that they returned again, or, almost as often, had failed to do so. No desert had ever witnessed more passing trade than this one, nor claimed more lives. To make the crossing six times was considered the limit of a camel driver's working life, and very few managed that number. The watering holes were far apart and hard to find: to miss one meant almost certain destruction for the whole caravan. The market value of a slave who survived the journey and reached the Mediterranean coast was increased a hundredfold, for the vast majority of the countless thousands of chained wretches who set out under the harrying whips left their bones to bleach along the way. Small wonder the tumbled expanse, silvery and full of shadows, seemed also so full of ghosts.

By the fourth day, the sense of infinite remoteness, of being in a world entirely cut off, was heightened by a feeling that the voyage would go on for ever, a thought that was pleasurable at times, but could also plunge me into deep gloom, depending very much upon the time of day. Particularly trying were the afternoons when the horizons, usually so wide, seemed to close in with a draining heat that sapped the body dry but gave the tormenting flies renewed energy. It was then that insect bites on legs and ankles itched like the torments of hell, so that it was almost impossible not to scratch them, and when the cracked and dried-out linings of nostrils and throat throbbed and ached the most, when lips bled in spite of the coatings of protective grease, and when eyes, inflamed by the unrelenting glare, refused to focus on a page, and oozed slow tears.

The freezing desert nights and the cold grey mornings with a howling harmattan trying to blow the tent to kingdom come before I could get it stowed were less hard on me than on the boys, for I could pile on several shirts with a nylon cagoule over the top, and I had my good warm sleeping bag, as Boubacar was always pointing out, half in admiration, half in envy. He and Mohammed rolled themselves up in the sail at night, which was part of the reason it had so many holes in it, and why we so seldom carried on sailing through the hours of darkness. On the rare occasions we did make a night passage, they lit a fire in the clay bowl and took turns to crouch over it. Madame coped with both the cold and the heat by always wearing several dresses one on top of the other, and had many layers of shawls and blankets to pile over her at nights. It was the hardness of the sacks of rice that eventually wore her down, until one day she became convinced she was very ill and Boubacar was worried and asked if I had medicine to make her better. I gave her two aspirin which worked wonders, and afterwards she kept begging for more, 'to show her friends at home what "*Madame Blanc*" had given her' as she told Boubacar. Alas, medicine, even aspirin, was in too-short supply for souvenirs.

Food would have proved the biggest problem for me, without the generous parcel from the Swiss. In theory I like fish and rice, which was the unvarying thrice daily meal of the pirogiers. We bought fish for just a few coppers from passing fishermen, and varied and lovely fish they were too. I especially liked a species the size of mackerel that, like them, were silver with stippled backs, only in bright reds and yellows. Not that I had much chance to study them before Madame was cutting off the fins and gutting them while they still wriggled and flopped about the boat. I was happy to pay the whole of the paltry sum for the fish in order to have them fresh daily, but we always got enough to last into a second or even a third day, by which time they were stinking and certainly toxic. The real reason I eventually gave up even trying to eat fish and rice, however, was the fat used so generously in cooking it. It was a vegetable product called *carité* which is obtained from the fruit of a tree after a tremendous amount of pounding and kneading. The resulting thick yellow grease smelt worse than anything I can describe and tasted like something that had long gone off.

Boubacar and Mohammed had thrived on the diet since birth, but Madame was used to more variety, and there came a day when she too turned up her nose at fish and rice. I then proffered the packet of macaroni from the Swiss parcel which was duly cooked, and all three of them ate quantities of it, professing themselves delighted with the change. But as it had been liberally dressed in the same horrid grease, and well larded with bits of putrid fish, I found it no better than any of the other uneatable meals.

In Africa the saying goes 'If one eats, all eat'; so it was not easy to consume my stores without sharing them, and as there was not enough to go round as well as to keep me alive, I had my main meal in the tent at night. It was seldom more than a small tin of tuna or processed meat or cheese, with a few crackers and perhaps half a tin of corn, and one or two pieces of dried fruit. I had also been given a packet of milk powder and some muesli and I had that for breakfast with a mug of coffee, while the others had their fish and rice. The rest of the day I managed on peanuts which I had bought in Gao and which I did share, so that they failed to last the whole journey.

Every inch of the boat was impregnated with a greasy black grime that came off on everything, so that clothes, books, luggage, all one's possessions in fact soon bore the same grimy patina. There were spikes and splinters everywhere too, so that wounds and scratches were all too easy to come by and provided another focus for the flies. With mere physical existence so demanding, and every task and movement such an effort it was not surprising that I slept well at nights.

The tent made all the difference, giving me the necessary hours of solitude to recharge my energies. In spite of the wind filling the interior with sand, I only once used the outer cover, being unwilling to be cut off from those superlative skies which I could see almost in their entirety through the mosquito netting of the inner tent. Also, being in visual contact with the outside world was less worrying than if I had only been able to imagine what might be there. So it was that I had a good view of the mad marabout who came at midnight and stood over the tent for ten minutes, screaming imprecations. It was a night when we had stopped near a village which had seemed faintly hostile towards us. Boubacar trusted no one who was not related to him, and normally we tied up for the night far from any civilization. When I was awoken by the crescendo of loud shouts I was frightened, thinking it might be an attack by the villagers. The solitary white-clad figure waving a stick wildly around his head loomed up before I had decided on any course of action, so I just stayed quite still where I was, and hoped the boys would come to the rescue. The fact that no one came in spite of his screaming tirade somehow reassured me and, tired as I was, I think I closed my eyes and had almost drifted back to sleep before he had even moved on. In the morning Boubacar told me that he was a well-known feature of the middle Niger, an itinerant marabout preaching Islam to

141

backsliding Moslems between Timbuktu and Bourem; quite mad, but harmless.

The pump with which I rendered my drinking water free of harmful bacteria was still terribly hard to operate so I went over to drinking the Niger's water purified with tablets which the Swiss had also given me. Bathing in the Niger was to run a serious risk of bilharzia, but I never considered not doing so, as it was the only thing that made the afternoons bearable. Everyone enjoyed bath time and took it very seriously, adding huge quantities of lather to the Niger. I had several opportunities to study Madame's technique, as after the second day she didn't feel the need to remove herself quite as far, but marched only a short distance from the pirogue with her red potty, the nylon scouring pad and the large bar of yellow washing soap of the sort I could dimly remember being used in my childhood when clothes were washed with it on a corrugated scrubbing board. Madame would execute complicated manoeuvres beneath her layers of clothing, removing various skirts and lengths of cloth and managing modestly to divest herself of all but a single wrap that covered her from armpits to mid-calf. She would then get to work vigorously beneath this with her scouring pad and soap, and sitting massively in the fringes of the Niger would rinse off and, with difficulty because of the rolls of fat, bend her head forward until all the complicated little plaits were under water. On emerging she would pinch her nostrils together from above and blow vigorously, a practice everyone but me followed several times a day. Madame was in fact some years older than I, though she looked considerably younger as her face bore not a single wrinkle – probably the result of never creasing it with a smile. I thought her a very stately personage, and one day, when we had stopped to trade at a small nomad camp, a man of about sixty with twinkling eyes and a large silver earring in one ear took quite a fancy to her, holding her in what seemed to be a very pointed conversation and casting unmistakably ardent glances at her. Madame looked coy and pleased, and I thought she was probably blushing too. Just as we were leaving, her admirer bowled two huge water melons across the mud as a parting present for her.

Set against all the hundred-and-one irritations of the journey was the abiding miracle of our ribbon of bright water, and as long as I continued to believe that it would eventually bring me to Timbuktu, I never seriously wished myself anywhere else for long. The bird life alone was enough to keep me busy with the binoculars for most of the day. Without a bird book I couldn't hope to identify much of what I saw, and although this bothered me (it being so ingrained a habit of Westerners to need to identify things) I still derived tremendous pleasure from simply watching, and noted down over forty distinctive breeds, from a huge bittern-like creature to an unmistakable little Senegalese firebird. Those I didn't know I felt free to coin my own names for, such as 'rosy-bellied lapwing', 'fresh-water oyster catcher', and 'long-winged Niger river gull'. In one place I noticed that the lovely pied kingfishers, common as sparrows on this river, nested in burrows tunnelled out of the muddy banks, as sand martins and puffins do, and as I had not read this in any book it felt like making an original discovery.

The river was never empty and was always changing as nomads arrived with a great ferrying of their gear and animals onto islands or across to the other bank. I tried to find out what I could about them from Boubacar, but it was not easy. The most distinctive people after the Tuareg were the Bozos, itinerant fishermen who built as their bases little villages of distinctive gable-ended huts, where they dried most of their catch. The products of their year-round labours were sold in all the markets of West Africa. As the river fell, leaving shallow lakes cut off from the main flow, they would harvest all the fish in them in one concerted action, several families working together and sweeping the lake clean with their nets. They were superb boat-people, with a natural balance that came from living on the water since babyhood, and it was common to see a tiny mite of no more than four or five, standing with legs wide spread on the bow platform of a pirogue, poling it along against a fearsome wind, skilfully utilising every ounce of his puny strength. His father, busy with the nets in the stern of the pirogue, didn't need even to glance up, he trusted the child so absolutely.

The cattle-owning nomads seemed to have the same relationship to the agriculturalists as I had observed in the south. When the ancient rice paddies had been harvested, the herds were welcomed in to fertilize the ground for the next season's planting. In other places it was not true nomadic life I was witnessing but a sort of transhumance – a seasonal movement of flocks to another region – while part of the tribe, often the elders, remained to tend what crops there were. In these cases the domed woven-mat tents of the herders would be pitched alongside the simple *banco* huts. No one was living above bare subsistence level, and often the banks were innocent of even the thinnest strip of arable land. Often too, there were abandoned *banco* villages where the river had changed its course and inundated the dwellings, or, more often, where the fertility of a particular sliver of land had failed, or where the small fields had been smothered by great drifts of blown sand.

Contact with the real nomadic people was rare but exciting. There was a quality about them almost like deer on the hills, something free and wild but essentially non-threatening. There was a poignancy too, for I knew that I was in at the death of something precious and exceptional, something that we needed to learn about before we destroyed it. What I was seeing were the last throes of a way of life that had achieved a perfect balance with the environment which supported it. Where man has exploded all over the planet, multiplying at a rate to threaten the extermination of all other species, burning the forests, poisoning the land, the seas and the rivers, and threatening all the lovely wildernesses, these people sought only to continue the life they had known for centuries. They had cared for the marginal land that maintained them by being aware of its limitations. They had not over-grazed it, nor over-produced; they had moved on when necessary, and adapted to the climatic changes by seeking new grazing grounds until the cycle of the rains returned.

Now the teeming millions of Africa, who no longer die from famine or disease, press in upon them on all sides. Their fragile grazing lands are increasingly swallowed up in millet fields which will become the deserts of tomorrow, since they are not suited to that use. The nomads seem a people without ambition other than to live and to enjoy what they have, and what could they not teach our success-orientated society if only we knew how to ask them the right questions before they are forced to live by our standards.

I couldn't ask anything. I had to build a picture from the fragments I gleaned as the pirogue moved on unhurriedly, north-west, south-west, on the turning twisting stream of the Niger. Sometimes men appeared on the banks in robes of yellow, bright blue, red, or jade green, gorgeous against the dull ochre of the land, their women the perfect foil, all in black. Boubacar had a cardboard drum which he locked with a sliver of metal and a minute lock. In this he kept his trading goods, tea and sugar mainly, and a few cigarettes. When we were sailing midstream, boats would come shooting out from the shore, several men paddling hard to intercept us. They would hang onto the sides of our boat for the lengthy haggling and exchange, having to paddle back afterwards several miles to where they started. Sometimes when we were poling slowly by the bank, a woman, hung about with barbaric silver jewellery, would walk beside us bargaining until the price was right, when we would stop. Boubacar would put a tiny glassful of sugar into a scrap of torn-off plastic, with an even tinier amount of tea knotted into a corner of it, having first added an extra pinch for good measure.

One day I saw a small boy, hardly more than eight years old, driving a great herd of fast-moving cattle through a dust storm, quite alone on the fringes of the desert. He was an heroic little figure naked but for the short bright-red cloak flying out from his shoulders. He ran fleet-footed behind the cattle, stick in hand, his head back and his mouth open in a yell of command, looking for all the world like a young warrior from an Etruscan vase. Boys had little time for babyhood in this world, but they could handle responsibility, and do the work of men.

We passed several large villages in the latter part of the voyage, their colour varying from grey to deep chocolate brown, depending on the clay from which the houses were built, and there we would often see young children practising boating skills. Special sorts of reed canoes had been made for them, or rather half canoes, for one end was swept up in a prow shape and the other was simply cut across. They were only about three feet long, and fiendishly difficult to keep from rolling over. Any child that learnt to master one of those couldn't help but develop superb balance. It pleased my western notions of sexual equality to see the occasional girl learning to manage one of these tippy craft rather than being forever bent over the dirty pots or the laundry.

The closer we came to Timbuktu, the more the sand encroached upon the river, and we began to see increasing numbers of camels, some with one of their forelegs doubled under and tied, in order, Boubacar said, to prevent them from eating the rice. The double-trunk doum palms were everywhere now, elegant but no use for food, only for wood and mat-making; though the children sometimes chewed at the large red fruit for the scraps of astringent pulp beneath the hard skin. Although the land looked so barren I knew that there were fertile areas around Timbuktu where wheat was grown, and that soon I could look forward to eating bread again.

Timbuktu had once been nothing more than an oasis where a tribe of Tuareg had established a permanent camp. By the middle of the twelfth century, when the trans-Saharan trade began in earnest, the strategic position of this fruitful oasis, so near to the point where the Niger bites deepest into the desert, made it a favourite first halt for caravans struggling back from the North African coast, as well as an excellent starting point for the outward journey. Soon markets sprang up there, merchants moved in, and Timbuktu established itself very quickly. The Tuaregs, who had no appetite for town life, moved out, but they always regarded it as their city and periodically rode in to demand tribute, a custom they maintained well into the twentieth century until the French finally put an end to it. They also found rich pickings in harrying the caravans making their way to and from the city, and the fear of encountering the Blue Men of the Desert became one of the major hazards of travellers in the Sahara.

After being so anxious to arrive, the final approach to Timbuktu happened all too quickly. The last day afloat began with a brilliance seemingly designed to fill me with reluctance to leave the world of the river, which I now felt I had known for ever. Never, it seemed, had the morning dawned so fresh and jewel bright, with white sand, jade water, bright green edges, and skies pink and baby-blue. A perfect wind, clean and fresh, carried us swiftly along the twisting winding course. We sped down the last reach, Boubacar hanging out with the crazy sail as though we were competing in a regatta. It was perilous stuff – any bit of the crazy cobbled gear could go at any moment – but still we held on, tearing along mid-river, both boys enjoying the excitement, and Madame, as impassive as ever, doing her duty with the bailing tin.

With a sudden change of direction, we swing in fast towards the northern bank. Down comes the sail, and all too abruptly we close with the shore, an unattractive stretch of dry crazed mud, littered with bits and pieces of twentieth century debris – scraps of broken rusted winches, chains, wire, and a couple of beat-up vehicles. This apparently is where I am to be put down. Evans, who has done duty as a ship's locker for ten days, festooned with bags of produce and drying clothes, is carried ashore, a bicycle once more. I can hardly believe the moment has come. Too late I realize how fond I've grown of this little ship's company. All I've left them is my straw mattress, bequeathed to Boubacar for when he gets married. Madame didn't even get her aspirin for a souvenir. The boys are anxious to make the most of their favourable wind, and with only a brief '*Au revoir, bon voyage*' they are off, sailing on up the broad stream of the Niger, while I turn my face inland towards Timbuktu.

# 14

# Timbuktu

*'Or is the rumour of thy Timbuctoo*
*A dream as frail as those of ancient time?'*

AS I STRUGGLED to cover the last few ridiculously tortured miles to
Timbuktu, I felt a great sense of unreality about being almost
within sight of the 'mysterious city'. Some myths are never totally
exploded. Like Samarkand, Petra, Troy and Palmyra whose secrets
have also long been laid bare, an aura stills clings to Timbuktu that
continues to excite the imagination. It has stood for centuries as
somewhere so impossibly distant as to be virtually unattainable, and
few people even now would hazard a guess as to its exact location.

The great days of Timbuktu were over long before any western
man had clapped eyes on the city. Thanks to the vigilance of the
coastal Arabs who controlled the trans-Saharan trade, the interior
of Africa remained inviolate from European competition. By the
mid-eighteenth century Europe was equally determined to penetrate
those mysteries. Since 1550, when the report of a captured Moor –
one Hassan ibn Mohammed el Wazzan el Zayyati was published –
nothing but rumour had emerged. The Moor, renamed Giovanni
Leoni, or Leo Africanus, after the pope who realized the extraordinary importance of the man's travels in those fabled lands, had
been persuaded to write down his experiences, and it was upon his
descriptions of vanished glories that the curiosity of later generations
continued to feed: 'The rich King of Timbuktu hath in his possession

many gold plates and sceptres, some whereof are 1300 ounces in weight, and he keeps a well-furnished and splendid court ... In travelling he rideth upon a camel, but all his soldiers rideth upon horses ... Whosoever will speak to the king must prostrate himself at his feet and then taking up dust must sprinkle it upon his own head and shoulders ...' No one outside Africa could know that the wealthy ordered world described by Leo Africanus had been reduced to a state of anarchy and separate warring tribes; but such were the volatile and dangerous conditions that Mungo Park and his successors found at the end of the eighteenth century, when the rush to seize land in Africa had begun, and when France and Britain both had their eye on this particular part of it.

By 1800 not one Christian had succeeded in making his way to Timbuktu, or if any had, none made it back again to tell the tale. Mungo Park tried in 1795, and again in 1805. And although by then the course of the Niger was as much an object of the search as the mysterious city itself, it was the latter that continued to exercise the popular imagination, and Park himself called it 'the great object of my search'. He came within nine miles of it on his second expedition, when he was sailing down the Niger determined to follow the river to its end, wherever that would prove to be, and at whatever cost. There is no doubt that he would have won the race to Timbuktu had he not decided upon the course of shooting at any natives who appeared hostile. At the Kabara channel he fired on a group of Tuaregs and was forced to continue downstream, thus missing his one opportunity.

An American sailor named Adams who had been taken into slavery by Moors seems to have been the first non-Moslem to reach Timbuktu, sometime around 1812. An uneducated man who had undergone several years of frightful sufferings before rescue, his tale was not unnaturally a little confused, and contained many inconsistencies. The reason he was not generally believed however was that he described the mysterious city as a miserable dirty place, and no one was prepared to accept that.

In 1826 Gordon Laing, a Scottish officer, became the first Briton to enter Timbuktu, after achieving another impressive first in crossing the Sahara from north to south. He was a courageous and gifted explorer who, although still only thirty-two, had already travelled extensively in West Africa, making many inspired and, as it turned out, correct deductions about the Niger's probable course. Of the discoveries he made on his final journey, or what he learnt of Timbuktu, however, little is known, except for what was contained in a few brief letters. Fanatical Moslem Tuaregs hacked him to death just thirty miles from the city as he was setting out on the return journey, and his journal, left behind in Timbuktu for safety, vanished and has never yet reappeared.

Two years before Laing's expedition the Geographical Society of Paris had offered a prize of 10,000 francs to the first person to return to Europe with a first-hand account of Timbuktu. And in 1828, just two years after poor Gordon Laing had so narrowly missed it, this prize was claimed by an obscure twenty-six-year-old Frenchman. René Caillié had been possessed by the idea of Timbuktu since boyhood, and he prepared himself for the venture rather better than his predecessors by learning Arabic, studying the Koran and adopting Arab disguise. Unlike Laing, he had no official position, no sponsorship, and hardly a soul knew of his intentions. But like Kipling's mariner, René Caillié was a 'man of infinite resource and sagacity', and possessed moreover the sort of charm that made all manner of people anxious to assist him. To account for discrepancies in his Arabic he concocted plausible stories about having been kidnapped as a child by Christians, and seems to have been ever ready with fresh invention to avert the threat of discovery. In spite of the constant danger of blowing his cover, he was indefatigable in recording what he saw and in noting down the names of villages he passed through. Had he been caught while writing this journal he would undoubtedly have been killed on the spot as a spy, but it was as well that he had this tangible proof of his travels. When he returned to France after the usual horrifying privations of an extended desert crossing, he found many of his countrymen disinclined to believe his story, as he possessed neither the birth nor the breeding which the nineteenth-century Establishment preferred for its heroes. He was eventually awarded the prize, but when the

150

French were considering mounting an official expedition to the area, poor Caillié, eager to return to the scenes of his triumph, was not selected on the grounds that he was 'not qualified'.

The publication of René Caillié's journal did little to end the speculation about Timbuktu. Although travellers who followed him were able to corroborate his account, many people, particularly the disappointed British, still stubbornly refused to believe that he had actually been to the city, despite all the evidence. Others were eager to see for themselves, and in any case there were still many questions left unanswered.

In 1830, the Cornish brothers, Richard and John Lander, filled in an essential part of the geographical jigsaw of West Africa. Continuing downstream from the point where Mungo Park had met his death on the desperate journey twenty-five years earlier, they finally solved the problem of the Niger's exit. Rather touchingly the Landers were also able to recover Park's Bible and his logarithm tables.

It was now high time for a more scientific approach. Britain, eager both to capture profitable trade agreements, and to gain information to further the abolition of the slave trade, decided to mount another official expedition. One of the men chosen to gather the minutiae of accurate geographical and ethnographical know-ledge was the German, Heinrich Barth. Very different from the inspired amateurs who preceded him, Barth was a paragon of learning, with a prodigious gift for languages, and of immense physical strength. He lacked Mungo Park's enthusiasm and gift of description, and a touch more humour would have done him no harm, but he was certainly indefatigable. After spending five years on the task, he produced an impressive five-volume account of his travels and discoveries which played no small part in Britain's decision not to concern herself immediately with this part of Africa. Of Timbuktu, which he entered in 1853, and in which he stayed reluctantly for four months, he formed an even lower opinion than he did of Gao 'You will have heard of my arrival in this ill-famed place' he wrote to London. 'Patiently am I awaiting the hour of my departure, which I hope may not be very far.'

But Barth's description of Timbuktu as a rubbish-strewn mouldering clay heap of little importance did almost nothing to change
the hold it had over people's imagination. Travellers still attempted
to make their way there, and were either murdered by Tuaregs or
fell prey to the many fates awaiting the rash in that most inhospitable
of habitats. In the meantime, the rush by the developed nations to
grab chunks of the African continent continued. The British, busy
with the colonizing of the lowest and richest part of the Niger, in
what is now Nigeria, left the deserts to the French, who were
perhaps more temperamentally suited to them. In 1894, the tricolour
flew over Timbuktu and the days of the Foreign Legion and decades
of skirmishing with the Tuaregs had begun.

In 1960 Mali regained its independence, and the Timbuktu I was
approaching was once more under the aegis of the descendants of
the emperor, Mansa Musa, who had set out to visit Mecca in 1324,
carrying so much gold that he had debased the currency of Egypt
as he passed through scattering largesse. But as I made my way into
Timbuktu it was my paltry largesse that everyone was after. I
was following in René Caillié's footsteps, he too having made his
approach by river, though coming from upstream. His pirogue,
stuffed full of slaves, had been able to proceed up the canal that had
been cut from the river in the fifteenth century to create the port
of Kabara. Arriving two months earlier than he had, when the level
of water should in theory have been considerably higher, I found
only a few puddles in the bottom of this canal.

The way was terrible, dry crazed mud being the best of it, and
the worst, sand of so perniciously soft and sticky a consistency that
I couldn't make twenty yards without a rest. The five to ten miles
a day that the slave caravans had managed seemed reasonable to me
now. Lining the dry canal was a ribbon of refugee shelters as awful
as any I had ever seen, mere scraps of cloth and rubbish cobbled
together into the semblance of dwellings. Having to stop so often
invited endless importunate approaches from young and old. Desperately hot and running with sweat, I was in no mood to cope
with the hundreds of hands stretched towards me in the ceaseless
demands for 'cadeaux'.

152

Far more alarming were the attentions of youths and boys and even some of the men who were also walking towards Kabara, and who accompanied their aggressive demands with barely veiled threats to which it was necessary to respond with some vigour before they would leave me alone. The inevitable comparison arose with the predatory Tuaregs of Laing and Caillié's day who had preyed upon all travellers between the river and the city. Fortunately there were one or two who came and helped to push Evans, so that eventually I reached the high-and-dry port of Kabara, and the broken blistered stretch of tarmac, the first I had seen since Tillabéry, which stretched like a royal carpet towards Timbuktu.

It was easy now. I sped past the mid-way point, called 'None can hear their cries' because that was where the worst of the Tuareg massacres of caravans had taken place. There is only an airfield there now where Air Mali, more usually known as 'Air Maybe', operates its erratic flights. I didn't experience the sense of let down that my famous predecessors had on their first sight of Timbuktu because I was forearmed with Caillié's and Barth's accounts, and had a much better idea of what to expect. What I saw was exciting, because it seemed not to have changed at all since those nineteenth century reports. It was still a town fast-disappearing beneath the sand that surrounded it on all sides; a town of crumbling houses where no one seemed to have any employment, except to sit, just as they had done then.

The first priority was to find an hotel. There were two, the very expensive Sofitel which was quite outside my budget and was almost empty, except for sharply dressed local young men who occupied the bar stools but bought nothing, merely lying in wait for the rich tourists who so seldom came. The other was the older Hôtel Tomboctou, which was very run down but just affordable, its small windowless cells costing a little over £12 each. This place was more aggressively besieged by traditionally dressed Tuaregs, who spent their nights in desert camps and their days hanging about in the hope of encountering a chance visitor. They thrust their jewellery and weapons upon any hapless traveller they encountered with an abandon that made the Agadez Tuaregs seem quite restrained. There was no question of using the hotel's garden with its views of the desert as all the chairs were occupied by the Tuaregs, and it was imperative to get inside as quickly as possible to escape their importuning. My room led off the dusty garden, and, hot though it was, the door had to be kept closed, for a dozen pairs of Tuareg eyes were fixed upon it like desert hawks. The washing facilities of the Hôtel Tomboctou were decidedly unattractive, and the meals were worse. Over the bar hung a faded poster with the message FOR SUCCESSFUL MEETINGS CHOOSE NICE, which wasn't a bad comment on the place.

In the dim gloom of the fifteen-watt electric light bulb, my cupboard of a room pressed in on me on all sides, so that I longed for the open skies above the river and the desert. But what finally decided me to dispense with the shelter of the Hôtel Tomboctou before I had spent a single night there was that when I lowered my weary body onto the greasy bed, some sharp pointed object pierced my flesh, and tearing back the sheet I discovered an enormous thorn protruding from a horrid stained mattress that looked as though it might contain many more unwelcome surprises. The incident was a blessing in disguise, providing the necessary catalyst to get me out of a place where my ever-lurking claustrophobia had finally caught up with me, and where I would have lain awake in misery all night.

Instead, I had the pleasure of wandering around a sleeping Timbuktu by night, and making its acquaintance in perhaps the way it should be seen, when imagination has the freedom to conjure up something of its past. Silent and quite empty except for the occasional flitting bat and sinuous cat, the narrow alleyways were half in heavy shadow, and half illumined by soft moonlight falling on heavy studded doors set in the low façades of pale stone houses. The exotic barbaric shape of bristling stucco mosques rose massively around every corner. Beyond the last of the houses another, tented city, like a besieging army, stretched away past the low-walled burial places into the edges of the desert. I have never been in any town that was quite so still. In the four or five hours I strolled about there, or sat half-dreaming among the shades of the mosques in which Caillié had written up his notes, I heard not a single dog bark, nor a child cry. It could have been a ghost town.

By daylight the same streets could be seen to be in an advanced state of decay, with sand piling up everywhere, threatening to engulf them entirely. The lodgings of Caillié, Laing and Barth, distinguished by black commemorative plaques, were mere gaping shells, and the mosques, which were neither particularly large nor impressive, were also in poor repair. The yawning black gaps of midnight proved to be where houses had collapsed altogether, crushing their occupants in the fall, I was told. Tall clay beehive structures in the streets were ovens for baking flat round loaves of wholemeal bread, always gritty with specks of the ubiquitous sand.

There were seven separate quarters of Timbuktu, each with its own mosque, but all quite small. The various trades and guilds, now things of the past, had kept to their own parts of the city, but although I spent the best part of four days wandering through the streets, I could not determine where one quarter ended and another began. Most of the buildings in the twisting alleyways were of mud-brick, but there were also several streets where the houses were built of good desert limestone and had a modest elegance of proportion, enhanced by the ornate heavy wooden front doors armoured with metal studding, and the carved grilles in the tiny windows. These streets, wider than most of the alleys and distinguished by an occasional tree, unbelievably beautiful in the dry dusty setting, looked as though they had seen better days. It was said that previous generations had disguised their houses under a tattered exterior so as not to excite the avarice of the marauding Tuaregs who periodically raided the town to exact tribute. Those same Tuaregs who had once scorned life in the city were now refugees there; it was their tents encircling it, doubling the population.

A very few houses, mostly the stone-built ones, had been recently repaired, and looked as though they might reveal a more luxurious interior, but the ones where I was invited inside, or caught a glimpse into as I passed, seemed little better than caves; everything that might have made for a degree of comfort, like tiled floors and plastered walls, having disappeared long since. What remained of Timbuktu was not the ruins of palaces and pleasure domes of which the Victorians had dreamed. Concentrating on the gold, the nineteenth century had forgotten that Leo Africanus also wrote, 'There are numbers of books brought out of Barbary which are sold for more money than all other merchandise'. In its heyday, Timbuktu was as famous for saintliness and learning as for trade, and what was mouldering away here was the shell of a modest sober town of merchants and scholars; an Oxford of the desert from which both trade and scholarship had long-since fled, and where it seemed as if an alien people had come in from the wilderness, like birds and foxes, to make their nests among the crumbling homes of the former inhabitants.

Towards dawn, on the night when I was wandering alone around Timbuktu, musing on Thackeray's delightful lines:

'In Africa (a quarter of the world)
Men's skins are black, their hair is crisp and curled;
And somewhere there, unknown to public view,
A mighty city lies called Timbuktu.'

I had the good fortune to meet a young man called Amadou, who was cook to a Frenchman in charge of building a large new hospital there. Amadou, who clearly thought I was in need of protection, suggested I should come and meet his employer, whose breakfast he was just about to prepare. As a result I not only enjoyed my first cup of real coffee since leaving Niamey, but was also offered the use of a room in the large comfortable bungalow. It was out on the southern edge of town, among a scattering of nomad encampments and other modern buildings which housed the offices of international aid agencies and their directors. This kindness made all the difference to my visit, and was not out of keeping with the traditional courtesy towards travellers who reached Timbuktu – all my famous predecessors had enjoyed protection and hospitality in the town, even if some of them got clobbered when they left it.

A comfortable bolt hole made all the difference to coping with the attentions of the younger inhabitants of Timbuktu who, from the age where they can just about stagger upright, are instructed by their mothers to pursue all white-skinned people, and demand '*cadeaux*', a circumstance that makes it difficult to linger in the way the place warrants. The smallest children attacked in numbers, chanting '*Ça va? Ça va bien?, Ça va très bien?*', their voices growing shriller and shriller, as they grabbed and thrust hands into bags or pockets. Even the tough and ruffianly guides were unable to offer their clients protection from them. Instead, the very few tourists who found their way to the city were instructed to be firm and to deal with the children themselves. On two occasions, hemmed in on all sides, poked at and taunted, I hit out at these young tormentors with my small notebook, and managed to land a cuff. Passers by, rather than remonstrating with me for striking a child, applauded heartily with a '*Très bien Madame*' and the small horrors duly fled. On the rare occasions I did see a Timbuktu adult attempt to drive off young children, it was done by throwing stones at them.

The youths who offered their services as guides I found even more obnoxious. In any case, a guide was totally unnecessary in a town that could be seen in its entirety in less than an hour. To enjoy the freedom to loiter peacefully was all I wanted, but to achieve that required protection from both guides and children. This came in an unexpected way. Before I quite realized it, I had collected an entourage of about a dozen boys of between ten and thirteen who accompanied me, either altogether or a few at a time, wherever I went. They had all become my 'friends' through the simple expedient of refusing to go away again after trying to take me round the sights. '*Madame,* I show you *la maison de Gordon Laing*'. All the boys knew about Gordon Laing and rushed up the ruin to poke their heads through the little window at the top, rolling their eyes as they drew a finger suggestively across their throats: '*Voila! Très mauvais les Tuareg, non?*' At first I tried to drive these boys off also, but when that didn't work, I told them they were welcome to walk around with me if they wished, but there would be no question of payment. The ones who only wanted money soon departed, but a hard core remained; boys who found me a welcome diversion and enjoyed asking questions. I enjoyed their company too – once a school

157

mistress always a school mistress – and they were a help in keeping away the rapacious infants.

All of my young friends went to school in the mornings, where they learnt their French, except for Malik, who each day claimed that his master was sick, and although I had my suspicions about this, and cross-questioned him sternly, I wasn't able to budge him from his story. Ahmed, another boy I saw a lot of, a leggy child like an ungainly colt, did occasional washing for the wife of an American evangelical missionary, and one afternoon as we passed her house I exchanged a few words with her over the gate, while Ahmed went in to collect something he had left there. The hostile way she talked to him made me feel she was under siege. 'You can't trust any of them,' she hissed in an aside to me. 'They are all thieves.' By this time I felt rather proprietorial about 'my boys', particularly Malik, Ahmed, and another regular called Ibrahim, a boy full of spirit whose frequent skirmishes resulted in his outgrown clothes becoming ever more tattered. I resented her attitude more than her sentiments. Possibly they were all thieves; there wasn't much opportunity for boys to work for a future, or to choose a career in Timbuktu. From the first I had been puzzled to understand what possible economy the place could have; none was apparent, most people seemed to spend the whole day sitting in front of their houses, or playing table games in the sand. Jean Yves, my host, said the building of the new hospital had provided the only source of work in the town, and that was almost completed. There was a small aid-funded irrigation scheme for growing rice near Kabara, and a few gardens for vegetables. Otherwise there was nothing but the endless circulating of the same money, year in year out.

I had one further glimpse of the Timbuktu of legend before I left, this time in broad daylight. I was walking in the northern quarter of the city with Ibrahim, on what was to prove the eve of departure, when I heard the loud complaining cries and snortings of camels. Round the corner a string of very rough strong-looking baggage animals were being forced reluctantly to kneel in the sand by unkempt men in archaic short tunics who seemed to be answering the camels in their own language. There was a wildness about both men and animals, a feeling of them belonging to another world, and by the great tombstones of what looked like greyish quartz strapped on either side of the camels, I realized they had just come in from the salt mines of Taoudeni – a place so deep in the desert that few maps agree on its exact location. Yet it was these great slabs of greyish granular salt, from those self-same mines, that had changed hands in Timbuktu in the days of its greatness, pound weight for pound weight with gold, so valuable was it to the salt-less lands lying to the south and west. It was the very stuff on which Timbuktu's wealth was founded, and to have seen even this tiny remnant of the legendary trade seemed a fitting souvenir to take away with me.

# 15

# Getting Away

BY THE FOURTH DAY of my stay in Timbuktu, much of my time was spent in trying to find a way out of it again, this being, as Barth had discovered, as notoriously difficult to achieve as getting there. I had come right round the great buckle of the Niger, and my route was now southwards towards Djenné and the country of the Dogon. I wasn't able simply to load up Evans and cycle off because, apart from the horrid desert that hemmed in Timbuktu on all sides, the formidable barrier of the inland delta also lay in my path. An area the size of England, the delta is flooded for half the year, and is criss-crossed by small rivers and interrupted by innumerable lakes for most of the remaining months. As no all-weather road crosses it – just vague tracks meandering between small remote settlements – unless I wanted to make a wide detour to the north, missing out the whole fascinating region, the river remained the only feasible route, as it has been since earliest times. I needed to find a pinasse to take me as far as Mopti, a hundred miles south, after which I would be able to resume my travels by bicycle.

It is almost impossible however, to get news of boats in Timbuktu, so far from the river, and before he had put me ashore, Boubacar had suggested that the easiest way would be to go overland to the port of Diré, where he lived, and from where he could help me find a pinasse bound for Mopti. Not that this was to prove much easier, because to get to Diré meant first going inland to Goundam, and unless I wanted to spend a week or more pushing the laden

Evans through sixty miles of very soft sand, I needed to find motorized transport. I tried exhaustively and ineffectively to hire a taxi. All my Timbuktu boys appeared to have brothers, uncles, fathers or friends who were driving to Goundam the very next day, and I haggled and agreed prices a score of times, only to find none of them materialized. Jean Yves said it was always like that, and suggested I ask the Aid people if they had a truck going, but there too I drew a blank until the evening I was invited to dine with the local Malian organizer of UNICEF.

During supper, another guest said he knew of a pick-up leaving for Bamako that very night, and he was sure it could be persuaded to take Evans and me as far as Goundam. A dozen Malians then demonstrated how quickly and efficiently things could be done in Timbuktu once the will was there. Within an hour, after only the briefest of goodbyes to my kind host, and none at all to my dear Timbuktu boys, Evans and I were aboard a truck bucking and pitching across an infernal terrain in a motion that threatened to tear all my limbs out of their sockets. I feared for the safety of my bicycle, but was glad that it was the strong young man whose place I was occupying who had the job of hanging onto it.

It was still pitch dark when I was put down in the rough compound of the local forestry officer of Goundam, and a place was found for me to spread my sleeping bag and try to recover a little from the fearsome jolting. Lac Faguibine was not far away, a huge and reputedly marvellous body of water that is host to enormous numbers of migratory birds. Shivering in the early morning air over coffee and rice cakes in the compound a few hours later, the forester reminisced about escorting Prince Philip to the lake some years before. 'Oh he is a wonderful man;' he said to a visiting colleague. 'He does not care for people. He spends all the royal English money on wild animals'. I too would have liked to see this lake, but one of the hardships of travelling is having to make choices; you cannot go everywhere at once. It was not a good time to visit in any case, the forester told me, the water being so low that it was impossible to get close enough to enjoy a good view of the birds.

The day continued cold and grey with a strong wind carrying

clouds of dust, so that I had to tie a scarf around my head and face Tuareg-style in order to be able to breathe. As I was cycling out of Goundam, a youth rushed out of a shack to take my name; it was necessary he said in case I did not arrive at the road's end, a sentiment in keeping with the day and with the empty, dreary land I rode through. The track to Diré was just rideable, though tough, and I covered the twenty miles in a little over three hours, by which time the wind had dropped and the sun shone brightly once more.

Diré was a far larger town than I had expected, and was surrounded by hundreds of acres of rice fields created by recent massive irrigation – a scheme which has many detractors among ecologists, who feel that an age-old system of natural balance has been destroyed without sufficient thought. They claim that so much water diverted from a river already fallen to well below its usual level, coupled with the disastrously low rainfalls of recent years, could have widespread and catastrophic consequences.

At the police post where I went for the necessary stamp in my passport, I was bought a brochette by the elderly officer in charge. 'But if you want another one you pay for it yourself.' he said, in case there should be any misunderstanding. He was a notorious womanizer, I learnt subsequently, but I had rather suspected as much from the suggestive leer with which he offered me, 'for free', the key to a tin shack in the compound, where I could stay if I did not succeed in getting away by boat that day.

Not a stone's throw from the police post was a *pinasse* with a line of men wading out to it, sacks of rice on their heads. I hurried down to find the owner, and a man was pointed out who, in spite of being black looked so exactly like a character out of Chaucer that 'shipmaster' seemed the only possible title for him. The effect was partly due to his stocky figure clad in grey robes, and the flat turban with a strip of it hanging down like a medieval cap. But it was also something to do with the way he conducted his business; he appeared so calmly in control, so unmoved by the bustle and commotion around him, as if he had all the time in the world to issue his commands. He inspired confidence, and I felt favoured that he was prepared to take Evans and me, even if, as usual, the price was many times greater than any other passenger would pay. It would not be a fast passage, he warned. He would stop in each port to unload goods; but five days would certainly see us tying up in Mopti, and anyway, he doubted there would be another boat, as the river was so low and dropping fast. Having agreed the price, a man seized Evans and carried it into a pirogue and we were poled out to the *pinasse*. By the time I was settled aboard with Evans tied in securely, I had about seven separate palms to drop coins into, and more to follow as I went ashore again. 'We sail in fifteen minutes – without you, if you do not come,' warned the shipmaster, as I rushed off to get provisions with the aid of two small boys to show me the way.

I had enquired around for Boubacar as soon as I had arrived in Diré, but the speed with which I had found myself a boat had driven all thoughts of him from my mind. And suddenly there he was beside me in the *pinasse*, dressed in a fine orange shirt printed all over with huge electric-blue kingfishers, and wearing an even more brilliant smile. It warmed my heart that he seemed so genuinely glad to see me. Word had got about that a white woman had been asking for him, and he had come post haste, he said. He was disappointed that I wouldn't be meeting his mother and his girl friend who had been told so much about me, but he agreed that this *pinasse* could well be the last, and that I must take it. 'You will be in Mopti in three days,' he said. I told him the shipmaster had said five. 'Who can say?' he laughed. 'You know now that all pirogiers are liars.' 'Not all, surely?' I joked. 'Oh yes,' said Boubacar seriously, 'They have to lie. If they told the truth they would get no passengers. When the money is paid, it doesn't matter, they have to stay with the ship, *Voilà!*' I don't think I shall ever hear a '*Voilà*' again without thinking of this happy Malian character and his Huckleberry Finn existence.

The engine was started up only an hour after the stated departure time which I, quite wrongly as it turned out, interpreted as being a good sign. Boubacar went ashore, and I was left to take stock of my new surroundings. Much deeper than a pirogue, the *pinasse* was built on the same general lines, though not nearly so graceful, and was about 120 feet long and 12 feet wide. The engine was in the stern, and the boat was steered by a wheel right up in the prow, with two stout chains running back along the outside to the rudder. It was divided into two parts by leaving the waist unloaded to form a deep well. Here the women cooked food for the whole ship's company, in huge iron cauldrons set on great wood-burning braziers. Aft of this well, amongst a plethora of assorted cargo, and partially hidden by the billowing clouds of steam and smoke were the quarters of the women and children. There were about two dozen of them, all related to the shipmaster, and, as he told me somewhat bitterly on several occasions, they were being fed at his expense.

Forward of the well, the cargo was piled up level with the gunwales, forming a bumpy uneven floor of sacks of rice. Under the sacks was another and far more exciting cargo – salt from the Taoudeni mines. Several hundred tombstones of the quartz-like stuff that I had seen being unloaded from the camels had been taken aboard from the spot below Timbuktu where I had been landed, and had I known of it I could have joined the *pinasse* there. It seemed fitting to be sleeping on this salt as we travelled towards the gold fields of the south, though less fitting that Evans and I had been allocated a space in what was the male portion of the boat. There were very few other passengers, however, since the dozen or so men with whom I had thought I would be sharing the space had all gone ashore when the boat set off.

I soon discovered that it was not nearly as pleasant aboard a *pinasse* as it had been on the pirogue. The tarpaulin roof spread over the curved bamboo poles came down to within a foot of the gunwale, severely limiting the view. I could see out only by lying down and peering through Evans' spokes. It was difficult to move about because the cargo was so high and the roof so low, and creeping about in the gloom, bent double, it was difficult to avoid blows from the bales, lanterns and miscellaneous items suspended overhead.

After half an hour's sailing there was a shout from the shore, and we stopped for police to come aboard and inspect papers. One of them asked me if I hadn't known it was not allowed for a white person to travel on a *pinasse*? I said I hadn't known this, nor had his chief told me of the rule when I was drinking tea with him just an hour ago. 'It is finished', said the man hurriedly, thrusting my passport back at me, and then I realized that he had been looking for a bribe, and that I had said the right thing. Ten minutes after the police had gone the boat stopped again, the gang plank was run out, and all the dozen or so young men who had been there before swarmed aboard, and I learnt the reason for their exodus. All Malians are supposed to carry identity papers, but seldom do, because they are difficult to obtain and very easy to lose. The absence of papers is a godsend to the police who, together with most Malian government employees such as teachers, civil servants and the like, are seldom paid wages. When someone is caught without papers, they are offered the choice of an official fine with a receipt, or a half-price unofficial fine, without receipt. The shipmaster said he too had to pay a large bribe every time the police come aboard, or they would find some way of making him wish he had. Nineteenth-century explorers had complained of much the same state of affairs in their day, so things have not really changed in these parts, except for foreign bicyclists, who are usually considered too lowly to be expected to pay.

The third stop came after only a further half-hour sailing, and proved to be the end of the day's run. The shipmaster's home was in a small walled village on the Western bank, and while we remained tied to the bank, he and his sons went ashore for the night. On board people gathered in groups around huge bowls of fish and rice, and I was passed a small bowl of my own. It was a distinct improvement on the pirogue's version of the same dish, though still not exactly a delight.

It was now quite dark and the tarpaulins were let right down to the gunwales and everyone prepared for sleep. The two young men who shared my space between two thwarts rolled themselves in thin flowered cotton cloths. I rigged my mosquito net to the bamboo poles overhead, let the air into my self-inflating mattress and wriggled into my sleeping bag. I couldn't pretend I was comfortable on the uneven rice sacks but it could have been a lot worse. By the light of the single dim hurricane lamp I watched the elderly man who, I decided, was the first mate, preparing for bed. He had a large comfortable looking mattress spread over a bamboo base in the forepeak, just behind the steering wheel, with a curtain to separate it from the part where I was. As soon as he was finished with his ablutions he coughed, and a woman came up to join him from the rear of the boat.

We did not set off the following day until 2 p.m., although the shipmaster had appeared several times on the foreshore, escorted by his wives and lots of children, all of whom seemed reluctant to let him go. When we finally chugged away he received a positively civic send-off, the entire population of the small walled village coming out to wave, while the wives wailed and wrung their hands. Quite a wind ruffled up the water and the shipmaster stood on the roof shouting down instructions to the first mate who in turn was giving orders to the helmsman. It was difficult to tell exactly who were passengers and who were crew, as several other men began shouting orders and issuing counter commands, until it seemed like a free-for-all. The shipmaster left them to it and talked to me instead. He told me he was very worried about the wind, because his ship was deeply laden and not strong. There was a sandbar at Tonka, he said, and with the river so low his ship could not get over it unless there was a flat calm.

Soon the Niger divided into the Issa Beri, the Big Water, which we followed, and the smaller Bara Issa, which meanders away through the thousand little lakes of the flooded delta lands before joining up again with the main river sixty miles further on. Tonka was as far as we got that day, indeed it was as far as I was ever to get on the *pinasse*, though I did not know this until four days later. On this bright sunny Saturday I was still full of western optimism; what did it matter that we had covered only thirty miles in two days, or that the river's convoluted course had brought us closer to Goundam than we had been at Diré? More passengers were joining the boat all the time; there would surely be more purpose to our progress once we left Tonka.

That night a wind came that put an end to any thought of getting under way the following day. It blew with a force that made me realize that the harmattans I had experienced so far had been nothing worse than a stiff blow. With the tarpaulins down we were protected from the worst of it, but even so dust and sand came flying into the boat in clouds, and all my equipment, including the nylon cagoule I wore, was permanently impregnated with fine grit. The men wrapped in their thin covers whimpered and complained in the biting cold. The morning was desolate, dark and grey, and the air unbreathably thick. After the bowl of sweetened rice, which was the best meal of the day, I struggled down the gangplank and went off to explore Tonka. Away from the shelter of the sloping river bank I met the full force of the wind and could barely stand. The surface of the surrounding sandy wastes was on the move, the air full of swirling debris. Tall trees on the outskirts of the town were stretched almost horizontal in a frenzy of tattered leaves. There was an air of unreality about the scene; as though nature was being a touch over-theatrical. It seemed uncannily like the lines on Cato's last stand at Utica:

> So where our wide Numidean Wastes extend,
> Wheel thro the air, in circling Eddies play,
> Tears up the sands and sweeps whole plains away.
> The helpless Traveller, with wild surprise
> Sees the dry Desert all around him rise
> And smothered in the dusty whirlwind dies.

Strange threatening shapes looming up through the murk proved to be only rusted defunct traction engines left over from French colonial days. Half filled with blown sand they were providing living quarters for the poorer inhabitants of Tonka. The town itself was composed of mud-brick shacks in sandy compounds, with a huge market in the centre. In the close winding alleys it was possible to escape the direct force of the wind, but the air was so filled with sand that it was like twilight. Apocalyptic figures on camels materialized suddenly as through a curtain. I passed a man holding onto a goat by its forepaw as though it was a child; presumably he could not find a piece of string. In a side alley a man fought grimly

167

to mount a camel that was equally determined to resist, and kept trying to bite him. Only by getting a grip on the creature's lower jaw and wrenching its head right round was the man able eventually to spring onto its back, and then it was up and away, vanishing in a moment into the swirling grey emptiness. Business in the main streets seemed to be carrying on as normal. There was a large camel market, with cows, donkeys and goats, and hundreds of stalls where everything from matting to dough balls, nuts to shrivelled unident-ifiable pieces of animal intestines was sold. Yet five or six yards was the limit of vision, and the whole scene was fantastic and unreal in the dim light and the choking dust.

By the second day of our enforced wait at Tonka, the wind had dropped considerably, but it was far from being the flat calm required for crossing the sandbar that lay in our path. The boat had collected so many additional male passengers that I soon needed to fight to preserve my space. Dark looks were cast at Evans, and there were mutterings about how it should be put on the roof, until I pointed out that I was paying the price of at least a dozen passengers, at which the grumbles diminished, Malians on the whole being fair-minded. It was not easy, however, sharing such cramped quarters with an ever-increasing number of men. Most of them were pleasant enough, though they showed an uninhibited curiosity in me and my possessions, and there was a dreadful amount of spitting, and not always over the side. A rather unpleasant marabout in a pink turban was the worst offender. He clearly loathed females, and my very presence inspired him to spit constantly, preferably at my feet. Then there was the frequent need for the men to urinate over the side, and I was always having to look somewhere else so as not to embarrass them.

One youth, a friend of the shipmaster's elder son seemed to feel a need to show off his manhood by scuttling across the sacks like a spider, squatting in front of me and shrieking in my face 'Donne moi, donne moi', while trying to grab at anything I had in my hand. These attacks continued until I lost my temper, and let fly a blistering tirade in English, repeating it in French when I grew calmer and could remember the words. Entertaining it clearly was for the bored passengers, and I thought darkly about how Caillié had been similarly abused on his river journey. It did me no harm however, in fact after that I was included in one of the tea drinking clubs, which were the sole entertainment aboard, and this gave me the excuse to go to the market again to buy my share of the tea and sugar.

When the third day dawned with no sign of improvement in the weather, rather than spend another day aboard the comfortless overcrowded *pinasse*, I wandered aimlessly about ashore. The shipmaster, his two sons, and the first mate also abandoned ship during the hours of daylight, and lay in a huddle close together on the bleak foreshore at some distance from the boat, in order, I thought, to escape the mutterings of the dissatisfied passengers. At the prescribed hours of prayer the shipmaster's small company spread their mats on the sand and performed their genuflections assiduously and at great length, otherwise they lay there semi-comatose, their robes wrapped tightly around them against the wind, which continued to blow strongly in spite of their prayers. Sometimes the shipmaster roused himself and called me over to have a conversation with him, but no matter what we discussed, it always came back to the subject of religion. We could agree on 'the one true God', but when directly challenged on the position of Mohammed, which was so central to his faith, we could not see eye to eye. Discussions on social issues ended in much the same way; if he complained of the terrible poverty in the country, I would point out that there were far too many children to feed and that was the root cause of most of Africa's problems. At this he would open his eyes wide in horror, and say 'But I am a Moslem, I have three wives and many children. It is God who gives, and what God gives he provides for.' I would counter this with notions of free will, and man's accountability, but even though I could see he was tempted at times to cover his ears to shut out such infidel notions, his fatalism was unshakeable. 'Everything is in the hand of Allah', including no doubt, this interminable wait at Tonka.

On the morning of the fourth day I awoke joyfully to the long-awaited sound of the ship's engine. The wind was still blowing, but the sun was shining brilliantly and we were slowly moving out into mid-stream. Then suddenly all was confusion as the wind swung the ship's bows and she was aground. Stripped down to voluminous shorts, into the river leapt the first mate, closely followed by the shipmaster in similar state. One of the sons and several other men followed, fully clad. Shoulder deep in the brown stream they pushed against the hull and pulled on ropes, screaming orders and counter orders, until, more by luck than judgement I felt, they had her moored again, pinned against the opposite, lee shore, and that was the end of all movement for yet another day.

Reading that day's entry in my journal, I see I came close to despair, thinking I would never get away from this god-forsaken spot. The spirits of the entire ship's company were at a low ebb, especially the shipmaster, who remarked bitterly yet again that all these female relatives were being fed at his expense. To lighten the atmosphere (or perhaps by way of sacrifice to darker forces) one of the live sheep we carried aboard, whose bleating had added to the nights' dolorous sounds, was taken ashore by the evilly-disposed youth and ritually slaughtered. Some of the raw liver was immediately served to the shipmaster, and the rest of the meat was stewed and distributed at the next meal.

The boat was so crowded by this fourth night that I found it quite impossible to sleep; and the shore round about had been used by the passengers of so many ships, similarly wind-bound, that hardly a foot of unsoiled ground remained. Something had to be done, I decided, as I lay there in the illusory privacy of my mosquito net. When the morning brought no change in the wind, and the shipmaster confirmed there would be no movement again that day, I decided that I must try and walk out. My map indicated there was a track of sorts, and the first mate confirmed that this was so, although none of the company had ever set foot on it because, local though they all were, their travelling was always confined to the river. Compass in hand (to the interest of the shipmaster who had never seen such a thing) I set out through the thorns and the sand of the broken terrain, and after half an hour I came to what looked like a passable track. Such a neat strip of order created through that jumbled hostile chaos seemed the most wonderful thing, and had me breaking into a Benedictus, out of a profound sense of gratitude.

Back I tracked, still singing, to collect Evans, and to settle up with the shipmaster. The repulsive youth had one last shot at dominating the proceedings, screaming at me that I had no right to go, and that I should pay the whole amount for the trip. The shipmaster, however, refused to accept a penny, saying I hadn't eaten enough to be able to reckon the cost, and he urged me to hurry, so that I might have a chance of reaching shelter before nightfall.

Annoyingly, my spare cooking pot was left aboard, as was my spare compass that had slipped down between the tombstones of salt, together with one of my two precious handkerchiefs. Keeping a grip on my possessions is always a problem on a journey, and although I take only what I think I cannot do without, things are constantly getting away, which shows that I could manage with even less. None of this was in my mind at that moment however, for I was setting off into the unknown, and although the joy of being free of the overcrowded *pinasse* was uppermost, I also felt a little scared about what I might find in the inhospitable territory before me. Then from the rear of the boat I saw the women and children, with whom I had exchanged only smiles. They were waving vigorously, their faces beaming with such friendly encouragement, that I departed with a light heart.

# 16

# The Inland Delta

ACCORDING TO MY MAP, the dirt track I had found went by a circuitous route to Niafounké, where, hopefully, dear Madame of the pirogue journey had arrived some days since. From Niafounké the map showed a seasonal track beginning on the opposite side of the river, meandering well over to the east before turning south and heading towards a proper road a hundred miles or more further on. The area the track passed through was underwater for more than two thirds of the year, and for the remainder it was liberally besprinkled with little lakes and rivers. Goodness knows if would prove a practicable route: I could but try.

Niafounké, I reckoned, was a good thirty miles away, and I doubted that I would get there that day, since it was mid-afternoon by the time I reached the track. The idea of a night's camping in the bush held no dread however; after the *pinasse*, just to be alone would be luxury. Before I had gone any distance the front tyre punctured, and as I was beginning to mend it a large truck roared by covering me in dust. It returned in a few moments, and a young man called down from the cab to ask if I needed help. Although I said I was perfectly alright, he thought I should ride into Niafounké with him, as night was drawing on. Such solicitude was very touching in a country like Mali, where most people have too many problems of their own to worry about strangers, but when I had accepted his offer and climbed aboard, I discovered that the young man was Senegalese, an engineer in charge of building a new hospital at Niafounké. He had been recruiting construction workers from nearby villages, he said, and the truck body was filled with them, so the still-punctured Evans was well supported in their midst.

Niafounké, with its tree-lined streets and sleepy colonial air looked civilized after the wilderness, but I was soon to find that the French influence expressed itself more in the orderly lay-out of the place than in any obvious comfort. I was put down outside the only place to stay, the Campèment, which was a very large dirt yard surrounded on all sides by low ochre-coloured buildings with tin doors and window shutters – more like a barracks than anything else. For a pound, I was given the best of the crumbling pink cells, which was quite bare except for a battered iron cot, its exposed springs thick with dust. There was no lighting or running water, just some noisome pit lavatories. The guardian's son, a young man of about seventeen called Allasane found me a grass mat to cover the bed springs, and a bucket of warm water to wash with.

Afterwards he and a friend escorted me around town to shop for necessities like supper and a candle. There was no restaurant, and since the market was closed the only food I could find was some tough meat from a street grill, some excellent warm flat bread, and a can of warm beer from the town's brothel. Sitting on the bed-springs in my crumbling cell, in the light of the single flickering candle, I tried to chew through some of the meat, but soon gave up and left it for my young friends. They meanwhile had been trying to find out what they could about my next day's route, but apparently no one they knew had ever made the journey to Saraféré. Some of their sources said it was impossible to get there because there was so much water blocking the way, others thought there was no problem. They stayed on and on, sitting on a low wall in front of my cell, chewing the meat and talking about their hopes and aspirations. One planned to be a doctor, the other wanted to go into commerce, but by this time they were both silhouettes against the starlight, and I could no longer distinguish one from the other. I was so tired that I could hardly follow what they were saying, so I shooed them away, and secured my cell for the night by placing Evans across the threshold.

173

With the help of my small camping mattress, the mosquito net and sleeping bag, the rusty cot springs were made comfortable enough to provide a better night's sleep than I had enjoyed since leaving Timbuktu, and dawn was creeping palely into the crumbling pink cell before I awakened with a start at the thought of the day ahead. The first thing was to check that yesterday's puncture repairs had held up. There had been four separate holes, all of them in fact caused by two vicious thorns, but in spite of having mended them in fading light, the tyres were still hard.

I made coffee and ate some bread and a few dates while I waited for Allasane, who had promised to come and take me to the river crossing. It was a windy grey morning with the enormously wide Niger a confusion of sharp white-topped waves. Fierce bargaining with a young pirogier and farewells to Allasane diverted my attention from the dangers of making such a crossing in a leaky old pirogue, and from the realization that no one else was going over. We were well out, tossing about like a straw, the wind blowing against a strong current and the pirogue taking in quantities of water, before I began to feel anxious. The skinny pirogier could not have been more than fourteen, and his assistant was about ten. That they were both amazingly tough and knew exactly what they were doing was not something of which I was totally convinced, however, until the nerve-wracking twenty-minute journey was over.

The eastern bank was another country altogether. Beyond a small cluster of miserable-looking huts there was nothing to be seen but empty flood plains of dried mud stretching away drearily into the distance. But at least it appeared that the floods had receded sufficiently to give me a chance of getting through to Mopti. Faint tyre imprints from a previous season were etched very lightly across the surface, and these marks were what I had to follow, the pirogier told me, taking me some distance to point them out. He had been made very friendly by the tip which thankfulness for the safe crossing had caused me to add to the fare.

I lost the trail almost at once, and had to cast about in circles before I picked it up again. This happened several times in the first two hours, and often I had to continue by compass bearing, hoping that I would pick up the tracks further on. Every so often the ground climbed up from the dried mud flats to a sandy plateau of doum palms, acacias and scrub. Areas of millet stalks showed that there had been a harvest some weeks before, but of the harvesters there was no sign, nor of any dwelling. I saw only one person the whole morning, an old lady who fled at the sight of me.

I was able to make good progress where the line of the route was clear across the dark reddish-brown flood plains. The sandy hillocks however were barely rideable, although the way here was plain and unmistakable, vehicles having churned up the delicate ground in a swathe of deep soft unstable sand. I sweated copiously trying to force my way along these paths, often choosing to go alongside them in the slightly firmer ground that was held together by vegetation. Then, at around mid-day, I realized the back tyre was flat, and stopped to make a repair. To my horror I discovered that the tyre was one mass of thorns, hundreds of them protruding from all over it, and when I looked at the front tyre, which hadn't yet gone down, I saw that it too was in the same condition. I pulled at one of the thorns and there was a depressing hiss of escaping air.

Concentrating so hard on keeping Evans moving forward through the sandy places, standing on the pedals, maintaining the momentum no matter what, I hadn't noticed the ghastly thorny ground-cover known as cram-cram; or the scores of other species of burrs and thorns with which every tiny plant, tree and shrub in this harsh habitat was thickly protected. Even my bootlaces and the exposed parts of my socks were covered thickly with burrs, and when I tried to pull them off I found they were so efficiently armoured all over that they stuck painfully into my fingers, and I had to remove them with pliers.

It was time for some serious thought. I had to remain mobile no matter what; there was no contingency plan to fall back upon, no hope of a friendly vehicle coming to the rescue. I was truly on my own. The Specialized tyres which had proved so good in sand were clearly useless for this thorn-infested region. I would change them for the despised Hutchinsons; although these offered so poor a grip they did have the benefit of a Kevlar lining which, in theory, should render them thorn-proof. I was also carrying two new inner tubes, so I need not consider tackling the enormous numbers of punctures. Not that I had anything like enough patches to repair the hundred or so holes which, at a conservative estimate, I reckoned there must be. Even with Kevlar tyres, I couldn't hope to get away without further punctures in this hellish terrain, and would need to husband what patches I had very carefully, as events soon proved.

I tried to work systematically, but the combination of burning sun, wind, dust and sand made it difficult, and I managed to collect a puncture in one of the new inner tubes before I had even finished pumping it up. The thorns must also be airborne, I thought in despair. I had to sacrifice some of my precious water to find this new hole, half-filling my remaining cooking pan, and running the tube through it inch by inch while I watched for the tell-tale bubbles. The most important thing in repairing a puncture is to find what caused it, as this is often a nail or a thorn lodged in the tyre, which, if not removed, will result in further punctures. I ran my fingers around the inside of the tyre again and again without finding anything, and was about to replace the tube when a vicious stab revealed the thorn stuck in the rim tape. Never had pain been more in the nature of a blessing, I thought; it was as if my guardian angel had rapped me over the knuckles, a thought that cheered me enough to celebrate by turning the used water into tea.

On the Hutchinson tyres I could only ride the flood plains, since they had no grip at all on sandy slopes, and I progressed more slowly, being very careful to keep out of the vegetation. There were times when the going was so soft that I could hardly make any progress, and I became very conscious of the strong easterly wind further sapping my energy. There was a nasty moment in the middle of a huge area of open mud flats when, trying to determine the line of the route, I dropped the tiny compass and couldn't find it again for a long time, although I knew it had to be within a few yard's radius, and before I did spot it I had begun to wonder if I was going mad.

In spite of the compass, I lost the path altogether, and did not realize it until I was hailed by a party of men cutting reeds in a thin ribbon of a river. They seemed to know which way I ought to be going, and poled their hugely laden pirogue over the few yards of water to where I was. They waded across a stretch of shallow water and glutinous mud and carried the panniers and Evans on board and then came back to help me. The old man who supported me was a leper, with fingers and nose rotted away. There are so many lepers in the Sahel, but at least they remain in their communities; they are not thrust out or sent to leper colonies.

I thought I had tipped them generously for the service, but they looked very disappointed that it was not more, and begged for medicine by miming the swallowing of pills and the administering of an injection – a rather sophisticated request, this last, I thought, in so primitive a place. I had strayed a good mile off the track it seemed, and the young boy in the party elected to take me back to it. I rewarded him with a handful of dates for which he seemed more thankful than the men had been for their money.

The way was more obvious after that; I even saw an old French road marker, a heavy pyramid of stone that wouldn't be washed away when the track was underwater. As I had seen no other vehicle passing in either direction, I still feared there might be some impassable obstacle ahead. Later I learnt that it was only because the rains had been so sparse that year, that I had been able to make the crossing this early; normally the area would have remained flooded for another few weeks, with only the sandy hillocks free of the water. For wheeled traffic such terrain could never be other than tricky! The next barrier was a smallish pond, with an attendant ferryman who came to meet me and pushed Evans through the soft surrounding sand. His pirogue was the most primitive I had yet been in, more rope sewing than wood, and with a layer of hay inside to provide a footing. The man seemed so friendly and sensible that I thought I would let him determine what a ferry charge should be, and held out a selection of coins for him to choose from. What he took was about what I would have paid in England.

Soon after this, I glimpsed fairy-tale pinnacles and minarets, towers and battlements, and, unbelievable though it seemed, there before me in this inimical wilderness was a walled and gated city, all rosy red in the late afternoon sun.

Saraféré was so pretty from a distance that it was bound to be in some sense a disappointment, although the fact that it was there at all, exactly where the map claimed it should be, was wonder enough for me after the rigours of the way. It wasn't all that marvellous close to; but that a people who lived at a bare subsistence level found the time and resources to beautify their small city was touching. The mosque was fantastically pinnacled and decorated in the exuberant Sahelian manner, but the walls of the city had been in part an illusion, created by the long battlemented sides of the mosques and the taller houses. It certainly had its fair share of rubbish heaps, malodorous pits and ditches, but many of the houses were two-storey and carefully built, with beautifully carved doors and window grilles, and all, even the smallest dwellings, had patterns imprinted in the *banco*. There was something too about the layout of the place on its twin hills, that if not exactly planned, was harmonious and probably lent Saraféré its special charm. I would have loved to have seen it afloat during the wet season, like a Venetian city in the lagoon.

Two charming young boys left their flock of goats and helped me to push Evans through the soft yielding sand to the ferry over an arm of the Bara Issa, the eastern and lesser branch of the Niger, which I had last seen just after Diré. The channel ran through the town, between the twin hills, cutting it into two halves. There were lots of people around on either side – water being always a focal point in a dry climate, the element that makes life pleasurable rather than merely bearable. Everyone stared at me with disbelief, some women even breaking into embarrassed giggles. An interfering old fool tried to bully me into paying some vast sum for the ferry, although it was clearly nothing to do with him. I shook him off, and gave the pirogier the same coin as the previous ferryman had taken, with which he seemed perfectly happy. Still in a state of bemusement, I would have liked just to sit on the bank like everyone else, enjoying the expanse of water and slowly taking in the scene, but I was proving much too exotic an attraction for the townspeople, and two young men quite rightly said that I should go with them to the *arrondissement*, where the *'chef d'administration'* had his office and where the official *Campément* was. Mali is still organized on the old colonial lines, with government-appointed administrators in every region, and Saraféré was the centre of this particular area.

The network of rest houses, also left over from French colonial days, is well thought out in Mali, a roof usually being available within a moderate day's journey. The problem is that for the most part they are all just like this one was – a crumbling cell with nothing at all in it (except for the shrivelled corpses of spiders) and absolutely no amenities. Had water been available, I would really have been better off in the wilderness in my tent, but of course wherever there was water there were crowds of people too, so I couldn't win. However, *'le chef'*, whose residence adjoined this dismal rest house, very kindly loaned me a leather folding bed/chair and a stool for my candle, and promised to send over some dinner in *'quelque minutes'*, which meant three hours later, by which time I had almost expired.

Of the crowd of boys and youths who had joined the procession escorting me to the *chef*, two had been chosen by him to see to my needs, and the others were chased away. The younger one, Ali, fetched water, and bought bread and tomatoes and candles in the market for me, while his brother Mosi, borrowed a little charcoal brazier and a teapot and set about making Tuareg tea with ingredients I supplied, regaling me, in the now familiar pattern with the problems of his life. He was hoping that I would hire him to guide me on the next day's journey, because once, he said, a Dutchman had come to Saraféré in the month of June when the way was dry, and he, Mosi, had guided him to Niafounké, where he had been given so much money as a reward that all his family had bought new clothes. He had hoped ever since for another 'red ears' to come along. Alas for him, this 'red ears' had no intention of hiring a guide, and I longed only for him to depart, so that I could strip off and have a wipe over with a flannel.

When it was quite dark, a servant brought dinner in several vessels. There was curried spaghetti, bread, a tiny piece of chicken, and a gritty salad of green stuff that I thought was probably risky considering the water source it would have been washed in, but which I ate anyway as I was so hungry. Sitting in front of the door under the huge stars, with the twinkling lights of the cooking fires all around, relaxed and restored by the food, I felt a great sense of peace and thankfulness sweeping over me. Having come safely to so remote a place made me feel small and vulnerable, yet at the same time protected and very happy; emotions not uncommon to travellers who have left most of the trappings of civilization behind, and who discover how much fuller life can seem without them.

The *chef*'s wife came to invite me to their house for tea, bringing the servant with a huge bunch of keys to lock up my cell first, in case of thieves. This impressive display of efficiency lasted only as long as it took to discover that none of the keys fitted, at which point it was decided there were no thieves in Saraféré after all. The *chef*'s house was almost as bare and comfortless as my cell. A solitary smoking hurricane lamp spilled a dim light into the large room, whose unpainted mud walls reflected none of it back. When my eyes adjusted I could make out children lying asleep on rush mats on the floor. The only stick of furniture was a hard chair on which the *chef* sat, a rather bored and unhappy-looking man. He told me his appointment as the administrator of this district was considered almost a punishment, because it was so far out in the sticks. During the months when the land was flooded, he said, there was no problem with transport, everything went by boat, but the last *pinasse* carrying supplies from Mopti had got up the Bara Issa a week before, and now the river was too low to bring another until after the next rains in about four months. The track that I would be travelling the following day was not yet dried out enough for motor vehicles, but he thought it would be fine for a bicycle. He also thought I should have fewer problems on the route from here on, and that the worst was behind me. He was not right, but it is often better not to know what lies ahead.

I had several ponds and lakes to cycle around at the beginning of the next day's ride, and wherever there was water there were birds too. Herons launched themselves into the air with their characteristic spring as I drew near, and flew off on slow measured wingbeats, while egrets, too intent on fishing to bother about me, stretched out their snake-like necks over the water; all of which made the wilderness seem a little less daunting. The terrain was at first somewhat easier than that of the previous day, but certainly no sinecure; in some places cattle had trampled the mud while it was still wet and left a surface almost impossible even to walk over. After four and a half hours of hard work my mileometer showed only 18.4 miles, and at that point an enormous thorn pierced the sidewall of the rear tyre and I had to stop for repairs. There were now only seven patches left, and I was relieved that other chunky thorns lodged in the front tyre came out with no accompanying rush of air.

I was not feeling particularly well. My throat, sinuses and chest had been cauterized for some weeks now by the parching, searing winds and the perpetual irritation of blown sand and dust; but today they felt particularly raw. The previous night I had noticed how hoarse my voice had sounded, and how it hurt to talk. Now it also hurt to swallow, and what with my cracked lips and nostrils I was well on the way to feeling sorry for myself, a dangerous emotion in my present position, where I was exposed to so much possible calamity.

I stopped at lunchtime to brew tea but found I could eat nothing except for a piece of the crystallized ginger that had lain forgotten in my bag since the Channel crossing. After weeks of a fairly monotous bland diet, the exotic taste exploded on my palate, conjuring up visions of silken hangings in marble palaces, with fountains splashing in the background: more importantly, it also seemed to possess the power to get me going again. Some catalyst was certainly needed, for the way by now had become quite appalling, and it got even worse, with sand so soft that I stuck in it for minutes at a time. After that the ginger took the place of the exhausted whisky.

At one small town I had to cross a river on an incredibly narrow mud-brick bridge, no more than the width of a wall, and a crumbling one at that. I cannot think how I managed not to fall in. On the other side, like a Pied Piper, I attracted the entire population of the town's children, who started to pursue me in full cry, pouring out of their homes and out of the school in ever-increasing numbers, and in spite of the restraining shouts of their parents and teachers. There were scores of them, all egging one another on, so that it was difficult to adopt my usual ploy of hiring a few to get rid of the rest. I felt extremely intimidated, even more so when one of the boys nearest to me cried 'Regardez le fou Madame. Il vient aussi' and I saw that a great shambling dribbling idiot of a boy, making loud unintelligible noises was shuffling along fast behind us, overtaking the other children who scattered from him in fright. I too found it all most alarming, so that I lost my grip on the situation entirely. I should really have stayed in this town, where there was a rest house, but instead I could think only of getting out of it as fast as possible. Some of the bigger boys pointed out the track I should take from the profusion of paths that presented themselves, and I scattered so much largesse in my eagerness to get free that, like Mansa Musa, I might well have had an influence on the town's economy.

But in the end it was 'le fou' who got the biggest tip, and earned it, because he refused to let me get away, but shuffled fast down the track after me for a long way, mouthing his weird urgent sounds, until his very persistence convinced me that I was going the wrong way. By the time he had helped me manhandle Evans through the bush to the right path, I had ceased to be intimidated by him, realizing that he was neither dangerous nor an idiot, but only dreadfully afflicted with several cruel handicaps together with the chronic speech impediment. When I had paid him, and had managed to convince him that he could come no further with me, he stood there wreathed in great beaming smiles, making sure that I continued in the right direction, while I was almost too overcome to see where I was going.

The ground for a mile or so around any village, where over cultivation and the hooves of cattle had turned it into desert, was much harder going than anywhere else, especially as all villages were perched on low hills. As I was making my way up one such sandy incline a donkey long since drowned, and hanging where the floods had left it, high in the branches of a thorn tree came into view. For a long time the hide-covered skeleton with its gaping holes and grinning skull met my gaze every time I raised my head. In order to shut out the ghastly sight I kept my eyes on the ground, and I think I must have sunk into a sort of daze for a while, because when I next raised my head the tree and the donkey had disappeared, and I was wheeling Evans along the main street of a very poor-looking village. Ahead, in the distance, the sun was glinting on a pond or a river, and I remembered that I must refill my empty water bottles. I was just looking round for a well when a man came up to me, took hold of Evans and said '*Vous êtes fatigué Madame, restez ici*'.

I staggered after him into a school yard where stood a bright yellow pump 'A gift of India to the people of Mali', and there in the shade of a tree a chair was brought for me to sit on. I felt quite ill by now, and knew that soon I must rouse myself and take some medicine. But for the moment it was enough just to sit and drink glass after glass of cool water that didn't first have to be laboriously pumped through a filter.

# 17

# Winning through to Konna

I LAY UNDER MY mosquito net in a small walled garden full of low dark-green pepper bushes. At the far end was an ornate little mosque, the only building in the village that was not strictly utilitarian, and which was lent even greater flamboyance by the sun setting redly behind its pinnacles and minarets. I kept my gaze fixed on it in order to avoid the many faces appearing and disappearing over the garden wall, young faces mainly, wide-eyed with curiosity, craning for a glimpse of the strange white woman and her red bicycle who had stumbled into their remote corner of the world. At my back was the wall of a crumbling *banco* hovel, windowless and full of dust, in which the man who had decided I needed looking after, Kola Bouri, had first tried to install me. There was no doubting now that I was ill, and if I was going to expire during the night, I had decided that I would prefer to do so under the stars.

I didn't carry a thermometer, nor did I need one to know that I had a high temperature and a nasty chest infection, probably the result of all the spitting on the overcrowded *pinasse*. I had begun a course of antibiotics, and could do no more now but rest and hope that the medicine would work. Kola Bouri had volunteered to buy a hen and get it cooked for me and had asked for 400 CFAs. I had given him a 1000 CFA note, and later he explained to me that the additional 600 had been used for the oil, wood and salt with which to do the cooking. The bird had been brought for my inspection, first alive and squawking vociferously, and a little later dead in the bottom of a bucket, and I had felt the familiar quick pang of conscience that something so vibrantly alive was transformed into a limp bedraggled corpse.

It was a good five hours later, when darkness had put an end to the peep show and I had at last fallen into an uneasy sleep, that Kola came to wake me up to eat the hen. I was feeling decidedly sorry for myself, aching all over, and the last thing I wanted now was food; but he insisted. Groaning with the effort, I got myself into a sitting position, lifted the lid of the pan, and felt about gingerly inside. What I pulled out was a lower leg and foot, the claws still attached. In my sick state, it seemed as horrible as a human hand or foot would have been, and I dropped it back in disgust. Poor Kola, it was undoubtedly a fine bonus to be handed a whole cooked hen and told to do what he liked with it, but I am sure, poor as he was, that he would have preferred that I had eaten at least some of it.

My temperature was down by morning, when Kola appeared with some horrid flaccid rice cakes soaked in something he called 'cow oil'. I stashed them away to dispose of later, not being able to bear the thought of causing further offence. I felt weak but more or less in my right mind, and the various pains in chest, throat, and ears were much improved, all clear indications that the antibiotics were working. I was not tempted to spend another day in the unhygienic little village; it would be wiser to press on towards civilization, I felt, where I would certainly improve faster with some decent food and a few comforts.

Kola walked me through the unlovely outskirts of his village to the river I had seen, the Koli Koli, another large tributary of the lesser arm of the Niger. I was now through the most tortuous section of the river's meanderings through the lower part of the inland delta, but as an indication that the rigours of the journey were by no means behind me a tyre punctured on the short walk to the ferry.

The next serious obstacle was a small lake across the track, with no boat to act as ferry. Had I waited, a young girl would have carried everything across for me, but I didn't realize that and struggled over with Evans on my shoulder while she took the panniers, both of us wading fully clothed up to our waists, while an elderly woman who was gathering millet stalks tut-tutted in the background. So fierce was the wind and the sun that my clothes were bone dry again in ten minutes.

There were villages on top of low hillocks at about two-mile intervals, each no more than a cluster of little huts enclosed by thorn hedges, and all surrounded by a sea of sand too deep to ride through. There was no one much about except for groups of older women pounding millet in companionable circles. The younger people and the men were away working in distant fields, or taking their flocks to graze. Sometimes I caught sight of them in the distance, tiny figures in an immensity of space. The women were not alarmed by my sudden appearance as people further north had been, and at one small place an old woman who spoke a little French came over to tell me that the track improved further on. I was pushing on as steadily as I could, hoping to find food and shelter at Korientzé, a town marked on my map as a regional centre. But although it proved to be larger than Saraféré, it was not market day, and I found only a cup of Nescafé, two oranges and some pieces of stale bread. There was nothing for it but to embark on the remaining forty miles to Konna, where the tarmac of the main Malian highway ran.

My way now lay around the southern side of Lake Korientzé, where a vast agricultural plain had recently been harvested. The lake was soon out of sight, but the plain stretched out seemingly forever, a flat featureless dreary expanse, not unlike parts of the eastern counties of England have become since the trees and hedges were ripped out in the interests of so-called efficient farming. The relentless wind blowing strongly in my face was also reminiscent of bleak English fenlands in winter, but when I stopped and sat on a rare solitary rock to eat my oranges, I saw with a sudden shock of delight how intensely beautiful was the sky over this ugly landscape. Unpolluted by any hint of traffic haze or industrial smog, it blazed a scintillating blue, with long tattered banners of wind clouds streaming across it.

At some point in the hot unrelenting slog of the afternoon, the land changed back to dry savannah – small trees and scrub on an undulating laterite soil, but still with the debased over-grazed over-cultivated sandy areas spreading out from every village. If any children were around when I became totally bogged down in the sand, I called to them, and they would come and push Evans. Four or five small boys and girls, barefoot and dressed in rags and tags of western clothing, could manhandle it along as quickly as I could walk, and we would enter the village at what became the head of a procession. There the men would take over Evans; once I was handed a stick to hold, so its owner could have both hands free for the handlebars, and the others were quick to point out that I could use it if I wished to drive the man along. It was clearly considered an honour or at least a welcome diversion to wheel this red bicycle, and in the competition that ensued I often lost sight of my original young helpers whom I wished to reward.

In this way, with a good deal of laughter and banter to lighten the labour, I covered about half of the forty remaining miles. There was momentary elation when I reached the start of the proper road – a wide unsurfaced track with telegraph poles running alongside it. There were no wires stretched between these poles; they had been cut during a coup twenty-five years before, I was told, and never replaced. But the bare poles set at regular intervals expressed a sense of sophistication nothing short of miraculous after the primitive world I had come through. Unfortunately they also heralded the end of the friendly helpful villages, and the euphoria vanished altogether when I realized that the road was even less rideable than the tracks had been. Being above the flood level of the delta it was in use for most of the year and carried regular traffic, and nothing carved up the surface of the fragile Sahelian ground faster than motor vehicles. It was half past five now, and I wasn't making even two miles an hour; there seemed little possibility of being able to reach Konna that night.

Instead of a soft bed and a hot meal, I was beginning to contemplate another night in the bush when, as the light began to fade, a vehicle came slithering and bucking through the sand behind me, the first I had seen since Niafounké. It was a bush taxi modified from an old pick-up, the roof piled high with assorted bundles, and the roughly constructed body visibly bulging with people, animals, hens and baskets. We were just on the outskirts of a village that straddled the road, and the taxi stopped to let people out and to take on others. The driver called over to ask me if I wanted to travel with them, but I said 'No' without even considering it, for I was running a temperature again by this time, and a little light-headed. Another line from T.S. Eliot's *Four Quartets* kept ringing through my head like an exhortation – '*Not fare well, but fare forward voyagers*'.

The taxi went on, but a little way out of the village it stopped again, and the driver sent over the young man who did the loading to plead with me in French. They didn't want money, he explained, but the road was too hard for a bicycle. Even if I didn't wish to ride with them all the way to Konna, then I must at least let them give me a lift out of this sandy section, for it grew even worse in a little while. You can ride on top with your bicycle if you are worried about it, said the young man, and at that point reason reasserted itself, and feeling moved almost to tears again by all this solicitude I climbed gratefully up onto the roof, holding on with one hand, and clutching Evans with the other as we plunged and rolled over the remaining miles into Konna. There was no question of getting down again when the sandy stretch came to an end; for one thing it didn't end, and for another, I had lost the initiative, and giving in and letting someone take over was fatal to any thought of further effort, as well as being the most blessed relief. I thoroughly enjoyed the ride through the velvety darkness, with the stars bright, and the wind making me feel cool for the first time in what seemed like an age.

The *Campément* at Konna, to which I was delivered, was a bustling place, every one of its twenty little cells filled with '*commerçants*' from Mopti, come to do trade in the market with things like electric torches, plastic toys and other western goods made in Taiwan. Standing in the dark courtyard with candlelight spilling out of the open doorways around the perimeter, I had glimpses of robed figures, of sleeping mats laid on mud floors and bales and rolls of bedding that made it seem very much an ancient caravanserai, an effect rather diminished by great blasts of relayed sound coming from a sort of mud-brick village hall across the unlit street where a film show was in progress. As all the cells were occupied, the guardian offered me the use of his for a slightly inflated price. It was about eight feet by four, a real bed with a foam mattress taking up most of the floor space, and the owner's clothes and shoes spreading over the rest. Running along the top of the two longer walls were banners with lettering more than a foot high, each reading 'BIENVENUE AUX DELEGATIONS' – almost as though I had been expected. Above the bed, a psychedelic tapestry of Jesus as the Good Shepherd kept company with photographs of boxers cut from magazines. The guardian, removing some of his possessions to give me more room, explained the decorations by saying that although he was himself a Moslem, he thought all religions were good, and that he was also very keen on sport. It was as a sportswoman he welcomed me to his room, he said, and would do all he could to make my stay enjoyable; could he for instance send out for supper for me? I had been fantasizing about a simple plain omelette ever since the antibiotics had begun to bite, and my appetite had returned. The guardian said he would do his best.

An hour later he was back with an omelette he had cooked himself because such a gastronomic nicety was not available in Konna. It was flat like a pancake and swimming in a plate of sizzling oil. With it was a salad that I reckoned I could eat with impunity since I was already on antibiotics, and a bottle of green fizzy drink, jewel-like in the light of the candle. Being so ravenously hungry, and not having had much to eat for several days, I was probably not a reliable judge of its quality, for it seemed to me a feast. One of the traders came to visit me and to practise his English while I was mopping up the last of the oil with the bread. He took one look and went off, returning shortly with a large mug of rice pudding and milk. It too was delicious, and even without a spoon I managed to down it in a trice, after which a series of monumental yawns which I was unable to smother cut short the trader's visit.

I had an unexpected ordeal to go through before I could at last sink into blissful oblivion. The guardian had heated a bucket of water so that I might wash, and he carried it for me into the *Campément toilette*, where he left me, mounting guard outside since there was no lock. The candle lit up a cavernous chamber several times the size of my cell, and absolutely thick with cockroaches, their shadows vast and nightmarish on the dark walls and ceiling. In the centre of the room was an open pit from which came so powerful a smell that I would have fled immediately had there been no other considerations. I could not leave however until a suitable time had elapsed, otherwise this kind considerate guardian would be offended, so I began to count, reckoning that five minutes would be the least I could get away with. As I counted, I thought about how I would also have to pour away all the lovely hot water, and this seemed such a sacrilege that I took what in retrospect I consider the bravest action of my life: my flesh creeping with the thought of the cockroaches and the pit, I took off my clothes, and poured jugful after jugful of the water over myself, until it was all gone.

# 18

# Mopti

WHATEVER ELSE THIS journey had offered so far, it had certainly proved that there is nothing like a period of discomfort for burnishing up perceptions, and making even quite ordinary and familiar things seem newly discovered and delightful. Last night there had been the delectable omelette, today it was the rediscovery of the heady delights of bicycling along an empty asphalt highway, which I reached soon after I had been waved off from Konna by the kindly guardian and the *commerçants*. It was the road that connected Gao with the capital, Bamako, and had only recently been constructed by a combined German and Canadian team. It was nothing special, and already it was breaking up in several places through lack of maintenance, but after the 300 miles of brutal and virtually trackless terrain I had just fought my way through, its wonderful unyielding surface was pure bliss.

One of the presents I had been given for my journey was a tiny computer that fitted on the handlebars, providing me with information such as what time it was, how fast I was travelling, how far I had gone, and what my highest speed had been. Small boys coveted it more than the bicycle itself, and I rather enjoyed it too, particularly the speedometer function. The flashing digits took my mind off things when the going got tough, a reward for that extra bit of effort as another 0.5 m.p.h. was recorded. During the previous weeks, however, it had served only to illustrate the slow painful progress as, battling through the sand, I had watched the digits flicker between 1.4 and 1.5 m.p.h., and the occasions I could show a 2 m.p.h. were short-lived triumphs. I had almost forgotten that the bicycle could be more than a pack mule. Now on this empty highway, with a strong wind at my back, I felt almost as though I was flying, and the m.p.h. fairly whizzed up the scale to such dizzy heights as 20, and even topping 30 on downhill stretches. I was filled with the exhilaration of movement; the tyres hummed loudly on a high triumphant note, and I joined in with a Jubilate.

This love affair with speed came to an abrupt end thirty-five miles further on, where the Mopti road left the highway. Mopti had once been little more than a few hummocks of land in the middle of vast rice fields. It was the French who realized the geographical importance of a settlement so close to the main flow of the river, and turned it into the main trading port of the Middle Niger by building an eight-mile causeway to it across the flood plains. Along this narrow dyke the tarmac continued, crazed and potholed, and no more than the bare width of two vehicles, and on it a shuttle service of battered taxis hurtled across in both directions, like bats out of hell. Had the French, in their civilized fashion, not also planted a line of great trees on either side, where it was possible to ride just clear of the tarmac, I doubt if a bicyclist would be able to get to Mopti in one piece. Even so, I was in great danger from the taxis' sudden swerves as they pursued their rash and headlong progress, and could spare only brief glances for the strings of figures with donkeys and cattle winding their way across the enormous expanses of the largely dry paddy fields below. There were Bozo fishermen too, clearing the last shallow ponds of their harvest of tiny silvery fish, but I retained only distant simplified images of them, frozen in mid-action like Lowry figures translated into another landscape.

Coming suddenly into the bustle of Mopti at the end of the causeway was a shock. After the days in the empty monochrome wilderness, the riot of colour, the noise, the over-powering smells, and the press of people had my senses reeling, so that finding a place of refuge to collect myself became an immediate priority, taking precedence even over the food and drink I had been fondly contemplating. It is always difficult to find your bearings in a strange town if you don't have a definite objective, and the constant importuning of aggressive young men who come and stand in front of you, blocking the way, and demanding to know where you are going, doesn't help.

I already knew that there wasn't a wide choice of places to stay in Mopti. There was a *maison du passage* for the Peace Corps volunteers in from their villages, where strangers could sometimes find a bed for a small charge. I had planned to do this so that I could find out something about the area from the volunteers at the same time. The young Americans assigned to Mali, however, found life so hard and unrewarding in their villages that the hostel was always full of them flocking to the fleshpots of Mopti. I quickly vetoed the few cheap places near the mosque, for although by this time I had become quite used to the over-taxed open drains of West African towns, those of Mopti's oldest quarter were so bad that I found it impossible even to cycle there. The medium-priced *Campément* was certainly no bargain by western standards, but accommodation has a highly inflated value in Mali and under normal circumstances I would have settled for one of its dark dingy rooms. After the days in the delta however it would not do. It wasn't that I was desperate for what I considered luxury – I could quite well do without the silk sheets and the sunken bath. But I craved a clean, uncluttered room, with lights that worked, unlimited quantities of running water and no cockroaches. I wanted a place where I could close the door, and quietly recover my equilibrium without a string of people coming to make demands on me; and since those requirements were considered positively opulent in this part of the world, they came only at the top end of the market.

Entering my room was like walking into paradise, except for the mirror in which I saw myself for the first time in weeks – a very brown, desiccated person whom I did not at first recognize: I had not remembered looking so old. Poor Evans looked even worse, thick ochre dust clogging every cog and sprocket, and I marvelled that we had been able to spin along so well that morning. I threw the clothes I had been wearing into the shower basin to be soaked and pounded underfoot as I stood under the wonderful cascade of warm restoring water. Afterwards I put Evans under too, and watched it slowly change back into a smart red bicycle. Still reluctant to leave the lovely flow of water, I took the rest of my equipment in with me, and scrubbed it clean of the dust which smelt of dried excrement.

Festooned with dripping panniers, tent, mosquito net, sleeping bag and the laundered clothes suspended from lines made up from bits of nylon string, spare boot laces and elastic bungees, the room was no longer a paradise and it was necessary to seek refuge elsewhere until I could take it all down. I had noticed the Bar Bozo on my way in, an unpretentious little *banco* shack with a white-washed shaded terrace, standing on a slight eminence overlooking the harbour basin. It soon became my favourite spot in Mopti. The Niger divided once again at this point, and the port was just at the entrance to the Bani, which flowed southwards off the main river. The Bar Bozo was therefore very much at the centre of things, and provided an excellent viewpoint from which the flavour of the whole place could be absorbed. Sitting at ease in a cane basket chair, an ice-cold beer on a low table in front of me and a meal of Niger pike on its way, I was conscious of a deep contentment, and couldn't think of anything more that I required of life just then.

Below, pirogues plied to and fro across the harbour to save people a 200-yard walk around it; others criss-crossed slowly up and down, often with boys wielding the poles, practising their water skills, and the black slender shapes constantly formed new patterns on the water, like a slowly turned kaleidoscope. The brown water was a foil for the glorious strident colour that was everywhere: bright robes and head scarves against shiny black skins; rich jewel-like fruit – mangoes, oranges, papayas, bananas, pineapples, limes, tomatoes – piled up on low stalls around the harbour walls or in the overflowing baskets in an abundance I had not seen since Niamey. After the dry thorny wilderness, Mopti seemed to me like one huge cornucopia. Even the few crumbling colonial buildings across the harbour were decaying without any hint of melancholy. The whole town wore an air of colourful ease.

Beneath the old customs house, a dozen big *pinasses* were hauled up on the dried mud foreshore, their cargoes of precious salt slabs carefully stacked alongside, but my *pinasse* was not amongst them. When I had parted from the ship's company on the drab wasteland by Tonka, the owner, who must have felt a shade desperate by then with all those mouths to feed and no sign of the wind abating, had said in response to my wishes for their safe arrival in Mopti, 'The threads of our lives separate here, so what happens to us is no longer your concern'. Being of a different culture I did not feel the same and would have been delighted to see them arrive. I would also have been pleased to retrieve the cooking pot I had left aboard.

Near the boats, on the causeway that joined the islands, were market stalls where the desert salt was being sold. Small quantities of glittering fragments were heaped on scraps of paper, as though it was truly a precious stone. Above these stalls floated the delicate ethereal pinnacles of the mosque, which, since it was barred to infidels, I need not make the effort to visit, but could enjoy from a distance, where it undoubtedly was at its loveliest.

The fish market, Mopti's only other feature of note was adjacent to the bar, and the pungent aroma of the mounds of small dried fish spread out on sacks over an acre or two of ground that had for years absorbed the excess oil, masked all other scents. It was one of the smells of Mopti I enjoyed, reminding me as it did of the days that seemed so long ago now, when the Niger had been my highway, and when, from a straw mattress on a pirogue, I had seen a part of this harvest being gathered by Bozo fishermen.

Around the edges of the water there were people engaged in the sorts of activities that the more affluent world conducts in private. The most intimate acts of personal hygiene were carried out in full view. It was as though by preserving silence and keeping their backs turned firmly towards the shore it was possible for people to pretend they were quite alone, even when separated from the next person by no more than a foot. Cheek by jowl with the bathers were women soaping howling babies, or cleaning pots and pans, or washing clothes, just as I had seen in all the small villages that lined the Niger. There were also scenes of great animation near my hotel on the main river, where the sand was firm and all the cars, lorries, vans, motor bikes and bicycles of the city were taken into the shallows and scrubbed. That the people of the Sahel felt the same need to divest themselves and their belongings of the awful dust of their environment as I did, gave me a sense of affinity with them. But however the people of Mopti used the Niger, their delight in it was clear. Whether they had just finished washing their bodies or their cars, they immediately scooped up the same water in their hands to drink, or to wash their faces, and they did so with a great relish. They revelled in the water, though how they avoided contracting serious diseases from it was a mystery.

Among the bathers was one solitary Bozo, casting his small round net in the fringes of the water, and in spite of the raw sewage and every other sort of rubbish floating there, he was pulling in a few small silvery fish at every cast. I had been inwardly shuddering at the thought of the contents of that water, and wondering where the hotel supply came from. But watching the fisherman hauling in his modest catch, I was suddenly aware of how pollution comes in many guises. In the West we are able to turn our backs on our rivers as the deadly work of poisoning them with industrial waste, chemical fertilisers and other modern pollutants goes on. The Niger on the other hand is central to the people, indeed without it there would be no life at all in the whole vast region. The river might appear grossly unhygienic and misused, yet so far a balance between man and nature has been maintained: as is amply demonstrated by the continuing harvest of fish.

Two days in Mopti and I was a new woman, restored to vigour and ready to continue my exploration of this fascinating country. I had eaten well in the excellent cafés in town at a fifth of the price charged by the hotel, and with all the wonderful fresh fruit and bread available there was no problem about fixing breakfast in my room either. What with the beer and three meals a day, my trousers were no longer hanging quite so far down my hips.

I had located 'pièces d'attacher' in the market for repairing the least damaged of the multi-punctured inner tubes – sixty patches it had taken, sold singly and at a ruinous price, and I hoped profoundly that I would never have to put the tube to the test. But it was comforting to have a spare again, especially for the trip into Dogon Country, where I was now bound.

The Dogon people were a race of peasant warriors who had dwelt beside the Niger until some time in the twelfth century, when a wave of Islamic reforming zeal swept through from the north. Wishing to preserve their animistic beliefs and practices, the Dogon fled to the rocky fastnesses of the Falaise of Bandigara, a great sweep of precipitous cliffs about a hundred miles long and about thirty miles east of Mopti at their closest point. There, until the present day, they had preserved their unique religion and customs in an equally unique habitat, tending their gardens, and producing a distinctive art that has become the most sought after in West Africa. Since by all reports their way of life was once again seriously under threat, this time from the pressure of twentieth-century tourism, I was at some pains to try and find a part of the Falaise which had not been subjected to such exposure. I certainly didn't want one of the guided tours that the aggressive young touts of Mopti had been urging on me. On the other hand it was an area where the iniquitous Tourist Police were active, and they could be very heavy-handed with travellers who wandered around without a guide. After consulting what authorities I could find among Peace Corps workers, I decided to bicycle to the southern end of the cliffs, to a small town called Bankas, where I planned to leave Evans and hire a guide to take me on a tour of some of the least-spoiled villages.

I left Mopti early in the morning, well in advance of the death-defying taxis, and had advanced only a short way along the asphalt highway in the teeth of a strong harmattan that was speedily undoing all my recent efforts with soap and water when I was hailed by the driver of a bush taxi who guessed I was bound for Bankas. He suggested that in this wind it would be more comfortable to travel there in his taxi, a point of view I was happy to endorse. As far as saving effort went, however, I might as well not have bothered, because we drove only fifteen miles to where the dirt road to Bankas left the highway, and there in a depressed little village we waited until sufficient passengers arrived to make the trip financially viable –

less than full to bursting point was considered running at a loss.

We sat on rickety stools in the shade of a tree, a mild source of interest to the handful of villagers who were about. A painfully thin but pretty little girl, whose hair stuck up all over her head in the usual crop of short pigtails, had put down her tin bowl of washed clothes and stood regarding us solemnly, her legs crossed beneath the scrap of material that wrapped her from navel to mid calf and was her sole clothing apart from a string of beads. A young woman, similarly dressed but with the addition of a cloth around her head watched too. There was a large-headed little baby tied on her back, who was almost certainly hydrocephalic, a stick-like child with closed runny eyes thick with flies. He was moaning faintly as he tried in vain to pull himself round under his mother's arm to reach her empty flaccid breasts. Several small bony boys in tattered scraps of western clothing or cotton tabards which were all holes walked up and down the road, stealing a glance at us as they passed. One of them, who was about eight or nine and had a shy gentle face shaded by a crocheted baby's hat, came and sat himself down a little distance away, beaming sweetly in our direction. I asked the driver, Amadou, what their interest in us was, and he said they were just hungry. All of them carried small tin bowls or plastic containers, as did the boys apprenticed to marabouts, who are sent out to beg for food as part of their training, in the intervals between committing passages of the Koran to memory. There are many such koranic 'schools' all over Islamic Africa, but these boys were not attached to any holy man; they were simply destitute, Amadou told me, and reduced to begging for a living.

Mali was full of such children, because everywhere harvests were failing through drought, locusts, or worn-out soil. Amadou himself was Dogon and these people were Bambara – the largest group in Mali – but it didn't matter which tribe people came from, conditions were much the same. Everywhere in Mali there were people walking along by the side of the road who had just abandoned their village, he said. What he was describing was the terrible urban drift of the Third World, as he saw it from within. He was at some pains that I should understand it, and as I wished to hear what he had to say,

I continued to sit there long after it became clear that no other passengers would come that day, and that he would spend the night there sleeping in his taxi, while I continued by bicycle to Bankas.

Peoples' reserves were gone, he said. The goats they kept as insurance to sell when the bad times came, when the crops failed, had already been sold to see them through earlier disasters. After that, when a fresh catastrophe struck, they had to move at once or they would die. The old and the very young were left behind, and the rest of the family set out on the road, going from village to village looking for food, for work, for any way of staying alive. If they found nothing, they would move on again, and again, until they died, or reached a city. Those who were left survived as best they could, usually by begging like these boys with their bowls, many of whom were now the main support of their mothers. Amadou called the sweet-faced boy over and took the cover off the small red plastic bucket he held. Inside was a tiny solitary rice cake, as cold and flaccid as the young woman's breasts. 'That he will not eat,' said Amadou. 'All day he will keep it in case he gets nothing else, then at night he will go home and ask his Mama if she has eaten that day, and if she says "No" he will say "Here you are Mama, I have already eaten."'

I surrendered my lunch of tomatoes and bread to this child, more than rewarded by the way the small trusting face lit up as I placed the offering in the jaunty red bucket, which seemed more suited to seaside holidays than to begging. Before I headed off I saw him sharing a piece of the bread with another boy, and thought again of the saying, 'In Africa, if one eats, all eat'. Crumb by crumb, they were making the bread last, licking the specks from their fingers with every sign of enjoyment, but also with a sort of reverence for the food that made me remember what had struck me about people's attitude to the river at Mopti. Desperately poor though they were, and in a dying land, they were aware of a quality in life that much of the affluent West either forgot long ago, or never knew.

There were about fifty miles to go to Bankas, and as I was almost immediately in a different landscape there was plenty to hold my attention and to take my mind off the poverty of Africa, the heat and the head wind, and the soft surface dragging at the wheels. Hills appeared on either side as the road wound up towards the plateau. Alongside was a river, mostly out of sight in a ravine or hidden by bushes and undergrowth. The land appeared very solid after the delta, with outcrops of sandstone and a darker coloured earth, and with some fine leafy trees to provide a change from the ubiquitous acacias.

About halfway to Bankas, as I was toiling up the steepest part of the climb, the lever which controlled the gears suddenly ceased to function and I was stuck in a ratio too high to pedal. Had I been less tired, I would have dealt with this by making a simple temporary adjustment to the rear mechanism. Instead, I took the faulty lever to pieces, and many of the forty or fifty tiny springs, cogs, washers and ratchets that made up the complicated little gadget had already disappeared in the sand when a pick-up van drew alongside and stopped. The driver was an uncle of Amadou's, and had been told to look out for me, and to make sure that I arrived safely in Bankas. He demanded twice as much money to take me from this half-way stage as Amadou had asked for the whole journey, but he compromised when I said he could keep the cogs and sprockets, which he had been collecting for me from the sand. I knew I should never be able to reassemble them into any meaningful arrangement.

The light had been fading fast when I was busy with the repairs, and now with the sun setting behind us, we drove into our ever-lengthening shadow, and I fell asleep squashed between Uncle and his fat jolly wife, who kept her arm along the back rest, cushioning me from the battering and the shaking. I was awakened some time later at the entrance to the Bar Faida, where I was to meet Bourema, a younger brother of Amadou, whom I had been given to understand was a splendid and knowledgeable guide. Even in the dim gleam of a few hurricane lamps I felt an immediate instinctive mistrust of him. He was a very tall, loose-limbed young man, with a weak mouth and a receding chin, and he moved with a studied carelessness. He was fashionably dressed in expensive denims, and in spite of the darkness was sporting sunglasses, which gave the impression that the hidden eyes were shifty. But since I had been so impressed by his gentle and perceptive brother I didn't feel like dismissing him out of hand. Hiring a guide is clearly like undertaking mechanical repairs – not something to contemplate at night, when fatigue has warped the judgement.

Bourema danced attendance upon me in the cluttered yard of the 'hotel', fetching a meal of stringy roast chicken and blackened potatoes, and making sure no one else could get anywhere near me. He discussed the tour and made lots of calculations on scraps of paper, which I couldn't read in the dim light. Sums of money were casually mentioned, amended, argued over, amended again, and before I was aware of what I had done, almost by default, I found that I had hired his services for a week at a rate of at least twice what I should have paid. What was worse, I broke all my own rules and advanced him a considerable sum in order for him to buy provisions for the journey.

Bourema left the moment I had given him the money, and I retired for the night, feeling distinctly uneasy about the arrangement. My bed was on the dirt floor of a lean-to shack of millet stalks which I shared with two tethered sheep, calmly munching their supper in a corner. The light of the smoke-blackened hurricane lamp cast a dim rich glow over the scene, and with stars glinting brightly through the generous gaps in the roof and walls I was reminded of Giotto's setting of the Nativity, and the uneasy feelings I had about the guide and the journey ahead faded into the background.

# 19

# Dogon Country

BOUREMA TURNED UP THE next morning with a donkey cart, and we set out across a wide sandy plain towards the great wall of the Falaise which shimmered insubstantially out of the hazy distance. Groups of bare-footed, brightly clad young women came hurrying towards us, carrying on their heads baskets of the small shallot-like Dogon onions which were introduced here by a Frenchman about a hundred years ago, and which are now famous throughout West Africa. The onions grew on the plateau above those far cliffs which meant that the girls had been carrying their loads for ten miles or more, and with the day already uncomfortably hot, sweat poured freely down their faces as they loped on towards the market at Bankas.

There are Dogon villages on all three levels of the land. Those which cling to the ledges and terraces of the towering Falaise itself are the original strongholds, taken over from earlier races who found security there from hostile tribes and wild animals, long before the Dogon came. On the plateau above, the first true settlers planted crops in secluded fields and gardens, and later, after the Dogon had ousted these people and times had become more peaceful, they were able to establish permanent villages both there and also on the plains below the Falaise.

These plains, across which we were painfully jolting, were once densely forested and teeming with wild life, but now, like so much of the Sahel, after decades of tree felling and over-cultivation they were fast turning into an irrecoverable desert. Sterile white sand drifts lay across the harvested millet fields, and the soft tracks that intersected them. It was no place for wheeled traffic, and the poor little donkey, constantly belaboured, was having a tough time.

Halfway across we stopped to visit a village around which stood many huge leafless baobab trees whose bizarre appearance was increased by their being festooned with fruit the size and weight of cannonballs that dangled from long thick stems, at a height to brain the unwary. They were also hooped with regular white bands where the thick fibrous bark had been removed for the making of rope, which made them look like a strange type of lamp post. The village must have had a good water supply for it was the most prosperous-looking I was to see. The façade of its temple was freshly painted with totemic symbols and animals, including an enormous snake, a symbol of life, made to look as though it was entering the shrine through a hole and emerging again near the summit.

The Dogon religion is a rich and complicated form of fetishism, centering around ancestor worship, and would require years of study to understand in all its subtleties. Almost no stone in a Dogon village is without significance, expressing an equivalence in the cosmic world, and there is almost no piece of ground that does not have its taboos, or is not furnished with a phallic-shaped fetish stone, brown from centuries of sacrificial blood that has been poured over it. A fetish is not worshipped for itself, but for what it represents, and the power that centres around it increases from the accumulation of devotion and offerings. Since chickens are the cheapest and most plentiful form of domestic life, they are the commonest sacrifice, a circumstance which makes it impossible to obtain eggs in Dogon country.

The dwelling houses were all flat-roofed, for the family sleeps on the roof in the hot weather. As staircases are unknown in Dogon country, access was from the outside by way of a notched log that splayed out into an upright 'Y' shape. Almost all the houses in this village had some sort of yard, though most were very small; the chief's was ornamented with a pair of large wooden doors, finely carved with male and female ancestor figures. A few of the houses had traditional fronts made up of rows of niches. There were eight niches in each row to represent the eight primal ancestors, four male and four female, through whom all life, human and animal, had come to earth and through whom everything was sustained. Death, which had made its appearance along with the ancestors, together with the gifts of speech, fire, metal, and so forth, had been balanced by a form of resurrection, so there was a belief in life after death and in an omnipotent, though rather shadowy, presiding Deity. The niches were shrines for housing memorabilia of a family's ancestors, together with sacred 'covenant stones', mementos of dead infants, traditional medicine ingredients and the like.

Bourema hurried me past these niched façades, saying they were the dwelling places of the village sorcerers, and very dangerous. Although a Dogon, he professed to despise most of their beliefs, while seeming inordinately afraid of them. The religion as he saw it was much nearer to what the West used to label 'black magic' -a vehicle for irrational fear and dread. His world was ruled by sorcerers, most of them it seemed intent on causing harm, sickness and death, and whose evil influence could be fought only by the efforts of a stronger sorcerer. There was no finite 'good and evil' for Bourema, only 'power'. He believed that everywhere, masquerading as ordinary people, there were sorcerers looking for victims to 'suck out the soul to feed upon it'.

The most distinctive buildings in the village were the granaries of which there were hundreds, for just about everything is stored in them, not only grain. Whether it was intended or not they were wonderfully animated little structures, each one totally individual. Like stout little sentry boxes of smoothed *banco*, splaying out a little at the base, they were raised on low piles of stone which resembled feet peeping out from under a robe. Several small square wooden doors, often exquisitely carved, were set into them like facial features, and they were finished off with a pointed roof of thatch with deeply overhanging eaves, and with a few long sticks protruding at an angle from the apex, like feathers in a jaunty Tyrolean hat. The total effect, especially when viewed over the surrounding walls of a village, was of an army of benign four-sided gnomes confronting an opposing army of baobab trees. They were so delightful that it would have been worth going to Dogon country just for them.

We stopped for lunch at a village at the foot of the Falaise. It was a place visited by many tourists because a motorable road brought it within reach of those who had only a day or so to spend, and as a result it was rather squalid and full of plastic bags and other twentieth-century litter blowing about the sandy streets. Tough goat meat was the only food on offer, and with the freshly severed black head regarding us with a faint smile from the top of a wall, and the flies buzzing around in profusion, I found I had no appetite.

The visit wasn't improved by a furious row which suddenly flared up between Bourema and the proprietor, to the great interest of the other young men hanging about there. Such events are rare in the Sahel, which is so pacific that it is considered by many that the people had the stuffing knocked out of them during the French occupation. But I was to witness many acrimonious scenes during the time I spent with Bourema. He owed money everywhere, having for months failed to pay the village elders the fees required for bringing visitors, or for the cost of their food and lodgings. Subsequently I learnt that Bourema's problems stemmed from drugs, and had reached the point where no one in Bankas would trust him. I suspected something of the sort, since he was subject to sudden and bizarre swings of mood, and each day, usually around three in the afternoon, he would either sink into a fit of depression or fly into a rage, ranting and raving and even shaking his fist under my nose until, just as suddenly, he stopped, begged my pardon, and became perfectly reasonable again.

Bourema took me away from the unpleasant scene before I could find out what it had been about, and we set off on a stiff climb to visit a village high on the Falaise. This settlement was largely deserted, the former inhabitants having moved to an easier life on the plains below. Only an old holy man remained, the Ogon, who officiated at funerals, but whose chief function was to stay in the place of the ancestors. It was a very good site to explore because all of the three main periods of cliff dwellings could be clearly seen.

The oldest levels of occupation were on the highest ledges, where a pygmy race that has now entirely disappeared had established their simple shelters – touching little relics, no more than rough walls of *banco* protecting the entrances to a series of low natural caves. This small-statured race of hunter gatherers left no other mark of their passing, except that on the flat rock surfaces above the caves, where the sheer walls of the Falaise soared up to the jutting overhang, were the most wonderful rock paintings of formalized stick-like men hunting various sorts of game. They were quite different from the more naturalistic rock carvings I had seen in the Aïr but equally charged with a sense of mystery and awe.

Just below the pygmy caves were clusters of slender towers, mostly square-cornered but occasionally rounded, all beautifully proportioned and set on ingeniously engineered terracing. They were the work of the Tellem, the people who had presumably displaced the pygmies and had been, in their turn, entirely absorbed or annihilated by the Dogon, who had the advantage of iron weapons. The Tellem were a Bronze Age people who planted the first gardens on the plateau, and to judge from their architecture, their engineering, and the few shards of pottery that remain, they had a highly developed culture. Their beautiful little towers, on which the Dogon had clearly modelled their granaries, will probably outlast the villages of their conquerors, because the Tellem positioned their buildings so cunningly that the great overhang at the top of the Falaise directs the annual rains in great spouts and sheets away from them. They also knew how to mix a *banco* that was harder and more durable than concrete, the secret of which was lost with them.

The sacred places of the pygmies had been used for the same purpose by the Tellem, and are still used as such by the Dogon today – a practice of continuing worship which has been followed in many places in the world, and accounts, I think, for the profound sense of the numinous which is to be found at such sites. If ever there was a natural setting for a holy place, it was here, at the summit of the terracing which looked out over the huge amphitheatre of the plains, with the pygmy paintings glowing like icons on the sheer face of the cliff. Here on a small level area was the sacred dance floor where the most important of all Dogon rituals, the funeral, takes place. When a Dogon elder dies, wonderfully carved tall masks and special drums are brought from their hiding places and an elaborate rite is enacted. At its climax, decked in mask and funerary trappings, the body is hauled up the cliffs to a narrow platform, where the finery is removed, and from where the corpse is lowered into its final resting place in a hidden cleft.

Several times in Dogon country I was offered a performance of this funeral dance if I was prepared to pay for it. It would probably have been beyond my means, but I wouldn't have wanted to see such an imitation anyway. Westerners tend to be excluded from the real thing because they cannot be trusted not to take photographs, something Dogons believe will destroy the efficacy of the ceremony. Though I never saw a Dance of the Masks, I had a small consolation early one morning, when from my sleeping place on a roof in a remote village I saw several old men in robes and Phrygian caps dancing slowly backwards and forwards before a stone, to the music of drums and simple pipes, and as they advanced and retreated all the animals of the village – the sheep, the goats and the cattle – trooped out past them towards their grazing grounds. I had no idea what was being enacted, but that didn't matter, it was one small glimpse into Dogon life.

Eight centuries of protecting their practices from Islamic reforming zeal have not made the Dogon forthcoming with strangers. But on the other hand they are very poor, and although tourists do distressing things like taking pictures, they also bring money, so most villages welcome them. As a result, the traditional way of life is fast being eroded in the more accessible places. When renting out a sleeping space on the roof brings in more than could be earned in a month, it is almost bound to result in a questioning of established values. Children hang about the tourists, and little boys learning to smoke cigarettes are also learning that there are quite different standards and beliefs in the world from those embraced by their elders.

On the plateau I was able to see villages where Westerners seldom came. This is what I wanted, but it suited Bourema too, who preferred places where he was not known and could live on tick. There was little to eat, no sanitation, and nowhere to wash. Had I not still been on antibiotics for the chest infection, which was proving slow to clear, I doubt I would have thought it wise to dine on the salads of tomatoes and onions. Each night I slept under the stars on the roof of a house, with the wind blowing a gale around me and the unending chorus of goats calling like banshees all night. I was snug enough in my sleeping bag, though even with my small camping mattress I couldn't claim to be comfortable. The journey was beginning to take its toll, and with less padding on my bones to iron out the bumps it wasn't so easy to fall asleep.

Each day we wandered through a stony undulating landscape of ridges and shallow valleys, with here and there small ravines whose cliffs contained traces of the pygmy structures. There was little scrub left and even fewer trees, because every possible patch of ground, no matter how small or stony, had been pressed into service for the growing of millet. Every plot had its fetish stone where the spring sacrifice of a black goat was made to ensure the fertility of the crops.

The villages grew out of the landscapes with a lovely organic unity that masked their desperate poverty until one got close. *Banco* was hard to come by on the plateau, so the houses, like the low encircling walls, were of unworked unmortared field stone. The only piece of furniture I ever saw in these remote villages was a rough sort of bed, sometimes inside, sometimes outside on a raised porch. Clothes and tools hung from pegs driven into the walls between the stones, but most things were stored in the granaries, where they could be safe from predators, and this gave houses and village a bare uncluttered look. Cooking was done outside, or in a stone lean-to, on small fires on the ground. Water was nearly always brought from a long way off, carried on the heads of girls and women. The rough stone of the houses, together with the absence of anything but the most rudimentary of paths, the naked children and the patched and tattered gowns and tunics of the older inhabitants made me feel not so much that I was in a strange land, but in a previous age. At times it seemed positively neolithic, and the almost total absence of even such basic comforts as chairs added to the effect, as did the wealth of fetish stones, often unrecognizable until they were pointed out among the jumble of the unmade streets.

With the endless variety of the anthropomorphic granaries, no Dogon village could ever be totally unattractive or uninteresting, but some settlements we visited looked on the verge of collapse. It was clear that life on the plateau had been steadily deteriorating for years into an ever grimmer struggle for existence, as it became increasingly hard to wrest a living from the exhausted earth. Many of the young men had already left to work in the cities on the coast, and this broke the social cohesion and robbed the village of the labour to repair crumbling structures.

The chief delight of the plateau was the gardens. Small oases, green eyes in the wastes of dry stony earth, there was one wherever a small pocket of good soil was to be found close to an adequate water source. The gardens were worked intensively, so that the ground was completely hidden under a carpet of startlingly tender green. I never saw one when there were not boys and men constantly splashing on water from calabashes like human sprinklers. As well as the famous onions, there were mango trees whose fruit was just ripening, and papaya and tomatoes, so we were able to eat fresh food occasionally.

Some of the larger villages had a small mosque, a mere showplace, Bourema said, forced upon the people by various reformers. I certainly never saw or heard one used. Once I came across a little stone hut that was a Christian church. There was a carved black Madonna inside and a squat little Christ, like a replica of a Saxon carving, perched on a niche in the gable end. A woman came up in a rage at my having gone into this church, and I, in some bewilderment replied, through Bourema, that I had every right to, since I was a Christian, and fished out my cross to confirm the claim. She seemed to find it difficult to believe that a white person could share her religion, but eventually she invited me back to her house, where we sat drinking millet beer (a drink I detested) in her dirt yard, among the scratching hens, but since Bourema was in a decline and would not translate, we could only sit and smile at one another.

One day a string of boys in short white tabards, swinging rattles made of calabashes threaded on a string, came dancing all around us as we entered a village. They were in the middle of their week of circumcision rites, living in houses in the bush, and coming in each day for offerings of food. They shouldn't have been seen by a woman during this time, and the rattles were to warn all females to keep away, but probably I didn't count.

In another village a sorcerer offered me the chance to photograph him for a fee, and disappeared head first through the small door of a granary to get the things to prepare himself for the ordeal. I was tempted to record the waving disembodied feet, but resisted in case he caught me at it. When he pronounced himself ready, he was kitted out in a hunter's costume – hunters, like blacksmiths are, by extension, sorcerers because they deal in the mystery of life and death, fire and metal. Equally a sorcerer must be a hunter in order to capture the wild creatures necessary for his potions. Looking something like a Sherwood Forester in hat, tunic and boots, the sorcerer was also armed for the encounter with an ancient flintlock, known locally as a '*fizzy*' and possibly left over from some forgotten war, though Caillié mentions such Western guns being for sale in the market at Djenné. At his feet was his talismanic figure for additional protection, and to hide his face and protect his soul from the power of my camera he wore sunglasses. The whole effect was so funny that it was difficult not to laugh as he took up an heroic pose, the *fizzy* elevated to the skies and ready charged with gunpowder so as to go off the moment I took the picture. But when I persuaded him to remove his dark glasses, his face wore a sly and cunning expression that was not in the least comical.

Bourema's cousin had the self-same look, though I liked him in spite of it. He had only recently inherited his position as sorcerer, I learnt, on the death of his grandfather, and was now Keeper of the Great Doors, which meant he looked after the masks and totemic carvings of the village. By this time I had become totally confused as to what a sorcerer was. According to Bourema there were all manner of different ones, including a covert sort who wandered about in the bush at night, plotting evil, from whose invisible influence he had once fled in terror in the early hours, when we were sharing a hut just outside a village.

Cousin Doumo was home from his job as night watchman to the Yugoslav Ambassador in Bamako, in order to celebrate the new year. The Dogon calendar is complicated by having only five days in the week, so their New Year is unlikely to coincide with anyone else's, and this one fell in February. The celebrations were not impressive, just a large consumption of millet beer, and sudden sorties down a narrow alleyway to fire off *fizzys* at the home of the chief sorcerer. I had never seen so many ancient rusty muskets outside of period films, and although they were charged only with gunpowder I thought there was a high risk of the barrels bursting.

The real benefits of this visit was that Cousin Doumo allowed me to study the marvellous masks and carvings in his care, and that he was persuaded by Bourema to join us for the rest of the trip. His presence made all the difference, as he was able to diffuse Bourema's rages, keeping him mellow with great quantities of millet beer. Best of all, when the time came to descend to the plains, he led us down the Falaise by a secret Tellem route – a vertical cleft descending from an insignificant hole in the ground to the base of the cliffs, several hundred feet below.

I was the best equipped for the climb, having boots with vibram soles which gave a grip on rock worn smooth by hundreds of years of use. The other two went barefoot – Doumo with the superb confidence and natural ability of the born athlete, and poor Bourema with a courage that was impressive, given that he was both inept and scared stiff. It was certainly no place for anyone unhappy with heights, disappearing alarmingly as it did over smooth overhangs with brief glimpses of daylight hundreds of feet below. What made it possible were the Tellem artificial aids in places where the rock was too difficult or the pitch too long. Sometimes a chock stone or two offered a temporary resting place, or supported a series of the familiar notched 'Y'shaped logs, sometimes a spar with an end that hooked cunningly over a rock provided the means to swing out across a smooth rock face like a pendulum, to reach another 'Y' ladder. There was something inordinately satisfying about using

211

these cunning low-technology Bronze Age aids, established well over 800 years before, and still working so perfectly. No stranger who had come upon the route by chance would have been able to use it because key sections of the aids were removed after use, and much of the route was in darkness and had to be taken 'blind'. There were galleries leading off the main shaft which in times past would have provided a safe refuge from attackers. It was a place as redolent of the history of the Falaise as the sacred dance floors, and although I discovered later that the route was still a closely guarded secret, and I should not have been taken down it, I was very glad to have had the experience.

The last day provided one further glimpse behind the façade which the Dogons presented to strangers. Bourema and I were walking a sandy track at the base of the Falaise, on the way back to Bankas, when we were invited to visit a particular village. It was the imperative '*Il faut visiter*' that the man used, so it was more in the nature of an order than an invitation. He was the headman of Yabatalou, a small village perched half way up the Falaise, and apparently Yabatalou and its sister village on the plains below were both in real trouble – the wells had run dry. They were getting water from a difficult place, but soon that too would be finished. I was Western, maybe I had an answer?

So that I could gain some understanding of the extent of the problem, I was taken by the headman's brother on a tour of every part of the village, as though by seeing how lovely it was I might be persuaded to do something to help them. Ankoudia was a gentle, self-deprecating man, who had let his younger brother be chief because he thought him better fitted for the job. He was the only person I ever saw in West Africa stroke a donkey's ears as he passed.

We climbed from level to level, meeting various members of the five extended families that made up the little village. The atmosphere of co-operation and friendliness was probably no different from many Dogon villages, but because these people were open with me, I was aware of the close-knit nature of the community as I had not been elsewhere. It was a charming place, and far cleaner than any other Dogon village I had visited. Trees added interest; shade was provided in the flat places by matting roofs; breezes kept it cool and airy, and free of flies. The granaries were particularly jolly, and the houses better repaired and a little more comfortable than those I had been in on the plateau. Everyone was busy on a variety of activities, the men weaving baskets to sell, making rope, tending animals; girls and women sewing, pounding grain, preparing food. Only the small naked children were frightened by my white skin, a clear indication that tourists didn't go there, but they were soon taking turns to look through my binoculars, crowing with delight at what they saw.

At the very top of the village was the sacred dance floor and here too, to my surprise, I was taken, and allowed to look briefly at the drums, and the shapeless fetish hanging suspended near a marvellous pygmy painting of men with horses and monkeys. And just as before, standing on the other empty sacred dance floor, I had the feeling of being in a powerful place of worship.

Just below the dance floor, to which we had come by a particularly precipitous path, was a deep cleft where clear cold water dripped through the rock and collected in a pool. From there, presumably, or from a similar source, the water had once seeped through to the wells below. Skinny little girls toiled up and down the steep path, a round trip of at least half an hour. Water from the heavy buckets on their heads slopped over and soaked them as they felt their way down, step by rough step, and I quailed at the thought of the one false slip that could lead to a dreadful fall.

But that was not the worst of it. Still many months from the rainy season, the water in the pool was sufficient for only another few weeks, and when the last of it was gone, there was nothing the people of Yabatalou could do but leave. From the sister village on the plains below, people were walking more than a mile to fetch their water. Both settlements faced the possibility of having to turn their backs on something that was far more than just their homes. It was the core and root of their existence, the place of their ancestors, that had been in continuous occupation since the dawn of man.

Why had this state of affairs come about? No one knew, it was a recent phenomenon. In previous very dry years the wells had failed just before the rains came, but the level of this high source had never varied, I was told. They did not know where the water that fed their wells came from; it had always been there, it was part of their inheritance, the reason the ancestors had chosen this place. They did not know why the water was going away. But I knew, or at least I had a horrid suspicion that I did. The source of their water was rain seeping slowly drip by drip through the rock from the plateau above. On the plateau itself there had always been water shortages. With Western aid, several dams had recently been built in order to create reservoirs to collect the rain and conserve it. I had swum in some of these drowned valleys, and was now beginning to wonder if I had contracted bilharzia there. I also began to wonder whether the dams had diverted the source that had fed the wells of this part of the Falaise. One cannot hold back water in one place without affecting its flow somewhere else. Modern technology is so often a two-edged sword, and modern man is frequently unaware of the problems he creates when he sets about solving others.

All I could suggest was that they write to one of the aid agencies, who were so thick on the ground in West Africa, tell them their problem and ask for help. No one in the village could write, so I did it for them, using their own words, translated by a small boy, one of the few who could be spared to attend school, and whose French I understood better than Bourema's. I was almost in tears as he relayed the simple message. It began 'There are many children in our village, and their life is very hard.' It ended 'This is the place of our ancestors, it is not right that we should leave it.'

I addressed the letter to UNICEF because I thought they would care most about the children, and I enclosed my own observations. Several months after my return from West Africa, I received a copy of the reply UNICEF sent to the village chief. It stated that they did not deal with water in that area, but had passed the letter on to the appropriate government organization. I have heard nothing further, but there was very little time left to save Yabatalou.

# 20

# Djenné

BOTH EVANS AND I had departed from Dogon country rather the worse for wear. Apart from the broken gears, the last two tyres were now bald and fraying, and on the stony road from Bankas they punctured with monotonous regularity. I had severe doubts that they would last the 500 miles to Bamako, even on the tarmac highway, and there were no replacements of the right size to be found in Mali. I was in no better shape myself, though it was not my patched and threadbare clothes, nor even my dry cracked lips and nostrils, and my parched throat that were worrying me. The vague suspicion that I might have contracted bilharzia had by now hardened into near certainty; I was in quite a lot of discomfort, and although I couldn't actually see any blood in my urine, which was a sure sign, this was not surprising since the only place to pee was the great outdoors. My energy was at an all-time low, and whenever I glanced down, I saw the skin of my forearms was deeply wrinkled as though in extreme old age, and realized that in spite of the quantities of liquid I had drunk, I had become quite badly dehydrated. I knew that I looked pretty awful because people who spoke to me when I stopped to buy food at the roadside expressed surprise that anyone so old should be riding a bicycle. '*Mais vous êtes une vielle*,' they said on a rising note of surprise.

Djenné was meant to be my next goal: a place that had beckoned ever since I had first started to plan the journey. All early accounts of the great empires of Mali and Songhay speak of Djenné in the

215

same breath as Timbuktu – twin centres of wealth, commerce and learning. Of the two, Djenné was by far the older, possibly the oldest settlement in West Africa, and it was merchants and craftsmen from Djenné who, in the twelfth century, took their skills to the emergent Timbuktu to assist in its rise to prominence. By the nineteenth century, when Timbuktu held only a memory of its former greatness, explorers like Caillié still found much to admire in Djenné. I had hoped that, like him, I would find something there that had not been present in Timbuktu, some impression of what life might have been like when Leo Africanus could compare it favourably with the cities of Europe. But now, in view of the condition of bike and rider, it seemed necessary to give Djenné a miss, and press on with all possible speed down the highway to Bamako, where I could seek medical help.

So strong an influence is a mere signpost, however, to someone addicted to exploring far-flung places that, worried though I was, when I came to the stone marker bearing the legendary name I broke my sensible resolve and almost guiltily turned right along the dirt road to Djenné. The track soon became a causeway running straight as an arrow high above the flood plains of the delta, and so narrow that there was barely room for a bicycle and a car to pass, a fact that did nothing to slow the progress of the mercifully infrequent vehicles. I suffered no punctures on the twenty-mile traverse, but was nearly forced over the edge of the embankment on several occasions, and by the time I arrived at the crossing of the Bani, beyond which lay Djenné, I was beginning to regret my second change of mind.

This southern branch of the Niger was so shrunken and shallow that the modern car ferry couldn't use its engine, and was being poled across as though it was a pirogue, and several foreign vehicles were driving through the river to avoid paying the extortionate charge. When I queried the amount demanded – many times what locals paid – I was told 'You are rich, we are poor, so of course you have to pay very much'. I could appreciate the logic they employed, but was beginning to find it hard to swallow.

My indignation was soon forgotten, however, for on the other side, waiting its turn to cross, was a British army truck full of young soldiers on an African adventure course, and, wonder of wonders, the expedition was accompanied by doctors gaining experience in tropical medicine. They had lots of pills for bilharzia, and were only too happy to assist a fellow countrywoman, a cheerful man assured me. He suggested I took penicillin first, in case the infection was something less serious. It was very easy to pick up all manner of things when you got dehydrated, a condition which, he comfortingly assured me, was impossible to avoid in the climate of the Sahel. The *ad hoc* consultation alone was wonderfully restorative, as was the thought that yet again my guardian angel had steered in me in the right direction.

I was saved from having to stay in the horrible *Campément* at Djenné by a chance meeting with a couple of Canadian aid workers who very kindly offered me the use of their spare room. They lived on the upper floor of what at first sight appeared to be a well-preserved ancient palace, whose tall castellated stone walls, pierced with ornately shuttered windows towered above the low mud brick houses, lending an air of romance to the poorer end of town. It proved, however, to be entirely modern – built at the whim of a rich local businessman who had subsequently decided to live elsewhere. As it had never been properly finished, the inside was pleasantly ramshackle. There was no electricity, and although it boasted the first bath I had seen since the Ambassador's residence in Niamey, there was no hot water, and the plumbing never let you forget you were in Africa. A rather-beautiful Bozo woman called Fanta did the marketing and cooked on a charcoal stove on one of the balconies, among a welter of washing and household paraphernalia and two cocks with clipped wings awaiting their turn for the cooking pot.

The raised curved piece of ground on which the town stood had a depression in one part of it that was a lake for half the year, and for the other half a huge empty wasteland on which boys played football. From the palace roof I could look down on a wide expanse of flat grey roofs almost touching across the narrow shaded streets, broken here and there with compounds and small gardens of dusty trees and shrubs, in whose shade stiff-legged hens stalked and clucked. A flash of sun-bright water to the south was an arm of the Bani edging the town. Other rivulets, mostly dry by now, broke up the plains all around, with low hummocks in between on which stood villages and dark green orchards.

The bilharzia symptoms eventually disappeared with the penicillin, and my health improved steadily with rest and regular meals, but I was still short of energy, and spent long hours on the roof or the shaded balconies watching the life of Djenné pass by beneath. There was a precise moment each day, sometime between half-past five and six o'clock, when a distinct change occurred, as though someone had clapped their hands to signify that the play should commence. This was the best time to be on the roof, just as the heat relinquished its iron grip on the land, and the sky mellowed to a wonderful dusty yellow. For the first time since dawn, the sun itself became something other than a threatening presence to hide from, and hung low in the west, a few shades darker than the sky. Women came drifting back from the wells, walking like queens with the heavy pots on their heads. Flocks began returning with their shepherds from distant grazing, breaking up into twos and threes as they entered the city, making a run for their own compounds, snatching at any green leaf along the way, and calling urgently in anticipation of their evening feed.

From the great mosque, the voice of the muezzin added one more thread to the plangent symphony, swelled by a chorus of scolding mothers and the shrieks of young children having the dirt of the day scrubbed off them. Somewhere a drum blazed into life, the sound rolling and echoing across the empty spaces. The sun, now blood-red and huge, sank fast among yellow and pink clouds that rapidly changed to orange, red, purple, and then vanished as the great disc made its final plunge, leaving behind a faintly haloed rim on the dark horizon.

Immediately, as though the hands had clapped again, an air of calm tender domesticity replaced the earlier clamour and bustle. Cooking fires flickered one by one out of the gathering darkness with newly-clean children gathered expectantly around them, their faces beautiful in the warm light. Drums still throbbed – it isn't possible to be out of the sound of drums in Africa – but softly now, and joined by the hollow thud of the pestles pounding rhythmically in the huge wooden mortars, as older girls moved in and out of the pools of darkness helping the women with the preparation of the evening meal.

Later, wandering through the narrow winding alleyways, the rough *banco* walls cut off all but a thin sliver of the velvety star-filled night. Cavernous interiors glowed out of the blackness with the dark richness of Rembrandt paintings, where circles of people squatted around a single dish. Hurricane lamps cast pools of light on other groups sitting at their thresholds enjoying the cool night air. From the shadows hidden voices called '*Ça va?*' as I passed.

Apart from the similarity of its mud-brick architecture, Djenné proved quite unlike Timbuktu. Here the first thought was not 'What on earth do people do all day other than just sit?' On the contrary, Djenné was a hive of activity. From the narrow shaded alleyways doors opened into shadowy workshops or small court-yards, where potters, goldsmiths, silversmiths, blacksmiths, leather workers, makers of masks, carpet makers, embroiderers and others worked at their trades, using much the same primitive tools and methods as had been employed for centuries. Side by side with the traditional craftsmen were motor mechanics and radio technicians employing tools almost as primitive. When the bridge of my cheap alloy reading glasses broke, I sat in a dim cave of a room while a jeweller experimented with all sorts of different metals before he found one with which he could solder them together.

The 'Jenne' Caillié saw nearly 200 years earlier was substantially unchanged. 'The town of Jenne is full of bustle and animation; everyone is engaged in a useful trade ... they live very well and not even the children of the slaves go barefoot ... Everyday they have meat to eat with their rice ... Though their streets be unpaved they sweep them daily.' He was particularly impressed that he could blow his nose with impunity: 'I was pleased to find at Jenne that one might use a pocket handkerchief without fear of being ridiculed; for the inhabitants themselves use it, whereas, in countries through which I had previously passed, it would have been dangerous to suffer such a thing to be seen.'

My visit co-incided with the season for applying fresh coats of *banco* to houses, to replace what had been washed away in the annual rains. Some of these houses had two or three storeys and were embellished with ornate grilles and studded doors, and in Caillié's day they had belonged 'to the rich Moorish merchants who conduct the principal trade of the city.' But the majority were more modest, though still exactly as he described them – 'Very low, having only one storey ... they are all terraced, have no windows externally, and the apartments receive no air except from an inner court.' The clay for the replastering came from the street itself, a pit being dug outside every house under repair and water sloshed into it and stirred about until the right consistency was achieved. These pits left barely enough room to squeeze past, and were a great hazard to people like me who were too busy gazing at the animated scenes to watch their feet. Everyone involved in slapping on the mud by hand seemed to be having great fun, especially the children, all of whom seemed to be brought up in the work ethic of Djenné. There were seldom any, it seemed, who were not busy transporting something about on their heads, even the boys. Once I even saw a small mite, not two years old, remove all his clothes except for a bead necklace, and place them carefully on his head before solemnly marching off stark naked along an alley.

Perhaps it was because they all had work to do that only one boy attached himself to me in Djenné, a Bozo youth of about fifteen called Sori. It was a short-lived friendship because Sori's philosophy was too radical for me. To him a friend was someone who shared everything they possessed. I had many things he wanted – bicycle, camera, knife, spectacles, boots – in fact everything I had, Sori coveted. He said if he had anything I had wanted, he would have been happy to share it with me, and was saddened and indignant that I did not feel the same.

I met up with Sori by the great mosque at Djenné, which is reckoned by many to be the supreme example of mud-brick Islamic architecture. It was built in 1905 in the exact style of the eleventh century mosque destroyed (in a fit of pique it was said) by the Fulani ruler of Djenné, Cheikou Amadou, soon after Caillié's visit. Had Caillié learnt of its destruction it would probably not have distressed him unduly, since he seemed less than enthusiastic about the edifice: 'In Jenne there is a mosque built of earth, surmounted by two massive but not high towers; it is rudely constructed, though very large. It is abandoned to thousands of swallows, which build their nests in it. This occasions a very disagreeable smell, to avoid which, the custom of saying prayers in a small outer court has become common.' It was the only Sahelian mosque I ever actually entered, and I did so largely in order to get away from Sori who was badgering me. Often Westerners are not welcome inside mosques, females in particular, for as the janitor told the small group of tourists with whom I had gained admittance, in Islam women pray at home. Only when they are old like this person, said he, pointing at me – still a little shrivelled from the dehydration – are Moslem women to be found in the mosque.

Inside it was a sea of closely set roughly-finished pillars rising from an uneven dirt floor, with nets hanging between them to discourage the thousands of bats who sought its dim shade – perhaps Caillié, furtively writing up his notes in constant fear of discovery, mistook these bats for swallows. I found the interior reminiscent of swimming underwater among tough-stemmed seaweed, and, apart from its size and the magnitude of the labour it represented, was, like Caillié, not impressed. Its charm for me lay entirely in the exuberant and curiously fairy-tale nature of the lofty pinnacled exterior, which, with its unity of colour and texture, made it seem as though a benign giant had modelled it in play, much as a child builds a sand castle.

Djenné was full of surprises. One night there was an eclipse of the moon. It was quite unlike the same event in any western town where street lighting robs the night sky of its mystery and awe. Here the huge silver disc was a real and valued presence, and as the sharp rounded edge of the black shadow slowly engulfed it people danced through the dark streets to the sound of drums in order to drive off the malignant cat that they believed was devouring it. But

Djenné's best surprise was reserved for my final day there, when it was transformed into a medieval market town, the focus for the hundreds of small villages round about. From all directions across the plains came lines of donkey carts, pony carts, pack horses, and people on foot; all laden with heaped baskets of fruit, vegetables, nuts, fish, meat, bales of cloth, hens, guinea fowl, spices, unguents, holy texts, jewellery, and of course, quantities of the precious crystalline salt, broken into ever smaller quantities and gaining in value as it travelled. All morning the processions poured in, converging upon the huge open space in front of the mosque, until every part of it was jam-packed with humanity, and a pot pourri of powerful scents filled the air.

With the great barbaric mosque towering up behind this undulating sea of colour, it cannot have been all that different from the times when Djenné was a byword throughout the Islamic world for its wealth, its commerce and its learning. Certainly it differed little from the animated scenes Caillié described, though in his day the market was held daily. 'It is well supplied with all the necessaries of life, and is constantly crowded by a multitude of strangers and the inhabitants of the neighbouring villages, who attend it to sell their produce, and to purchase salt and other commodities. There are several rows of dealers both male and female. Some erect little palisades of straw, to protect themselves from the excessive heat of the sun; over these they throw a pagne (length of cloth) and thus form a little hut ... There are butchers who lay out their meat in much the same way as their brethren in Europe. They also thrust skewers through little pieces of meat, which they smoke-dry and sell retail ... Great quantities of fish, fresh as well as dried, are brought to this market, in which are also to be had earthen pots, calabashes, mats and cloth ... There are a great number of hawkers in the street selling stuffs made in the country, cured provision, colat (kola) nuts, honey vegetables and animal butter, milk and firewood ... I observed also some shops pretty well stocked with European commodities which sell at a very high price ... '

As I squeezed my way between the crowded stalls, buying the few prosaic items I needed for my onward journey I was thinking about what the explorer Barth had said concerning the advantage of the great wealth of empires like that of Mali and Songhay – that they produced a system that promoted industry at local level, so 'that commerce goes hand in hand with manufacture, and almost every family has a share in them.' The gold sources that produced the fabulous wealth of the Sahelian empires had long since dried up, and most of the network of trade routes existed only in the tribal memory of desert nomads. But I had watched some of the goods on sale in this market being made. I had seen some of the fruit and the vegetables growing, the animals being herded, and the fish being caught and dried. In a land of such appalling poverty as now plagued Mali, it was good to reflect that the system begun so long ago had not altogether disappeared from Djenné and its surroundings.

# Epilogue

# The Great Water

THE LAST TIME I was to sit overlooking a stretch of the Niger was at Segou, barely a couple of days' ride from Bamako and journey's end. I was the guest of a large family of Lebanese brothers who ran the Auberge near the waterfront, where I had turned up for a meal, ravenous and travel-stained after a week on the road. The brothers, who were full of enthusiasm for their adopted country, found the idea of someone exploring it by bicycle so jolly that they had very kindly pressed me to stay for a night or two. This was in such marked contrast to the attitude of a pair of American missionaries I had recently encountered that I accepted.

The journey down the highway from Djenné had given me a wonderful sense of the vast open spaces of the savannah, but had yielded few beds. Towns along the way were sparse and badly spaced for a bicyclist, and apart from the occasional meal of rice and peanut sauce at roadside shacks, my diet had consisted exclusively of Nescafé, tomatoes and rather dry oranges, enlivened by the last crumbs of crystallized ginger. The villages without exception had been desperately poor, and most nights I had pulled off the road and pitched my tent in the bush, where the thick scrub had provided cover. Lovely though the solitude and the birds had been, it had had its drawbacks, the main one as usual being the lack of water.

It was because I was desperate to wash off several days' accumulation of dust and sweat that I had called in at a Bible school I came to, on the edge of a small town that lacked any sort of accommodation and had precious little to buy. I found a pale, well-fed American missionary sitting in a pleasant garden outside a modern bungalow, and began fondly to anticipate a little welcome hospitality. But after a drink of wonderfully cold water from a rare refrigerator, I was escorted well away from the bungalow to a shabby concrete shack standing among others on some bare littered ground. It had a few battered desks in it and was, the American said, a classroom that was not in use at the moment, so I was welcome to spread my things out there and take a wash under a tap which the students used. I didn't exactly feel welcome, but it was too late by then to move on, so I put up my tent inside the comfortless little classroom, in order to escape from the general debris, the mosquitoes and the various sinister creepy crawlies that abound in Mali. The tap worked so at least I had my wash.

In the morning the equally pale and well-fed wife of the missionary accosted me just as I was leaving. She seemed to feel a need to explain why I hadn't been offered hospitality in their spacious bungalow. 'We never take people in from the street', she said, 'I mean, you just wouldn't know who you could trust, would you?' The words of Our Lord in Matthew came to mind 'I was a stranger and you welcomed me', and at the same time I had a delightful and unlikely vision of dozens of lone Englishwomen turning up on bicycles in this remote corner of Mali, but I volunteered neither thought as I feared the irony would have been lost on her.

So it was the warm acceptance and kindness as much as the luxury that was so agreeable at Segou, where I now sat contemplating the very place where Mungo Park, after far more privations than I had suffered, had first clapped eyes on the Niger. He begins the account in his journal with his usual punctiliousness: '*The Negroes call it the Jolliba, or the Great Water.*' But then the the excitement and the triumph of the moment leap out of the pages: '*One of my companions called out – geo affili – see the water, and looking forwards, I saw with infinite pleasure the great object of my mission – the long sought for majestic Niger, glittering to the morning sun, as broad as the Thames at Westminster, and flowing slowly to the Eastwards.*'

He was wrong about one thing I thought, as I strained my eyes

225

to see the opposite bank; the Niger at Segou seemed to me at least twice the width of the Thames at Westminster. But in all other respects my response towards that great sparkling expanse echoed his. How right he had been to put the importance of charting the river's course before everything else, even before the chance to be the first in Timbuktu – choosing the substance, rather than the frail dream, tempting though the latter had been.

For it was the great rivers of Western Africa, of which the greatest was the Niger, that had been the formative influence in the trading empires that had arisen in those vast spaces. Centuries before Timbuktu evolved from a nomadic watering hole, and long after Timbuktu had ceased to influence anything, the Niger remained the life blood of the Sahel. At the dawn of the nineteenth-century, when the land-hungry western world was casting covetous eyes towards the heart-shaped continent, those rivers were still the key to exploiting the considerable wealth that remained after the last of the great empires had broken up into warring factions.

In spite of Mungo Park's singleness of purpose and his success in establishing the great river's course, it was French not British gunboats that followed in his wake almost a hundred years later, to subdue the region. Strolling through the streets of Segou a further hundred years on, the evidence of French colonialization was everywhere, for this had been the centre of their administration before Bamako. It was a restful town, a place to linger in. The expansive classical buildings preserved an elegance even in decay, and tall trees scattered their dry leaves over wide dirt avenues and large empty squares. I could well have imagined myself in a sleepy provincial town deep in the French countryside, except that the familiar long sticks of bread were sold by black ladies squatting in the dust among all the colour and flamboyance of an African market.

On the river front, however, any mark the French had made in the way of concrete slipways, warehouses, and offices was entirely gone. This was a purely West African scene, more so perhaps than it had been two hundred years ago, when Mungo Park had found the country so dominated by the Moors. But the river still teemed with pirogues crossing backwards and forwards to the opposite bank just as he described it. At that time half of Segou had been on the northern side, where now there were only tracks leading over the flat sandy plains towards scattered villages. I crossed to and fro a few times also, simply for the pleasure of being afloat, and watching the scene from the water.

A raised embankment edged a long sloping foreshore. At one end were bright green gardens, each neatly separated from its neighbour by grass mats, with tall papaya plants providing shade. A long line of market booths, roofed with reeds, had little shacks behind them where the families slept among their wares, each with a pirogue tied at the waterfront below. Mats raised on poles protected a large boat-building and repair place on the foreshore where long slender pirogues were taking shape. While I watched, a row of little girls, each with a stack of enamel bowls on their heads, brought lunch of fish and rice to the men working there. Large areas of ground were covered with stacks of firewood, and there were towers of large dark pottery jars, each a replica of the others yet each subtly different; more were being off-loaded from donkey carts into pirogues for shipment, for this was the centre of the industry. Near the water's edge a woman was tending a fire under a huge iron cauldron of purple dye, while younger women ran backwards and forwards to rinse the treated cloth in the river, so that the shallows ran with shades of violet and mauve. All around the foreshore a sea of purple cloths was spread to dry. The same shallows were full of people bathing, washing their clothes, their pots and their babies; beyond them fishermen, balanced at one end of their frail craft, cast their round nets over the water.

There had been equally animated scenes on the waterfronts of Gao and Mopti, but here it was far more relaxed and domestic. People were not coming and going, they belonged here, it was the centre of their lives. Everyone in Segou seemed to have the time and the inclination to speak to me. They warmed to my interest in them and did not see me as merely a source of *cadeaux*. The children were relaxed with me; the men mending boats invited me to share their fish and rice; and the women dyeing cloth, seeing my curiosity, held up their stained hands and laughed.

Beyond the immediate narrow colourful margins, stretching away into the distance, eastward and westward, was the vast presence of the majestic river, the provider upon whom all this bounty depended. Untramelled by anything as mundane as a bridge, it appeared boundless, untamed, eternal – in truth 'a strong brown god' – and the idea of the lands it watered turning into irrecoverable desert made no sense at all. For a while Africa's twin spectres of famine and population explosion were absent. Nor did I think about them as I sat there watching the sun going down in a blaze of red and yellow, dropping dead centre into the flood.

# Equipment for the Journey

THE BICYCLE WAS, as usual, built by F.W.Evans of London, and although it spent quite a lot of the journey as a passenger, and suffered various mishaps, it proved itself a staunch and pleasant companion.

Madison Cycles supplied the Shimano Hyperglide gear system with push button shifting, and their excellent mechanic set it all up for me.

Luggage: Karrimor's front and rear panniers and bar bag, Iberian range.

Pump: a piece of equipment often overlooked. I took a Zéfal hp 2X. It had to work overtime on this journey, but made surprisingly light work of it.

Tent: 'The Tadpole' by North Face.

The mosquito net: by John C. Small and Tidmas of Nottingham. Also the head net to ward off attacks by virulent insects.

Mattress: three-quarter-length self-inflating, by Thermarest.

Sleeping bag: Karrimor's Superlight, used with a thin cotton inner, which could be washed frequently.

Stove: Optimus Climber, which runs on petrol.

Maps: Michelin 953 1/4,000,000 and IGN Carte International Du Monde 1/1,000,000 ND-31, NE-30, ND-30, ND-28/29.

Camera: Olympus AF-1 Twin

Film: Kodak Kodachrome Professional

Water Purifying: Katadyn pump.

Clothing: Rohan and Karrimor.

Footwear: Asolo Trekking boots, equally good for cycling.

229

Timepiece: Ray Leask of Bijou Jewellers, Blackheath provided the first watch that has ever survived one of my journeys. It was a Heuer Tag and even after its glass was cracked by a piece of flying debris in a sandstorm it still got me to my return flight exactly on time.

All my inoculations and health advice were given by British Airways doctors at their Regent Street clinic.